LIVING-ROOM WAR

MICHAEL J. ARLEN

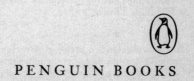

PENGUIN BOOKS

Penguin Books Ltd, Harmondsworth,
Middlesex, England
Penguin Books, 625 Madison Avenue,
New York, New York 10022, U.S.A.
Penguin Books Australia Ltd, Ringwood,
Victoria, Australia
Penguin Books Canada Limited, 2801 John Street,
Markham, Ontario, Canada L3R 1B4
Penguin Books (N.Z.) Ltd, 182–190 Wairau Road,
Auckland 10, New Zealand

First published in the United States of America by
The Viking Press 1969
First published in Canada by
The Macmillan Company of Canada Limited 1969
Published in Penguin Books 1982

LIBRARY OF CONGRESS CATALOGING IN PUBLICATION DATA
Arlen, Michael J.
    Living-room war.
    1. Television broadcasting—United States—Addresses,
essays, lectures.   I. Title.
[PN1992.3.U5A9   1982]   791.45'0973   82-3707
ISBN 0 14 00.6081 2   AACR2

Printed in the United States of America by
Offset Paperback Mfrs., Inc., Dallas, Pennsylvania
Set in Caslon

Except for the Introduction, "Kennedy in California," and
"Griefspeak," all the material in this book originally appeared
in *The New Yorker*.

FOR WILLIAM SHAWN

CONTENTS

AUTHOR'S NOTE

With three exceptions, the pieces in this book were all first published in *The New Yorker* during a roughly two-year period beginning in the fall of 1966 and ending in the fall of 1968. They appear here in the chronological order in which they were written, and though some of them have stood the test of time better than others, they appear here without additional comment or revision.

INTRODUCTION

TO THE

PENGUIN EDITION

I began to write about television in the fall of 1966 because William Shawn, the editor of *The New Yorker*, asked me to. The magazine already had a broadcasting column called "The Air," which had first been written by Ring Lardner, who briefly reviewed radio in the 1930s, and then by Philip Hamburger and Lardner's son, John Lardner, who reviewed television for a while in the late 1940s and '50s. But for a number of years the column had been dormant, unoccupied, abandoned. Even by the mid-1960s television was perceived, at least by most print people, predominantly in cultural terms—generally as the "vast wasteland" described by President Kennedy's FCC chairman, Newton Minow. The most notable television critic of that early period, the New York *Herald Tribune*'s urbane and acerbic John Crosby, entertained his literate readers by lambasting popular television programs for their all too evident lack of sophistication and low cultural ambitions, but for the most part few newspapers or magazines bothered much with the new medium—taking their cue perhaps from *The New York Times*, which steadfastly (and until quite recently) relegated all broadcasting copy to the next to last page of the paper, behind the classifieds and near the shipping news.

When Shawn suggested that I try my hand at writing television criticism, he was doubtless taking as much of a flyer on the new enterprise as I was. At thirty-five I was no newcomer to *The New*

Yorker, having published an erratic assortment of short fiction, essays, and journalism since the late fifties, but at the time I had no special feeling or fondness for television, beyond watching it in an ordinary way, and no prefigured theories or notions of how to proceed. Shawn himself had no theories or notions of his own, or at least he kept those he did have to himself. "Write about what interests you," I think is what he said, which remains—now sixteen years later—the only formal direction that this estimable editor ever gave me.

And so that's what I tried to do, and still try to do, though it took me a while to believe in the simple logic of that message. In fact, for my first column (which appears here at the beginning of the book), I produced the kind of thing I thought was expected of a television critic then: a strenuously urbane and mildly acerbic put-down of a standard piece of network dramatic waffle called *ABC's Stage 67*. But no sooner was it published, and I started looking around for my next target, than I realized that, if I pursued this conventional approach to television much longer, I was likely to do myself out of a job. For if the burden of what I had to say about television was that it was silly, culturally inferior, and not worth the trouble, why then should anyone bother to read what I had to say about it? So, I thought: What *interests* me about television? And the answer came back: the news, especially the Vietnam news—those strange, disconnected, generally optimistic news reports that spoke to us each evening of our increasing involvement in the fighting in Southeast Asia. Thus, the second piece I wrote (whose title, "Living-Room War," I borrowed for the book) was an early, even amateurish, attempt at taking a critical position on television's Vietnam coverage, and though many of my writings over the next two years were directed at a variety of non-Vietnam subjects, their principal focus remained Vietnam, for that was the principal (if often unadmitted) focus of America.

When I started, I wrote about the war as it was presented to us on the television screen—in our living rooms. By the late summer of 1967, I felt confined by my armchair perspective and so per-

suaded Shawn to send me to Vietnam for two months as a correspondent, from where I filed two longer reports: "A Day in the
Life" (an account of a CBS News team in action) and "Television
and the Press in Vietnam." Back home again, in 1968, I tried to
comport myself as a dutiful critic, but again grew restless at the
requirements of passive viewing, for much was happening in the
country. I went to Wisconsin that spring to write about the way
the networks were covering Senator Eugene McCarthy's maverick
presidential campaign. I was with Robert Kennedy and his staff in
California (from where I had already filed "Kennedy in California") when the Senator was assassinated. The final piece in the
book ("A Wednesday Evening in Chicago") was written from
the tumultuous Democratic National Convention in Chicago,
where once again, it seemed to me, Vietnam underlay everything
else.

A final word about television and Vietnam. From the vantage
point of the present, with the Vietnam war virtually everywhere
accepted as a national catastrophe (even by those who were most
enthusiastic about "winning" it at the time), it might seem obvious
that the war and television's coverage of it should have been suit-
able, indeed compelling, subjects for criticism. This *was* obvious
to those who, for one reason or another, were in a position to think
about such matters freely and to respond to them with humane
emotions or even common sense. But freethinking and common
sense were unfortunately not everywhere in evidence in the 1960s
(by what late date, after all, did commonsensical and decent
Walter Cronkite change *his* mind about the war?), and the fact is
that during the period covered in this book few national or mainstream publications found the voice to speak critically—or even
skeptically—of the war and of our war aims; and fewer still
seemed interested in examining the ambiguous effects of TV news
on our then steadily mounting military involvement.

I say ambiguous despite what social historians have often ex-
pressed in recent years on the subject of television and Vietnam,
which has come to be regarded in many quarters as the conventional version of events: namely, that the ghastliness of the war,

as revealed on the nightly news, provided the crucial leverage for the antiwar movement that helped end it. It seems to me that this perspective is neither more nor less correct than the equally one-sided view that prevailed among many intelligent people at the time: that television's banalization or routinization of the war had the result of numbing the audience into a state of acquiescence before government policy. At any rate, the truth is that television news in the 1960s rarely furnished scenes of bloody combat, while at the same time, the nightly reports provided steady, filmic imagery that was bound to suggest, if not sustain, a positive, progressive approach to what we were doing there. In the end, I believe that television in the Vietnam era performed, and performed quintessentially, the same paradoxical function that it has performed so many other times, though on less important occasions. That is, it served itself, and in the process helped march us deeper into the darkness, farther into the tunnel, while at the same time inadvertently providing fuel for the emotional fires at home that helped march us out again.

August 1982

LIVING - ROOM WAR

Stage 67 is the American Broadcasting Company's big effort this year to lure back to his darkened and cobwebbed TV set a species of recalcitrant gentlefolk referred to in the trade press as "the élite viewer." Much money has been spent. Much talent has been signed. Many ballyhoos have been ballyhooed. Words and phrases like "quality" and "culture" and "programmatic leadership" flutter out of open windows above Sixth Avenue and fall like stones upon the heads and shoulders of innocent bystanders on the street below. I saw the two shows shown so far, and they seemed fine. They were very professional—although I can't imagine what the élite viewer is going to do about all this. In the first place, the phrase "the élite viewer" automatically conjures up in my mind the figure of somebody like Baron von Krupp, which isn't helpful. In the second place, whoever the élite viewer may be, my guess is that he's been so traumatized by television entertainment in the past, cultural and non-cultural, that, except for football games, live coverage of Chiang Kai-shek invading the mainland, Errol Flynn in *Montana*, and an occasional debauch into *The Dick Van Dyke Show*, he wouldn't sit in front of a turned-on TV set at ten in the evening if the poet Whittier himself were scheduled to appear and read a selection of his poems. (Who knows? Maybe especially if the poet Whittier were scheduled to appear and read a selection of his poems.) But I think ABC has done a good job so far. Television people talk a lot about "quality programing," of course, and that tends to put one off, especially since they generally talk about it in a fashion, or in a language, that makes the teeth curl. ("We all need to prime the creative pump again to help produce the talents that will give us the cream now and the bread and butter later," a quality-program television exec declared the other day.) But what television people seem to be able to do nowadays, when they put their minds to it, and spend some money, and don't go out of their way to be foolish, is to turn out something that is at least creditably professional and workable as entertainment. At least, and at most.

The first of the *Stage 67* programs I saw was called "The Love Song of Barney Kempinski," which had been written by Murray Schisgal, the author of *Luv*, and starred Alan Arkin, an actor I greatly like, and was really, I thought, a pretty nice show. Admittedly, Schisgal has a tendency to slip into Schisgalesque, a quaint Basque village across the river from Saroyanesque, when he isn't watching the road carefully, and maybe "Barney Kempinski" had a little too much of that. And too many cute, fey, funny bits of business that didn't quite make it. Even so, the whole thing had a nice flow, some great shots of New York (what's the matter with having some great shots of New York?), a decent idea, and—yes, well, Alan Arkin.

The second offering, "Dare I Weep, Dare I Mourn" (I thought everybody had agreed to stop using titles like that), didn't have Alan Arkin, and was in many ways a cut below "Barney Kempinski," or maybe two cuts—less ambitious, less inventive, less "poetic." But it seemed to hang together better as entertainment. There certainly wasn't anything extraordinary about the story, which, one gathers, had been somehow extracted from a piece of writing by John Le Carré, and was set, naturally, in the Master's favorite locale, East Berlin—which, as everyone knows, is *the* contemporary, serious, on-the-cheap, Brechtian locale, where each day the drama of life and death, freedom and repression, democracy and totalitarianism, etc., etc., is played out against a stark gray metallic sky, and where you can always spot one of the principal Le Carré characters because it is always raining on him or has recently been raining on him or is just about to rain on him. James Mason played the No. 1 Raincoat (actually, it was an overcoat, but, as is customary, he never took it off), and I'm not going to tell you what the story was about, because it would sound sillier than it seemed at the time. The truth is, I think this sort of stuff is all right. It was very well done. All those things, such as sets and costumes and camerawork, that I get so fed up reading about in reviews were very well done. So go to it, ABC. And let me know what you hear from von Krupp.

LIVING-ROOM WAR

I read in the paper a while back that sixty per cent of the people in this country get most of their news about the Vietnam war from television, so for the past couple of weeks I've been looking, with admirable regularity, at the evening news shows put on by the three networks, to see what sort of Vietnam coverage the viewers are being given. If my own experience is any guide, I'd say that sixty per cent of the people in this country right now know more about the "weather picture" over major metropolitan areas than they could ever wish to know and a good deal less about Vietnam than might be useful. For example, in a random selection last week, CBS (*The CBS Evening News*, with Walter Cronkite) ran a three-minute film that showed a Marine company breaking off an unsuccessful engagement with some North Vietnamese (the Marines had been trying to get them off the top of a hill), that included a moving, emotional scene of wounded soldiers (ours) being helped, stumbling and limping, across a ravine, and that closed with a short interview with an out-of-breath, bright-eyed, terribly young Marine sergeant who said that it had been a tough fight but the Marines would push them off the hill tomorrow—they always did. ABC, which has its evening news show at 5:45 in the afternoon, didn't have any film on Vietnam (although it often does) but instead had a few minutes' account by Peter Jennings of the results of another Marine operation—Operation Irving (Operation *Irving?*)—a statement about a cessation of bombing in the demilitarized zone, and the latest battle-casualty statistics. NBC (*The Huntley-Brinkley Report*) had a three-minute film of some of our soldiers helping several dozen South Vietnamese out of an Air Force plane that had just returned them from a Vietcong prison camp. The former prisoners seemed (as one might imagine) in pretty miserable condition, and there were numerous closeups of scrawny limbs and of mournful, undernourished faces. Our own men looked strikingly large, healthy, and compassionate. CBS, again, showed a five-minute film of a company of South Vietnamese troops on patrol coming under Vietcong sniper fire. The technical quality of the film, as of NBC's, seemed remarkably good. You could see a handful of soldiers, under cover of some trees, firing into a line of trees that appeared to be several miles away. The rifle fire sounded clear and sharp. The camerawork was expert and agile. There was a sequence, very close up, of an American adviser asking someone over a field telephone to send in a couple of armed helicopters. You could hear everything the adviser said (he seemed calm and matter-of-fact, and he too was terribly young). Then there were more scenes of soldiers, crouching and standing, firing toward the distant line of trees, and later, up in the sky, far in the distance, the two helicopters. At the end, CBS correspondent Morley Safer came on to say that there had probably been only three or four Vietcong snipers, that nobody knew whether or not the southern troops had killed them, and that that was the way it often was in Vietnam.

That's the way it often is with television's reporting of the war, and it's hard to know what to make of it. The technique that goes into the filming—to say nothing of the arrangements for getting the stuff out of the field and into Saigon and over here to the networks within thirty hours—is often extraordinarily good. But what it all adds up to seems not nearly good enough, and when I write "seems" I mean "seems," because I certainly don't have any shimmering private vision of how this war ought to be reported. I do know, though, that the cumulative effect of all these three- and five-minute film clips, with their almost unvarying implicit deference to the importance of purely military solutions (despite a few commentators' disclaimers to the contrary), and with their catering (in part unavoidably) to a popular democracy's insistent desire to view even as unbelievably complicated a war as this one in emotional terms (our guys against their guys), is surely wide of the mark, and is bound to provide these millions of people with an excessively simple, emotional, and military-oriented view of what is, at best, a mighty unsimple situation. I don't for a moment suggest that the networks should stop showing film of men in combat—although I can't say I completely agree with people who think that when battle scenes are brought into the living room the hazards of war are necessarily made "real" to the civilian audience. It seems to me that by the same process they are also made less "real"—diminished, in part, by the physical size of the television screen, which, for all the industry's advances, still shows one a picture of men three inches tall shooting at other men three inches tall, and trivialized, or at least tamed, by the enveloping cozy alarums of the household. I should add that the networks don't always run combat footage in their Vietnam news reports; now and then they have human-interest stories (about a Vietnamese village, or an Army medic helping Vietnamese children), some of which are fine, if rather too smooth, and once in a very great while they'll come up with a whole program devoted to Vietnam. Saturday before last, in fact, I was all set to watch a show called "ABC Scope: The War in Vietnam" ("A report on Operation Market Time: the Navy and Coast Guard's attempt to stop the smuggling of Vietcong supplies and weapons"), but when the time came for it they showed us Jim McKay instead, standing in front of a gray screen and reading aloud the scores of all the college football games that had taken place since the fall of Constantinople. Then, on Sunday, NBC came along with a weekly program called *Vietnam Report,* which sounds good on paper, but which, the week I saw it, consisted in its entirety of Senator Fulbright expressing his views on Vietnam for about thirty minutes. I suppose I shouldn't knock as earnest an undertaking as this, especially when I think of Jim McKay and all those football scores, but it seems to me that Senator Fulbright's views on Vietnam are fairly well known by now, and that NBC, by having him repeat them at this time, was trying rather too evidently to appear as the Giant Communications Network Not Afraid to Air the Voice of Dissent but without incurring any bruises, or even any personal discomfort, in the role. Senator Fulbright was accompanied on the program by an NBC correspondent, Robert McCormick, who fed him some bland, leading questions about the "wisdom of our involvement," etc., and then appeared to vanish into thin air while the Senator uncoiled his opinions. (He was against our "involvement.") It all sounded very safe and institutional, and rather like a rerun.

On balance, it seems to me that CBS has probably been doing the best job lately of reporting on Vietnam, because in addition to having some especially enterprising photographer-reporter crews in Vietnam it has Eric Sevareid in Washington. Mr. Sevareid came on the other evening at the end of the seven-o'clock news and spoke for a few minutes about the political significance of recent military actions in the Mekong Delta, and I thought it was the most useful and intelligent few hundred words about the war I'd heard in two weeks of listening to television news reports.

SOME PROBLEMS

It seems to me that one of the troubles with most television documentaries is that they're concerned almost entirely with problems—the problem of air pollution, the problem of water pollution, the problem of Red China, the problem of the American Indian—which is all right up to a point, since there certainly *are* a number of problems that need to be confronted, and television, as we all know, is a Powerful and Pervasive Medium of Mass Communication, etc. But then when the documentarists actually set themselves to unwrapping one of these problems—I'm thinking of the *CBS Reports* I saw last Tuesday on prison reforms and, even more, of an "NBC Special" I saw a number of weeks ago on last summer's racial disturbances in Chicago and Cleveland—it strikes me that they usually go to such extraordinary lengths to provide "balance" (which seems to mean that if you allot five minutes of time to a Black Power leader, you must automatically allot five minutes shortly afterward to a white segregationist) and to convey an impression of significant "in-depth" reporting (which means dozens of interviews, some relevant, some pointless, each usually presented at face value, and stupefying amounts of on-the-one-hand-on-the-other-hand "objectivity") that the finished product comes nowhere near equaling the sum of its parts, and leaves the viewer feeling that the whole thing has been disgorged by a high-minded, cheerily informative, not very clear-thinking electrical machine. Besides, the great strengths of television journalism are, obviously, visual and emotional, and when you try to bend these strengths to a more literal treatment (as you often have to do, or should try to do, in order to be journalistically accurate), you run the risk—unless you're very, very careful about editing the various portions of film according to their different visual weights—of ending up with a piece of journalism that is simply not fair and truthful, no matter how much spurious "balance" it contains.

For example, in that *CBS Reports* about prisons there was some good footage of a rehabilitation program for prisoners in Connecticut—very uplifting, and reassuring to the guilt-ridden viewer—and shortly afterward there was a brief interview with a prisoner not in Connecticut, who described some of the miserable conditions that he'd encountered in different prisons around the country. Doubtless this was put in to let us know that things aren't quite as nice for prisoners everywhere as the Connecticut program might lead us to believe, but on film I don't think it worked out that way. The Connecticut material was visual and vivid. The interview with the man who had had the bad times was mostly verbal and unvivid. In other words, film is strong stuff and has its own dynamics, and you can't edit it as if it were prose. Picture magazines have always had trouble on this score (for instance, you can't print a dramatic photograph of a Negro boy standing beside a blazing storefront, drop a caption beneath it explaining that the fire was accidentally set by the local chief of police, and expect to achieve a completely truthful effect), and television has even more trouble, because its emotional impact is greater. Perhaps it's just not possible to illustrate with complete faithfulness, either in photographs or on movie film, a big, complicated, largely non-visual situation, such as civil rights or prison reform or many of the other subjects that television now pokes about in, since in most instances you can say only so much with pictures; at some point you have to qualify your way toward the truth with words, narration, facts—all that boring prose that tells you how something works, and why. But then, if television news departments are going to tackle these matters anyway (and they should), it seems to me they might set about it with a little more nerve and relevance—less concern for "balance" where balance isn't needed and more concern for accuracy where accuracy is. Speaking of relevance, in the course of that "NBC Special" on civil rights there was a classic interview with Chicago's Mayor Richard Daley on the subject of the white backlash. The reporter asked Mayor Daley to comment on the backlash. Daley looked very serious for a few moments—which must have taken a number of feet of film and a lot of NBC public-affairs money—and then said he didn't know of any white backlash.

The other morning, I roused myself at the sort of hour when a man can be made deaf by the sound of another human being crunching breakfast cereal, in order to watch a children's program called *Captain Kangaroo*, which had been recommended to me by a friend (some friend!) as "a really wonderful show." It seems to me that *Captain Kangaroo* is a really terrible show—vapid, pointless, silly, about as interesting an experience for a child as stubbing his toe. I know what you're thinking: What business has an old seafaring man, who has spent most of his last seventy-three years on the water and consequently knows little of the joys and terrors of family life, writing about what's interesting to little kids? I still think it's a terrible show. Kangaroo himself is played by a fellow called Bob Keeshan, whom one would normally describe as "pleasant enough"—and he probably *is* pleasant enough as Bob Keeshan. As Captain Kangaroo, he seemed half asleep and totally uninterested in what he was doing. Small wonder, too, since what he was doing was padding about onstage in what looked like a doorman's uniform, stopping occasionally to read a bland little children's story, stopping occasionally while a member of the cast sang a bland little children's song, stopping very often to deliver commercials, and, in general, giving every indication of trying to fake his way through a sixty-minute program on five minutes of decidedly skimpy material. May Allah believe me, I don't think children's programs should always be true, beautiful, inspirational, or spiritually enlarging.

I'm a great advocate of trash for young and old—good, honest, forthright trash. But this empty, empty, prissy, bumbling, sing-songy stuff is something else, and I can't see that it adds up to much of anything. Grown men ought to speak in their own voices when they speak to children, and they ought to pretend to be awake. That doesn't seem a lot to ask.

THE NATIONAL BROADCASTING COMPANY VIEWS THE MANILA CONFERENCE & FINDS IT PLEASING

I don't know what gets into a television-network news department that makes it think it has to stand so foursquare behind the government of the United States in all its comings and goings. Two Saturdays ago, I sat down to watch a half-hour news program on NBC described as "The Vietnam Weekly Review: The Manila Report," which I thought might tell me something about the Manila Conference, and possibly about Vietnam, and so what does one see but an NBC correspondent named Dean Brelis standing there in a natty corporation-lawyer's suit, with a look of high seriousness on his face, and delivering such information as "President Johnson was at Manila not as the leader of the conference but as just one member of an alliance." Come off it, NBC! Surely that's not really what a Giant Communications Company has to communicate about the President's relationship to the Manila Conference, or, if it is, it's hard to avoid the feeling that NBC either isn't telling all it knows or else doesn't know very much. After Brelis's appearance—for some reason, he also felt it necessary to equate the Chinese nuclear-missile test with the President's trip ("There were two milestones in Asia this week . . ."), as if we'd be uninterested in either one if it were presented on its own—another NBC newsman, John Rich, came on with an "analysis of the conference." Rich did mention the new commitments that Premier Ky had made, or had agreed to, on the subject of land reform and constitutional government—which, one had gathered from the papers, were among the more interesting products of the conference—but he did no more than mention them, and even then he managed to bundle them together with a "declaration" by the Premier that the allies would not invade North Vietnam. But the chief point of his remarks, which were squeezed into about three minutes, seemed to be that the world was now a better place to live in after the Manila Conference, because we had talked tough to the Communists. "The summit conference," declared Rich, in one of those authoritative, thoughtful, full-of-personal-character voices that television commentators employ when reading their more characterless sentences, "carries an unmistakably firm message for the Communist side. It spells out exactly how American and foreign troops would be withdrawn. . . . It goes a long way to answering Communist complaints that previous peace proposals have been too vague. . . . It also makes clear that the allies are solidly behind South Vietnam. . . ." Analysis? I wonder if NBC's television-news people really understand the degree of complicity with official government policy that they achieve by presenting government statements at face value and then simply *not asking* the questions that intelligent men are bound to be concerned about. I suppose they do, because they certainly have their fair share of intelligent people over at Rockefeller Center. Maybe the network feels that if NBC news were suddenly to take a detached tone toward the government, the Republic would founder and the viewers and advertisers would become disaffected—and maybe the network is right. In any case, at no time during that NBC half-hour did one hear the slightest discussion of our (to say the least) unusual proposals for withdrawing troops. At no time did one hear the slightest discussion of our (to say the least) unusual proposals for stopping the war. ("Give up and we will be fair" is the way James Reston described them later in a major metropolitan non-electronic daily.) At no time did one hear even the intimation of a murmur of a suggestion that President Johnson might have had some political interest in his Asian journey. John Rich concluded his analysis with the observation that "the road ahead is still a long one, but at least finally the route has been charted more clearly than ever before." We were then shown a long film about Australian troops in combat in Vietnam, which had been made by the Australian government. Those Australians are tough fighters—there's no doubt about that.

There are a couple of series I've been looking at recently that seem okay, each in its own harebrained way. One of them is called *Mission: Impossible* and concerns the activities of the Impossible Missions Force. Surely you've heard of it—a group of personable, well-meaning, energetic young people of draft age who tear about performing secret, dramatic, and obviously near-catastrophic undercover work for our government. The best episode I've seen so far was about a Carpathian terrorist who was trying to poison the Los Angeles water supply. (Now, why would a Carpathian terrorist want to do that?) In any case, the *Mission: Impossible* young people were on to him in no time, first shoving him into a modest little car accident and then, still unconscious, into a fake Carpathian prison. When the poor fellow wakes up, he naturally thinks he's in a *real* Carpathian prison, never having seen *The Ipcress File*, and doubtless assuming that all real, properly certified Carpathian prisons are staffed by six-foot-two, good-looking southern-California television extras speaking funny English, and— Well, you know the rest. Very tricky business. Very silly. Fine stuff.

The other series I've been looking in on is *Batman*. I can't say I'd recommend *Batman* for every night of the week, or for two nights every week, which is how often it's on, or even for one night every week, but it's a zippy program—sure-footed, full of nifty gadgets and ridiculous costumes, and with at least a couple of lines that could pass for wit on a foggy night. The last time I watched it, everyone in Gotham City was stirred up by a fellow called Egghead, who had apparently taken over the place by means of a "legal loophole." Vincent Price was Egghead, with a splendid high-rise head and wearing a beautiful white Tweedle-dum suit that Pierre Cardin ought to think about seriously. Batman was Batman. And at the end there was a fine rumble in a hatchery. One is grateful for small pleasures.

PETER HACKES TELLS US ABOUT
THE HAND-OVER-HAND
RESTRAINING SYSTEM &
OTHER STORIES

Before everybody has quite forgotten about the Congressional elections and the last Gemini space flight, I want to put in a brief and generally admiring word for the way the television networks have been covering events of this kind. I don't mean all those vote-analyzing computers and space-capsule mockups and reportorial task forces and assorted hoopla, although that's part of it. I mean the networks' at least partial willingness to set up their cameras at important events and then let them run; to provide, so to speak, cameras of record, despite a fairly universal fixation (which television usually abets) on entertainment and entertainingness—to take the risk, albeit occasionally, albeit very occasionally, of being *boring*. I certainly don't claim that television covers space and election nights perfectly—especially not election nights. And I'm aware that the networks still show an unremarkable preference for installing their cameras of record at Cape Kennedy instead of, for example, at Senator Fulbright's celebrated Vietnam hearings, during which the CBS and ABC cameras of record pleaded a sick headache, or something, and stayed home in bed. Even so, two Sundays ago, during the Gemini flight, I turned on NBC, and there on the screen was a little replica of the Gemini capsule, with a model of a man hovering above it, and in the background there was the sound of a couple of voices—the voices of the two astronauts. What they were saying to each other was indistinct, broken up by static—unrecognizable sentences delivered in engineers' flat monotones, the whole effect being a bit like what you hear from the back seat of a radio-controlled cab. Was it boring? In some ways, it was very boring. The voices spoke on and on, and on and on. How many people were paying attention to them, anyway? But it was marvelous just to have it there like that, and rather nervy—the way the *Times* is nervy when it suddenly erupts with twenty-five thousand words of a Papal encyclical, running in an unbroken, unreadable torrent of gray across three pages. Now and then an NBC correspondent named Peter Hackes, accompanied by an aerospace-company engineer, would break in to explain what the astronauts were doing. "Now, this here," he would say, picking up something that looked like a steam iron and gazing at it hopefully, "is part of the hand-over-hand restraining system—isn't it, Harvey? Harvey, perhaps you would tell us what *precisely* this is used for." And then Harvey would—great stanzas of arcane, strangely soothing technical description that could have been of interest only to other Harveys or to fourteen-year-old boys. I'm all for it. I think the networks do all right by us when they record, and don't get too twitchy about entertainment, and I wish they'd do it more. I wish they'd do it more on election nights, for example, instead of having all those straight-talking, straight-shooting reporters interviewing each other all over the nation and all over the networks' vote-counting rooms.

Speaking of vote-counting, there have been a number of complaints recently about network computers tabulating and announcing the results of elections in states where people are still standing in line at the polls, and, in general, about network computers taking all the fun out of election nights. I think the first complaint is serious and valid, and one hopes that next time the networks will arrange things so that they don't start releasing California "projections" from New York while the California polls are still open. As for the complaint of taking the fun out of elections—well, I don't want to sound too much like one of these Age of Communications swingers who find something just a little wonderful in every technological lurch forward, backward, or sideways, but I can't see that there's any absolute, intrinsic quality of fun in staying up all night to hear who's governor of Vermont, any more than there was in taking a horse and carriage six miles down to Boston Harbor to find out last summer's news from the Mother Country. Besides, it isn't as if the elections lasted all night long and the computers had somehow prevented them from running their full length. The elections, surely, are over and decided the second the polls close; after that, it's just a matter of counting. I do feel considerable sympathy, though, for campaign workers who slave like navvies for months and months, are finally assembled in the ballroom of the Hotel Van Meter with their hopeful smiles and their new hairdos and all those ribbons and paper cups, and are then told by Walter Cronkite twenty minutes after they get there that on the basis of 167 votes in the Upper Lompoc District their candidate has just fallen in the dust and everything is over. To wind up an election campaign at seven-thirty in the evening with the Old Tanbark bottles still unopened, the pressed-ham sandwiches still untrodden upon, the hairdos still in place seems a sorry, sad, un-American situation, and one that deserves a lot of attention from everybody, or from somebody.

You'd think that *Through the Looking-Glass* was so evidently a special piece of writing that even the most exploitative of television-entertainment moguls would be just a little diffident about pulling it apart at the seams and then stamping it slowly to death. Apparently not. A few weeks back, NBC hauled Alice in out of the public domain, flung her before one Albert Simmons, adapter, who was kind enough to straighten out some of the wrinkles in the story line (adding a character called Lester the Jester, making a light-opera villain out of the Jabberwock, and pretty well messing up everyone else), then dragged her off to Tony Charmoli, who provided some slick, "attractive," out-of-place choreography, and left her, doubtless with a peculiar smile on her face, at the feet of the NBC casting director, who instantly produced the likes of Nanette Fabray, Ricardo Montalban,

Jimmy Durante, and the Smothers Brothers for the key roles. Believe me, I don't think that classics should be kept under glass and not touched by human hands. But there aren't, really, very many things in the world like *Alice*, and it's just strange to think that there are all those highly placed people (such as everybody who had anything to do with this show) who have such a dim idea of what it's about, or who know and just don't care. Even Hollywood in its More Awful Days, when it barbarized the classics, at least barbarized them with some kind of lunatic style of its own. There wasn't any style in NBC's *Alice*—only ninety minutes of show-bizzy cuteness. It was a rotten show.

On the subject of Hollywood, the more I watch television the more it seems that TV "drama" is settling in at a level that the movies had reached around the 1940s. Then, as I remember, the "classic figures" of the old Hollywood, such as Griffith, Sennett, Lloyd, and Chaplin, had all died, retired, or disappeared; the best stuff, really, was being done by contract actors and directors who turned out genre private-eye movies, genre war movies, genre weekend-at-the-Waldorf comedies by the board foot for the old studios, and if you truly wanted to see a "serious" film you saw something with Ingrid Bergman in it, or *Mildred Pierce* (very serious), or, better still, James Mason and Ann Todd in *The Seventh Veil*, which was about as serious as one could get. Nowadays, in TV, the situation seems to be that the "classic figures" of the old *Playhouse 90* era—the Roses, Chayefskys, Frankenheimers—have all disappeared (to Broadway or to Hollywood); the best stuff, really, is being done by contract people who are turning out spy series, Western series, comedy series, etc., by the board foot for the same old studios, and if you want to see something "serious," and now "cultural," well, sometimes you can still see Ingrid Bergman on a *Hallmark Hall of Fame* spectacular, or a few evenings ago you could have watched Peter Ustinov in *Barefoot in Athens*, which was bad Maxwell Anderson in 1951, still is, and wasn't helped much by Mr. Ustinov's playing of Socrates as if for the benefit of the *Tonight Show* audience. Actually, the best dramatic show I've seen on television in several weeks was an episode in *Shane*—a simple story about Shane and the Starett family heading off to a dance in a faraway town that the girl has read about on a poster; they have a run-in with a small band of gypsy Indians (no shooting, though), and finally, when they get to the town, they find that there isn't any dance, the dance was last year, the town is deserted. But it all works out, and not in the usual, mechanical problem-solving way, either. It's foolish my trying to tell you about it. It was really very nice—a good story, told with feeling and skill and a minimum of slickness. And the performances—especially David Carradine's as Shane—were fine. It was so nicely done, in fact, that I called ABC the next morning to ask when they were going to discontinue the series—a fresh question, I admit. December 31, they told me. Too bad. Too bad.

MORLEY SAFER LOSES HIS BREATH
BUT FINDS HIS VOICE:
A MORAL TALE

The other day I was flicking my way around in the evening news programs—the usual stuff: a border incident in Jordan, Mamie Eisenhower visiting the White House, some fresh kids tipping a bus over in Los Angeles, a murder in Detroit, Gabe Pressman interviewing a West African delegate at the United Nations, all smooth, well done, old Harry Reasoner (I like Harry Reasoner) rapping it out so brisk and businesslike for CBS (Harry Reasoner doesn't fly all to pieces because a bunch of fresh kids tip a bus over in Los Angeles), and, down at NBC, Big Chet Huntley, the old pro, the gray eagle of Channel 4, Big Chet not bothering about buses today, Big Chet concerned about the Red Guards, but in an okay Texas-fatherly sort of way, it is all going to work out in the end (Don't worry, son—you, me, and your ma will manage somehow), everything according to form, really, Edwin Newman's firm, institutional voice now coming over from Germany, where he is interviewing Kiesinger, Kiesinger's firm, institutional voice replying, all of it so nicely near, so nicely far (how comforting to hear the winter winds and not to feel them), my kids tearing about in the hall—and I switch back to CBS, and there . . . and there is Morley Safer, CBS's man in Vietnam, standing in front of a thicket of trees, soldiers moving all around him, the camera taking his picture jiggling slightly, Safer not standing tall and staring purposefully into the camera, the way he's supposed to, but instead with his hand on his hip, out of breath, telling us about an action that some American troops have just been engaged in, a smallish encounter, two or three men killed, nothing extraordinary, but *Morley Safer is out of breath*, he is not reading from a little notebook, he has not written anything down, he is speaking with pauses, changes of direction in mid-sentence, occasional gaps between words, he is rubbing his face and moving his microphone about as if he'd just as soon not have to hold it, and pausing again, and going on, doing just fine. He does more than he thinks he's doing, because in addition to providing a good piece of news reporting he is providing the first sound of an individual human voice that many of us have heard on television for days and days.

Voices. Until not so long ago I used to think automatically that television was primarily a visual medium. One wrote sentences like that: "Television is primarily a visual medium"—"visual" being one of those contemporary, modish words that people (myself included) love to carry about in their pockets and to press whenever possible, each word so warmly glowing with contemporaneity, into the hands of friends and passers-by. But I'm no longer quite so sure about how visual television really is. Vermeer, for example. One stands in front of one of those marvelous démodé Vermeers at the Metropolitan and one knows—or one is fairly sure—that Vermeer is visual, and when they attach one of those press-a-button-and-hear-Dr.-Cathcart-describe-the-painting machines beneath it, one can even be fairly sure that Vermeer is "primarily visual." But television—well, it occurred to me the other day that if one had to choose, during most of the hours in which television stations broadcast, and certainly during most of the daylight hours, between having the sound on one's set turned off and having the picture turned off, it would somehow make more sense, be more useful, more intelligible, to have the picture off, because what you have so much of the time on television is static (almost still) pictures of people sitting down and talking. Sometimes they are seated in front of a quiz-show contest board, sometimes around a table, interviewing each other, or telling amusing stories of their early careers in show business, or of why it's important to have a manned-bomber program, or of cold fronts coming in from Canada. Even the soap operas, which stretch on for hours, seem to consist mostly of people sitting down and talking to one another. *George, you're trying to tell me something? . . . Yes, Beth. It's about Harry and Jane. . . . You mean, Ingrid knows? . . . Not everything. But when I saw Malcolm outside the planetarium, he said— Malcolm? I thought you were going to meet Fred.* Et cetera. Nothing wrong with this. A great many people obviously want the companionship of other voices as they pass through the day, with a sort of undemanding background picture thrown in to certify that the voices really exist as people (a bit like the Videophone of the Future that the phone company has been burbling about so happily since the 1939 World's Fair), and so why not provide them with it? But what voices? What people? Across the length and breadth of television, one almost never hears a living, breathing, real, first-hand, individual human voice. One hears a lot of other kinds of voices: the institutional voices of show-business people, the stylized voices of actors acting, the funnied-up voices of the people who provide dialogue for cartoons, the voices of quiz-masters, announcers—the omnipresent voices of Hugh Downs, in fact, and of all the hundreds (or is it millions?) of people who sound like him (or is it he who sounds like them?), so nearly classless, regionless, moderate, "well modulated," no sharps, no flats, no tricky chords, no tears, no fits, not even anger (you have to watch British television to see and hear people showing anger), a perfect middle C once struck and now reverberating gently and genteelly into time and space. It's possible, of course, that voices don't matter much on television—but possibly they do, possibly much of the time that people look into their television sets they look only incidentally because of what they think they see there and mostly because of the voices that call on them to look, the voices that beckon their eyes into the set and hold them there, explaining, talking, advising, cajoling, selling, talking, *talking*, representing so many things to so many people. (Man in 1966— *pace* McLuhan—thus still communes with man.) There are a few exceptions, as when Morley Safer stumbled into his own voice that evening. Eric Sevareid usually speaks in an individual voice, or seems to. Julia Child speaks in an individual voice, and so do a few others (William Buckley, to name several), but there are mighty *few* others. Julia Child came on the screen the other Thursday, working ten rounds with a poached chicken, and the sound of her voice—the voice of a living, breathing human being —was like a thunderclap in a hive of bees. The thing is, she doesn't have an extraordinary voice, just a real one—she plays all over the keyboard. She seems a nice lady, too—and she did all right with the cooking, although I thought the chicken took a couple of the earlier rounds.

First things first. That was a terrific football game the other weekend between the San Diego Chargers, Baltimore Colts, New York Giants, Buffalo Bills, Philadelphia Eagles, Green Bay Packers, Cleveland Browns, Oakland Raiders, Penzance Pirates, Baylor, Clemson, Auburn, Alabama, UCLA, USC, SMU, Artaxerxes High School, and the Royal Canadian Mounted Police, which was televised on everybody's favorite channels (with only occasional interruptions for glimpses of the Perth Amboy Surfing Championships, the Harrow squash finals, and what may or may not have been a Conelrad Early Warning signal) between the hours of noon on Saturday and evensong on Sunday. Viewers will not readily forget the brilliant passing attacks of Starr, Snead, Jurgenson, Brody, Namath, Unitas, Hadl, Jethro, Cathcart, W. W. Wiggins, Dinsmore, Burlingame, and Brevet Major de Peyster, or the exciting catches by veteran receivers Dowler, Mitchell, Ditka, Morrison, Renfro, Hayes, Loman, Henderson, Matthews, W. W. Wiggins, and Harry Joe Moon, or the dramatic runs by Taylor, Pitts, Perkins, Marshall, Smith, Kilpatrick, Huntington, Massoon, W. W. Wiggins, Lockmaster, Noble, and Cadbury (or possibly Basingstoke), or, indeed, the superlative place-kicking by Axelrod, Buckmayer, and Sarkis (Big Swede) Sarkisian, the veteran ninety-year-old Armenian kicking specialist, who, standing (as is his custom) with his back to the ball, his massive right heel encased only in his grandmother's Pucci scarf, lofted a fifty-four-yard field goal between the uprights in the last two seconds of play. Final score: 456–350. During half time, spectators were entertained by an on-the-field re-enactment by Chief Referee Abe Magruder and his staff of last week's ten most interesting clipping penalties, and by the Artaxerxes High School Band, which executed a series of tableaux adapted from the Book of Hours of Catherine of Cleves (and very nicely, too). The game will be reshown in its entirety on the Buzz Carter *Reshow of the Game in Its Entirety* program between the hours of Monday and Wednesday, after which viewers may turn to Victor Van de Velde's fascinating *Some Thoughts about Next Week's Game* program, in which Van de Velde attempts to guess all the plays that will be used the forthcoming weekend and interviews Buzz Carter.

All right, now. Everybody back to his desk. There have been a number of big shows in the past few weeks, such as *Blithe Spirit* (on NBC) and *The Glass Menagerie* (on CBS), that I feel I ought to say something about, but since the programs are over and done with—well, actually, when you come right down to it, they're probably not over and done with at all. I know people keep telling one about what a "voracious medium" television is, about how it "chews up scripts" and "devours material"—very digestive metaphors all—and I suppose that's certainly true, especially if you happen to be in the business of, say, turning out a 140-page script for *The Virginian* each week and seeing your show appear for one brief stretch of ninety minutes and then vanish into thin air. But do these things always vanish? It seems to me that often they don't, that the very demand for material that results in television's inhaling such immense quantities of stuff into its machinery also results in television's spewing it all back out, in a kind of never-ending circular outpouring of old and new— there's Hugh Downs as big as life this morning, coming to you live-alive-o *this very morning* from Rockefeller Center; you switch a channel and there is Felix the Cat coming to you (nearly alive) from 1938. It's not a point that I'd really want to lean too hard on, but it often seems to me that, given the fact that there appears to be so little easeful, fluid continuity today in life between past and present, there's more of this continuity to be found in television (albeit usually in a kind of harebrained way) than in a good many places where one might be more likely to look for it. You go into Brentano's (to say nothing of most other bookstores) and ask for last year's routine, interesting novel, and you probably won't get it. You go looking for last year's movie, and you probably won't find it—last year's play, last month's gallery show. There are revivals, of course. You can always find *Grand Illusion* playing in New York. (Sometimes, it seems, you can *only* find *Grand Illusion* playing in New York.) You can see *Annie Get Your Gun* at Lincoln Center. They are now making a big deal out of George S. Kaufman on Broadway. But there's something so formal and "historic" about revivals, a sense of a wall having been built between our world *here* and the world where *You Can't Take It With You* exists, or existed, and that somebody has almost literally gone up, up, way up and over the wall, has put all the stuff in trunks and suitcases and lugged it back to where we now sit, in dark blue suits and little strings of pearls, and look at it with the kind of stiff unease of people who try so well-meaningly to "make contact" with "old persons." Television devours—it does indeed devour. It has all that time and emptiness to fill, and so takes in anything and everything, but then it often keeps it and pays it out again a bit at a time: old, new, bad, good, back to back, this morning's space shot blurring blandly into Brian Donlevy ("Watch out, Sarge! That Zero's coming back again!") on Wake Island, last year's *Secret Agent*, this year's *I Spy*, Andy Williams, Walter Cronkite, Shirley Temple in *Heidi*, Greta Garbo movies, Rod Serling movies, Ann Sheridan riveting Liberty ships, John Wayne knocking down Montgomery Clift, Vietnam, James Cagney ordering the carrier *Enterprise* into the Coral Sea ("If Admiral Yamamoto acts the way I think he's going to act . . ."), *Donald Duck Meets the Führer*, and Johnny Carson. It's a bit like one of those small-town libraries (which probably don't exist any more) where there aren't so very many books (but enough), and there is no Henry James, no Henry Miller, where *Two Years Before the Mast* is to be found, but under "Boating," and where there are lots of magazines, old copies of *Time* current-events tests, and the complete works of Fenimore Cooper and Walter Edmonds (as a matter of fact, *Drums Along the Mohawk* was on TV the other night—the 1939 job, with Henry Fonda—and it was a fine, stirring Old Wave movie).

NBC's *Blithe Spirit* was okay too, although it was overcompressed. As for *The Glass Menagerie*, I thought this was very well done and had been excellently adapted and attuned to the detached intimacies of the TV close-up—even the commercials (for Xerox) were handled in a halfway decent fashion, and with none of this Amalgamated-Sprocket-pats-itself-proudly-on-the head-as-it-brings-another-fabulously-enriching-hour-of-culture-into-your-poor-benighted-lives nonsense. It was also interesting to really listen to Williams' first big-league play again; I'd forgotten how jerry-built the celebrated gentleman caller is (and what a *tour de force* it is to play him successfully, as I thought Pat Hingle did), and how "poetic" much of the poetry sounds, and how, in spite of such cavils, the play has one of those absolutely extraordinary single visions behind it, so that it truly touches one, even across that mesh of wires and film and magnetic tape. I know they probably revive *The Glass Menagerie* from time to time in theaters, but it was very pleasant to, so to speak, slip into it at home, between some Western and the eleven-o'clock news, as if we were all part of the same world.

I'VE GOT THOSE MAD ABOUT THEM, SAD ABOUT THEM, EDU-CAY-SHUNAL TELEVISION BLUES

The more I hear about the McGeorge Bundy Foundation's plan for lofting communications satellites into space in order to extend the scope of Educational-TV broadcasting, the more I wish it (and him) well, while at the same time allowing myself the tiny hope that one of these days somebody, somewhere (a rich ne'er-do-well, perhaps, should any of them still exist), will start another foundation—not a rival foundation, just another—for the support of Non-Educational Television. It's not that I'm against Educational TV. (I mean, how can one be against Educational TV?) But people tend to have these rather automatic ideas about it —that anything informative is therefore educational, and that anything educational is therefore good—with the result that most of the programs I've watched on Channel 13, the local Educational-TV station, seem to exist in a sort of sacred vacuum in which the producers and the viewers are so busy admiring the high-minded purity of each other's motives that it often seems that one could film thirty minutes of a seventh-grade geography class and title it "New Horizons in Geography" and Channel 13 would run it and people would sit before their sets fairly glowing with enrichment.

I certainly won't say that there aren't good things on Channel 13. They put on serious plays from time to time—Ibsen, Brecht—which are often well done and sometimes excellently done. They put on original plays, which now and then work out. I've seen some documentaries that I thought were good. There is always Julia Child, and doubtless there are others, whom I haven't seen. But even as I try to think of some of those "good" documentaries, I realize that I can't think of any that were better than what I've seen on network television. Not only that (which is maybe neither here nor there as criticism), but I can't think of any that made noticeable use of the supposed freedom that comes with noncommercial, "educational" work. A while back, for example, there was a documentary called "A Time for Burning" —about the difficulties of a Midwestern Lutheran pastor in trying to integrate his church—which received considerable critical acclaim for its fearlessness in showing a reactionary side in the Lutheran Church. In this case, the pastor had received so much opposition from his parishioners that he had been unable to manage the integration. The film was nicely done and it was interesting, but it had been produced under the auspices of the Lutheran Church, and—not to be unfriendly to a decent piece of work—it struck me as inescapably an establishment documentary. The establishment in question, the Lutheran Church, was admittedly trying to do something straight and true, and was not "afraid" to admit that there had been trouble in this Omaha church over the introduction of Negroes—only, it was simply incapable of presenting the trouble in any context other than that of the honest difficulties of good Lutherans, who are, *ipso facto*, good people. (For instance, there were plenty of sequences of integrationist Lutherans arguing against segregation but none of segregationist Lutherans arguing for it.) And so it was a cop-out. Another, and more recent, acclaimed Channel 13 documentary that comes to mind was one of those plight-of-the-educated-woman things, "Modern Women—The Uneasy Life" (why do they have such titles?), which *seemed* to be the kind of free-swinging contemporary program you can't do on network television (lots of *cinéma vérité*, motion, style, women talking out their honest feelings: their not wanting to be subservient, their wanting independence, etc.), and was not bad at all. Except that it didn't really say anything. Except that if you are going to bring up this subject of the plight of the educated woman in intelligent company today, surely you have to do more than state it. Except that there are, I should think, a number of fairly rough and disagreeable things that can be said on this subject, and that if you decide not even to try to say them, what you are left with is another seemingly serious, seemingly hip piece of ladies'-magazine journalism, and not much of an alternative to what the networks are doing.

The thing is, it seems to me, that whether you call it Educational TV or Non-Educational TV—whether, in other words, it's produced by networks or by noncommercial, NET stations—there is quite a lot of it around (more, perhaps, than one would think), and although I certainly wouldn't say, "Let's have less of it," I find it hard to be too uncontrollably gladsome at the thought of having more. One feels, really, that two great gods, Entertainment and Education, have risen up, and this in a way is okay, is the way things are, but they have kept out all the other, lesser gods: the gods of Wit and Unprofessionalism, the nasty gods, the gods that get into noisy arguments, the dissenting gods (David Susskind is not a dissenting god), the gods that say things in bad taste and recite poems and do things for the hell of it; the gods that exist in this "larger world" that television is always claiming to bring us—which still exists in books and magazines but does not exist in television, because the air isn't really available to everyone, and because it apparently costs so much to put together the equipment for broadcasting through it that one requires one of those great modern American institutions, a giant Commercial Network Television Establishment or a giant National Educational Television Establishment, but in either case an establishment, to run the show.

I think that one notices this lack of alternatives especially in children's programs. People fuss a lot about what kids watch on television. People fuss a lot about kids, which I guess is a good thing. They deeply want their kids to be "well educated," and so spend immense sums of money on new schools and go racketing around in the evenings to meetings where they discuss the hiring of teachers, the firing of teachers, the revision of the Alchemy Department in keeping with the New Alchemy—all very laudable—and in the meantime their own kids, who, it has been reliably calculated (and not by me, either, in case you were thinking what you were thinking), will by the age of eighteen have devoted more of their lives to watching television than to any other single activity except sleep, are home watching *Flipper*, which is a nice mechanical show about a dolphin, or *The Three Stooges*, which is a preposterous mechanical show about the Three Stooges. But, given what's available, I can't see that it makes very much difference what they're watching. Most kids' programs are either this amiable mechanical entertainment or the "educational" shows. Some of the latter are perfectly well done— I'm thinking particularly of such programs as *Discovery '66*, on ABC; *Wild Kingdom*, on NBC; and *What's New?* on Channel 13—but, even so, for all their well-doneness, and for all one's desire that one's kids watch *nice, good* things, and learn, and improve their minds, I can't see that these shows do much of anything for a child except enable him to pass the time. The other day, for instance, I watched a *Discovery '66* program. It was okay for what it was—a travelogue about Finland, with a number of pleasant (and, I suppose, informative) film sequences of fishing villages, and of kindly old grandmothers repairing fish-nets, and lots of pictures of kids, and *lots* of information about fish. One doesn't object to information about fish, but there was such an air of trivialization and complacency about the show! After all, Finland isn't all grandmothers and fish and little kids. Does life really have to be so diminished for kids to look at it with understanding? In the second place, you could *make* a story about grandmothers and kids, and even lots of fish, if you cared to make a story, and knew how, and you could tell it to a child, and maybe, conceivably (with luck), something inside him might be ever so slightly, lightly touched, and this would be worth the whole ball game, would be worth the Three Stooges rolled into one. But I can't see that any kid's imaginative life is much affected by *Discovery '66*, or by *Wild Kingdom*, with its beautifully modernist premise that as long as you only shoot animals with tranquilizer pellets everything remains unruffled in the Garden of Eden, or, in fact, by most of the "good" kids' shows that I've seen. Assuredly, one's children get no nightmares from them, but where do they get dreams from—*Huckleberry Hound*? I'll say this, though, for *What's New?*, the children's program on Channel 13. Although most of the time the stuff it presents is as routine and institutional as everybody else's, now and then it gets hold of a piece of film (I'm thinking especially of some Canadian Film Board footage on wildlife in the marshes) that does as much as a piece of film can do to evoke the life and wonder and beauty of this particular world, and just runs it, with no cutesy background music, no nonsense, no hosts or people in funny hats, but letting it speak for itself—a piece of film transformed by someone's care and sensitivity—and so one's imagination goes out toward it and connects. Come to think of it, that's what they used to say "education" meant—a drawing *out*. It still sounds right.

PERSPECTIVES

It seems like only yesteryear that my old dad would come shuffling into my study after dinner, seat himself shyly at my knee, and say, "Son, tell it again to me about the Axis Menace, the Giant Holocaust, the Dismemberment of Europe, the End of Civilization As We Knew It. Tell it again to me how we won the Big Two." And I would quietly put aside my paper, or my alembics, or retorts, or whatever I happened to be occupied with at the moment, and reply, "Old Dad, I reckon it was beautiful Greg Peck who won the Big Two for us—beautiful Greg Peck, who so bombed the bejeezus out of the filthy Hun; and Errol Flynn, whose impulsive, sexy counteroffensive swept all before it across the snake-and-mice-infested jungles of North Burma; and jim-dandy Brian Donlevy, who sank the entire rotten Nip fleet in the wine-dark waters of the Coral Sea; and, in fact, all those wonderful, well-groomed, good-looking southern-California boys and girls who enlisted as one man to do battle against that creepy, creepy bunch of guys like Sessue Hayakawa and Otto Preminger."

"Otto Preminger?" my dad would say. "Well, fancy that!" And he would give the V-for-victory sign ("Lest we forget," he used to say) and disappear downstairs.

The years went by. Summer turned into fall. Fall turned into winter. Winter turned into summer. One day, I remember, we were out in the orchard, and my dad looked up at me (in the snapshot, he is the one on the ground, I am the one in the tree; it was the way we always worked), and suddenlike he said, "Son, about that Big Two . . ."

"Yes, Dad," I replied. "Shall I tell it to you again the way it was?"

"I wish you would, Son," my dad said. "Fact is, the other evening I overheard you saying something mighty peculiar to your ma—about how the *real* reason we won it wasn't on account of Otto Preminger being such a creepy guy but on account of Curt Jurgens and Maximilian Schell—and who was that other general? James Mason?—wanting so badly to get back to their brandy cellars and ancestral hunting preserves, from which the Call to Arms had so cruelly ripped them."

"Dad, I'm glad you brought that up," I said. "A lot of new information has come to light that wasn't, it would seem, under the stress of conflict, available to our government or the Warner Brothers at the time. It turns out, you see, that, far from being filthy Huns, for example, or anything of the sort, over sixty-two per cent of the senior officers in both the German Army and Navy were university chaps—something, of course, we had no way of knowing then—and that they were naturally as privately disgusted, not to say, in some cases, actually *repelled*, by the loutish behavior of that fellow What's-His-Name—that rather rotten little guy with the mustache?—as all of us were. In fact, there are many people who now think that if good old Jurgens, Mason, and Schell had been able to get together and contact Greg Peck, or even Helmut Dantine, the war would have been over in no time at all, and without all that unnecessary bloodshed, killing, loss of life, and associated personal discomfort. I hope that clears everything up."

"Helmut Dantine?" my dad said. "Well, fancy that!" And he did his imitation of Martha Raye imitating General Tojo ("Know the past," my dad used to say. "Knowledge is power") and disappeared indoors.

Well, now. Time goes by. The stairs get steeper. Furniture is harder to lift. I don't go to the picture show so often any more. And my old dad—well, he has this thing about the army ants coming up from South America, and so he stays downstairs now practically all the time. But I watch TV a lot, especially the shows about the Big Two, and I guess it's fair to say that a whole pile of new information has come to light about the war, because the more I see of these TV shows the more I realize that it wasn't beautiful Greg Peck who won it for us, it wasn't even all those swanky, Goethe-reading panzer generals who won it for us. What won the war for us was the fact that in virtually every key position in the German and Japanese armies was a *comical* German or Japanese soldier. For example, take this show *McHale's Navy*, which I saw the other night. Here you have a big Navy guy, Ernest Borgnine, and a bunch of fun-loving gobs who are being held prisoner on a Pacific island by a Japanese major and a whole lot of very Japanese-looking soldiers. How do our guys escape? They escape by putting on a stage show for the Japanese major and his troops—you know, songs, dances, funny patter—which causes the Japanese major to laugh a great deal, and while he is laughing Ernie Borgnine sneaks up to a radio, which is on the table just behind the Japanese major, and signals for help to a nearby destroyer. It is a very exciting scene, although not quite as exciting as it might have been if the Japanese major hadn't been laughing so much, and at the end, while the Navy is shelling the island and the fun-loving gobs are escaping, the Japanese major quiets down for a moment, takes big Ernie Borgnine aside, and, with a straight face, says, "You'd be socko in Yokohama," and then they both collapse laughing—which is a nice touch, Borgnine doubtless thinking that someday this lousy, stinking war will be over and he'll get back Stateside and maybe start that motel, and someday his little girl will say, "Daddy, what did you do in the war?" and then, oh, my, he will have some pretty funny stories to tell.

Or *The Rat Patrol*, which says how it was with the War in the Desert. I guess it was exciting and pretty funny there, too, although naturally not without its perils and disadvantages, if you know what I mean. The way the show tells it, there are these four really neat-looking southern-California guys whose job it is to raise the very Ned with boring old Rommel's boring supply lines, and how they do it is to go varooming all over the desert in a couple of jeeps in search of the thousands of comical Germans whom the Field Marshal has evidently allowed into the Afrika Korps. Once they find one—in an episode I saw, there was a very comical officer in charge of a medical detail—why, our guys drive right up, kid around with the comical fellow, usually by pretending to be German, when, naturally, the comical German knows that they are really four neat-looking guys from southern California, and they *know* he knows, but they are all having such a swell time, what the hell? And then they swipe all his medical supplies. Boy, it must have driven poor old boring Rommel crackers!

My favorite show, though, is *Hogan's Heroes*, which tells about how it was in a prisoner-of-war camp run by the Nazis. It doesn't seem to have been too bad—at least, not in this particular camp, because it is commanded by a colonel called Klink (I mean, if you were being led off to a POW camp and you saw that the commandant was called Klink, you would know right away that there were going to be a lot of larks from then on) and by a funny fat sergeant called Schultz, and you would never believe the carryings-on that take place in that stalag. Chiefly, the Allied prisoners, led by this Hogan fellow, are always escaping. In fact, they have tunnels all over the camp, and a secret radio that operates night and day, and, why, sometimes a couple of the prisoners just sneak out of the camp and blow up a bridge and then sneak back to camp in order to share a few laughs with Sergeant Schultz. The reason they can do this, of course, is that Commandant Klink is such a comical fellow. Well, let's be honest —since he is a prison commandant, he is not completely comical, but he is certainly fairly comical, or fairly comical in terms of your average professional German-prison-camp-commandant type of person.

Some people, I know, would think that *Hogan's Heroes*, a funny show about prison camps, might be stretching things a little far. Some people, I know, have a lot of unbending ideas about this sort of thing. But not me. The past is always changing, is it not? Perspectives shift, move sideways, backward, forward, rearrange themselves. ("Remember the Maine," my old dad used to say. "Remember the Marne. Make not the same mistake twice, or even once.") A lot of people, I guess, don't understand about perspectives. My dad, for example. I bet he could learn a thing or two from watching some of these TV shows, but he never looks at the TV, except now and then at the eleven-o'clock news. "If the ants are coming," he says, "Tom Dunn will be the first to know about it." But then the other day, at teatime, I was looking at the early news when once again I heard the familiar footsteps entering the study.

"Old Dad?" I called. "Come in here. Walter Cronkite is telling us about the air strikes against the North."

"How are they?" my dad asks.

"We're bombing the bejeezus out of them," I say.

"Well, well," my dad says. "Those creepy guys again. I hear you have new information about the Big Two."

"You'll have to speak louder, Dad," I say. "Morley Safer is coming in now from the Mckong mudflats, and I have the volume up to better hear the proud thunder of our artillery as it argues against the evil whine of Vietcong bullets."

My dad sits down beside me, takes my hand, a pen, and a small bottle of India ink, and writes across the back of it. "Brief notes," he says when he is done. "The merest froth. No poems."

As he stands up to go, I read the back of my hand. "History speaks with a forked tongue for damned sure," he has written, although it is hard to read it in the flickering light, and a hand is no place to write on anyway. "If *Hogan's Heroes* garners 22.6 Nielsen Boffo in '66, explain inevitability or noninevitability of *Pleiku Junction* and *Hopalong with Uncle Ho* in '67, '77, '87? Give dates. Name names. Where were we then? Where are we now? Yrs. truly."

I call after my dad, but he has gone. It sounds pretty bad taste to me. A person should know better than to joke around about a war.

THE NETWORKS CONTINUE TO
GIVE US WHAT WE REALLY WANT.
WE ARE IMMEASURABLY GRATEFUL
& UTTER LITTLE CRIES OF HELP

The other Sunday evening, as innocent householders all over the nation were sitting around after dinner staring into the middle distance and generally minding their own business, the redoubtable cultural legions of the Columbia Broadcasting System came rushing out into the night, sabers flashing, bugles blaring, fifes fifing, holding aloft banners bearing many a strange and foolish flack-inspired device, and dumped onto the home screens a ninety-minute Very Big Deal Drama called "The Final War of Olly Winter," which—not to make too much of a thing about it one way or the other—was the most asinine and inept piece of cockamamie that I'd seen all year. Better make that retroactive to last year.

Olly Winter, the hero of the work, is an American master sergeant who is serving as adviser to some South Vietnamese troops in 1963, which isn't a bad idea to begin a play with—in fact, it's probably a fairly good idea, or would have been if anybody involved had bothered, or had had the skill, to actually try to say something or to express some first-hand feelings. As it was, "Olly Winter" was a ninety-minute uninterrupted cliché, and made one suspect that the chief reason for its existence was to provide the good folks out there on the farms and prairies with an illusion of topicality and "involvement," and to allow the playwright, Ronald Ribman, and presumably CBS, to spout a lot of empty-headed propagandish nonsense about the war, and War

Itself. "Everybody kills everybody. It's the world's greatest out-door sport," says Olly Winter. Or, "Somebody's got this thing [the Vietnam war] all figured out. Somewhere, somebody's got charts and papers which makes all this killing worthwhile." Or, "The only guerrillas I want to see are in the zoo," which is a line I'd have thought that even the Penumbra College Dramatic Work-shop would be a little diffident about using. Oh, yes. I nearly forgot. Olly Winter is a Negro—also a perfectly valid idea, especially when you consider the disproportionately large number of Negroes now serving in Vietnam. Only the chief reason for having a Negro seemed to be, once again, exploitative —to enable the people concerned to come up with a lot of second-hand, unfelt jargon about the plight-of-the-Negro, etc. Yes, I know, the plight of the Negro is real and hard. But the plight-of-the-Negro, etc., as pictured in things like "Olly Winter," is made of celluloid and cotton batting and comes apart in your hands. In fact, it's hard to believe that a bunch of supposedly savvy people could be as meretricious about it as they were in this show, with its maudlin, mechanical flashbacks to Olly Winter's maudlin, mechanical childhood and his poor, sad old mechanical mama. And there he is, Olly Winter (in another flashback), just out of the service after the Korean war, trying to get some information about a missing sister from some nasty, sour-faced white housing-project guard, and the guard is reluctant, if you know what I mean, to let him in, and so there is Olly clutching the strands of the cyclone fence that is keeping him out, out, *out*, and there it is—what a scene! (*quelle scène!*, Fr.)—all wrapped into one powerful moment: civil rights, the agony of the Negro, the free-ing of the slaves, the discovery of radium, the eruption of Mount Monadnock. Except that you have the feeling that someone has sneaked into the vaults at night and scissored the whole thing out of some ancient, equivocating, phony-gutsy Dore Schary movie of the 1940s.

Speaking of Dore Schary, the more I watch these big, phony network specials like "Olly Winter," the more they remind me of those fake-serious Hollywood things, such as *Pinky* and

Gentleman's Agreement, that the old Hollywood studios turned out. Oh, there are differences all right. Now and then on network TV someone will be permitted to murmur, "Damn," or be shown fleetingly in underwear—or, when a classy outfit like CBS puts on a classy show like "Olly Winter," before things get under way, instead of some tacky lion roaring out at you from the silver screen, or a bunch of pastel-colored searchlights, you get a relentlessly tasteful shot of a lovely little Giacometti sculpture group. But there are resemblances, many of them, between the nonsense put out by the old studios then and the nonsense put out by the networks now. And there are resemblances in the business structures that have produced it.

It's hard to remember sometimes that there was a period, not so long ago, when the big studios owned everything. They quite simply owned everything, and you couldn't make a movie in this country if you didn't make it through them—as an employee, on their terms. They owned the actors. They owned the studio lots, the sets, the cameras—the works, the whole means of production. What's more, in an exquisite arrangement, for years and years they owned the means of distribution, too; namely, the movie houses around the country. If you were a young director then and had a great idea for a movie, you could make it, maybe (if you had your own money), but you couldn't show it anywhere, because the big studios owned the movie houses. Television broke up the big studios, forcing them to sell off or rent out their means of production in order to reduce overhead. And the antitrust laws required the studios to divest themselves of the movie houses and, with them, the famous system of block booking, whereby the studios could turn out four hundred pictures a year—good, bad, awful—and the movie houses simply had to take them. Now, in the movie business, things are different. The remaining big studios are fat from television production, and from the sale of films to television, and from the financing of movie production. And as for the making of movies—well, it's still no piece of cake, but if you can get the money from a bank, or a studio, or your grandmother, you can at least *show* your movie. And, with luck, you may even be able to make it pretty much your own way. And what this means is that finally it begins to be possible in this country to make a movie animated by—not to sound too pompous about it—what one might call a single vision. It's hard to think of anything that's any good, in any field, that isn't, ultimately, the product of a sustained single vision. Making a movie animated by a single vision wasn't possible in the old Hollywood, where you had a lot of illiterate nickelodeon magnates, lackeys, second-guessers, hacks, and so forth mixing into each production. It is at least *possible* now for a director to get the money and then make his movie on his own terms, and no fooling around, either, with the First National City Bank's taking "final cut." But today in television there are a number of haunting parallels to the good old days when we sat stupefied at Loew's Seventy-second Street. The networks seem to own the means of production (namely, the facilities), and they seem to own the means of distribution (namely, the channels), and the people who run the networks still seem to be the same old nickelodeon magnates—only nowadays, of course, they're communications executives and have Italian tailors and Ad Reinhardt paintings and extensive collections of Scarlatti records—and they make the same kind of stuff for the same kind of reasons and talk the same kind of pap about giving the people "out there" what they really, truly want.

Fortunately, things aren't quite what they seem. In the first place, the networks don't own *all* the means of distribution. They do indeed own the major wide-band channels on the frequency spectrum, but they don't own the eleven-hundred-odd UHF channels that are now available for television broadcasting. In the second place, the proved success of the synchronous satellite (so called because of its ability, at the relatively high altitude of 22,300 miles, to revolve in time with the spin of the earth) makes the cost of relaying television broadcasts potentially much cheaper than it is at present, when broadcasts are relayed via underground cables leased from AT&T—and as much as fifty per cent cheaper even than a medium-altitude type of satellite, such as Telstar. And, in the third place, foundation money has increasingly become an accepted and energizing part of artistic life. Foundation money is really where the leverage is these days (think of what the Ford Foundation has just to *spend*, compared to CBS). And so outfits like the Ford Foundation and the Rockefeller Foundation are now beginning to step in and really throw their weight around. There's always a risk, I guess. One still can't be sure how the foundations will turn out. But there's sure as anything a risk in tossing away the major part of your frequency spectrum to a bunch of businessmen with an alleged fondness for Giacometti. At this moment I think the shadow of the big foundations over the TV scene is a fine thing and that any system, such as the one proposed by the Carnegie Commission, that would make it in any way more possible for individuals to produce and distribute their own individually conceived shows is great. And so what about the networks? For one thing, these new developments might encourage your average network execs to at least consider the possibility that their charts and ratings tell them only what the audience thinks of what's actually available—not of what might be available—and then some of the braver ones might cast an eye sidewise and a bit backward at what happened to the Ozymandias Studios. I mean, it will hardly do anybody much good for things to work out fifteen years from now so that every literate person in the country is watching some television Antonioni beaming out of a Ford Foundation-financed UHF channel while The Doctor Stanton is up there on Fifty-second Street running off old *CBS Playhouse* tapes for the benefit of the staff.

THE BOMBS BELOW GO
POP-POP-POP

It seems hard to believe that in midwinter of 1967, at a time when this country is conducting an air campaign against North Vietnam in an almost unparalleled context of national unease and international distress, a major television network could undertake an allegedly serious examination of this campaign and then come up with as childish and unaware and fundamentally chicken a piece of journalism as CBS did recently in "Vietnam Perspective: Air War in the North." By "chicken" I mean that CBS knowingly (they're not a bunch of kids over there) ducked out on something it shouldn't have ducked out on. I mean if you are in favor of the air attacks against the North, then come out and say so, and be intelligent about it. Or if you are against the air attacks in the North, then say that, and be intelligent about it. Or if, as a journalist, you want to say something about the whole situation, both sides, then do that—always a difficult matter—or, with honesty and skill, at least *try* to do it. CBS did none of these things. CBS took one of the most controversial and important political-emotional issues of the moment, made a few brief stammers at journalistic "objectivity," presented government propaganda for fifty minutes, then gave us some hurried, underweighted glimpses of the "opposition" for a final five minutes, and that was it.

The principal part of the program—a good three-quarters of it, in fact—consisted of a face-value, and therefore implicitly deferential and pro-military, "documentary" of the Air Force and

Navy pilots who fly the missions against the North, with occasional Defense Department footage of specific bombing raids. The point of view of CBS "reporter" Bill Stout seemed at all times to be unquestioning, and glowing with the kind of military-technological "tough-mindedness" that is presumably useful among military officers but is maybe not such a hot thing to have in a reporter who is supposedly telling us how things are. "A few days ago, these five-hundred-pound bombs were part of the flight-line inventory at Danang Air Base, South Vietnam" is the way the program opens, Bill Stout standing tall behind a neatly arranged line-up of bombs and missiles. "Goods on the shelf, ready for delivery to North Vietnam. By the time this report goes on the air in the United States, delivery will have been made. . . . All of it . . . designed to kill and destroy. All of it, according to the United States government, intended to shorten the war in Vietnam." Well, come on, now, Bill Stout. We know that's what the United States government intends. What one needs a news service for is to tell us how things actually are—and when a reporter gives us a sentence like that and then drops the subject, that, by implication, is how things are.

We were then shown the preparation and flying of bombing missions by Air Force and Navy pilots, with lots of *Twelve O'Clock High* sequences on weather briefings ("The weather in the Red River Delta, running four thousand broken, tops at seven thousand") and Intelligence briefings ("Good morning, gentlemen. Your target for this afternoon, as advertised, is . . ."), a long sequence in which the flight leader instructs his men on how to avoid a SAM attack ("I understand some of you have not seen a SAM attack before . . ."), and then some fine I-love-a-parade stuff, with planes whooshing off the runways and in the air (mountains, sky, clouds) and then down below the bombs making little un-noisy, faraway, almost pretty splashes (*pop-pop-pop*) of white and red on the dark green of the forest. Now, the last thing in the world I'd want to do is question the bravery or competence of these pilots, who, after all, have the job of fighting this miserable war for all of us; but to devote the principal part of what's supposed to be a serious study of a mighty complicated situation to this sort of our-brave-men-at-war type of coverage is, intentional or not, plain propaganda. Yes, of course, pilots like Air Force Colonel Sam Hill (whom we saw quite a bit of) are brave men, and there's no reason not to say so at some point. But if you present merely admiring sequences of this same Colonel Hill, brave, professional, old-pro-just-doing-his-job, for most of your program, you're in fact doing quite a number of other things as well. In choosing to spend your time this way, and thereby refusing to spend it in taking a hard, fair look at the disagreement over the consequences of the bombing—the military, political, and diplomatic consequences—you imply that a disagreement doesn't really exist, or that the causes for the disagreement are insubstantial, neither of which is true. In picturing the actuality of bombing as a remote, technological act (a "delivery" of "goods on the shelf"), when to at least fifty per cent of the people involved—namely, the deliverees—it is a near-mythic, deeply human experience, you make it that much more difficult, at a critical time, for your human audience to grasp in human terms the human enemy's sometimes complicated responses to what Colonel Hill is doing. And, worse still, you're leading people to *approve* of what he's doing (which is one kind of fact, and which deserves to be examined on its own merits) for the simple, specious reason that he's such a brave, professional, etc., man (which is quite another).

After the bombing mission, the men come back to the base. Here are reporter Bill Stout and one of the pilots chatting about it afterward:

> STOUT: Well, Colonel, what was it like?
> COLONEL: Real good mission. The weather was real good. We got good bombs on the target, and we had an excellent road cut by Otter Four. He got his bombs real well on the road.
> STOUT: Was it a road that you were after?

COLONEL: We had a road and a truck park, and we got our bombs all on the truck park, and Otter Four got his bombs on the truck park plus the road going through it.

STOUT (*concluding sequence*): Their exuberance is genuine —partly pride in the job they've done, partly relief. It's been a good day. No one was hit; they all came back.

Reporter Stout then interviewed the pilots on what they thought of the merits of bombing the North. Said Lieutenant Colonel Gast, an undoubtedly brave man, "I think it's shortening the war." Said Lieutenant Colonel Tanguy, an undoubtedly brave man, "I think we're going to have to apply more pressure." Said Colonel Hill, "I agree with you." Said Colonel Stanfield, "I think the North Vietnamese are as much a part of this war as the Vietcong, and to grant them any sort of sanctuary would tend to encourage them more than discourage them." At no point in these interviews did reporter Stout or CBS detach himself or itself from these views, or attempt to comment on them, or, more important still, attempt to put them in a more useful perspective, alongside equally weighted interviews with other, nonmilitary people. In fact, from the cheery, earnest way Stout put the whole question of the bombing campaign into the laps of the people who were doing the bombing (otherwise known as the "Ask the Man Who Owns One" theory of reporting), you'd think there wasn't anyone else around whose opinion on the subject carried quite so much weight—and maybe he's right. "It is," as Stout explained things for us (referring to the bombing campaign), "in the opinion of Americans, from the President to the pilots flying North, a critically important part of the Vietnam effort."

When, a few moments later, assuming an expression of high seriousness, Stout informed us that we were finally going to take "a look at the effectiveness of that bombing campaign," it seemed only natural that he first asked an admiral. The admiral hedged a bit at the beginning, but, under Stout's careful investigative prodding ("Do you think, Admiral, that the cost of what we're doing is worth the return?"), he informed us, "Yes, I do think that the cost is definitely worth it." Then Stout asked a general, who sat before a map, wearing lots of medals and looking very splendid. The general happened to be the general who is in charge of the Air Force planes that do the bombing, and the essence of his views, which were couched in a longish speech full of military- and business-English phrases about "continuing interdiction activities," was "I think we've had a major effect on the lines of communication." Then he asked General Curtis LeMay. That's right. Then he asked General Curtis LeMay, who was in civilian dress but very grand—actually, you had to look fairly closely to realize that he was in civilian dress—and who contributed to the general clarification as follows: "I would tell the North Vietnamese that we are going to start hitting their expensive and vital targets . . . and start out by eliminating Haiphong. There are many ways of doing it. . . . Then I'd start right out with what industry they have, their power plants . . . the transportation system . . . warning the people to get away. . . . If they want everything in the country destroyed, tell them we're going to destroy everything." Then back to the Navy and another admiral—Admiral Sharp, as it happens, who is in charge of all the Navy in the Pacific—who was a little sulky at first on the subject ("We, as military men, would like to see these restrictions removed, of course, but, as the unified commander, I recognize that in Washington . . ."), but was able to brighten up at least to the extent of advising us, "Well, I think the bombing is shortening the war, and surely if we stop bombing I think that would automatically prolong the war."

By now you probably think that CBS is another branch of the government, or of the military, or of both. Not a bit of it. After all, there are bound to be two sides to the bombing controversy, aren't there? If there *is* a bombing controversy, which CBS seemed just a little reluctant to face up to. Fifty-three minutes after the hour, with five minutes to go (not counting commercials), CBS unleashed the opposition, which consisted of a minute-long extract of testimony by Harrison Salisbury, very tweedy, unmedaled, his face only one among many faces, at a Senate hearing (at which no one on camera seemed to be paying him any attention) on the relative advantages and drawbacks of the bombing ("To my way of thinking, the one cancels out the other . . ."), and a short, prim little interview with the inevitable Senator Fulbright, who remarked that Secretary McNamara had said that the bombing hadn't appreciably cut down on the infiltration of men and supplies—an idea that the CBS audience was now hearing, fleetingly, for the first time that evening—and that "I don't think it's accomplished its purpose."

After a commercial, Stout reappeared briefly, referred in passing to the matter of civilians' having been killed by bombing ("Civilians always are killed in war"), and then attempted to truthify—a word I just made up and now present to CBS for the duration—the previous fifty-eight minutes of propaganda by admitting, without much conviction, that the bombing had only "partly" succeeded. Well, swell. One points out that CBS, along with NBC, is the major source of news and opinion for most of the people in this country. One points out that, at a rough guess, nine million people watched "Vietnam Perspective" that evening. One points out that we elect our government—so we say—on the basis of what we know and are given to know. One points out that one deserves a damned lot better.

One thing you could say for Henry Luce: when you picked up one of his magazines, especially *Time*, you really felt his presence. Think of it—all those pages, pictures, words, long series on snakes and Art and whatever happened to the Holy Roman Empire, and you felt the presence of this one man. And it's not just that he owned all these magazines but that he inhabited them. One looks out across the recent past at some of the forces that have fed, and may still feed, our heads and emotions—the great newspapers and magazines—and what comes to mind (a lot of the time, at any rate) is this larger-than-life presence of individual men. Hearst. Lorimer. Northcliffe. Bennett. Patterson. Luce. All of them different. Each of them, one gathers, at times maddening, brilliant, wrongheaded. But even now, just seeing these dead names on a piece of paper, one gets a feeling—at least a faraway ripple—of the immense gusto they shared. I don't know that gusto, immense or not, gets one a penny closer to truth or beauty, let alone to first-class journalism. But if a man has it, it gives you something of him; you pick up a cold, dead newspaper or magazine and you are dealing with a man, and what these lines are all about is that (it seems) we've surely passed through the heyday of the great newspapers, and possibly will soon have passed through the heyday of the great magazines, and so here we are, all happy boys and girls, in the era of television, electronic circuitry, electric information, the airwaves, the medium is the message ("Fear the Greeks"?), and one gazes out into the gray void mindful that one complained rather a lot about Press Lords in one's time (didn't one?) and there are no Press Lords out there now. Not there. No Lord Northcliffes high above the skating rink in Rockefeller Center. No Luces in Television City. There are others, but they seem different. Perhaps it's a good thing. Who knows? Perhaps it doesn't much matter.

In the meantime, the phosphor dots inside the tube glow brightly, beckoning our eyes. The voices call. All this television pours out at us, all these programs, entertainments, dramas, commercials, journalisms that seem to have been set in motion toward us by ghosts—ghostly computers, ghostly ratings, ghostly chairmen of ghostly boards, who sometimes have the same name and sometimes have different names, who pad silently about on the fringes of all our lives, making speeches at commencement time about the need for the "artistic community" and the "business community" to "get together," and whose thumbprint on the things they send out in our direction (their work? their product?) appears to have been so faintly pressed as to have vanished by the time they get here. What but a ghost—a ghostly computer, at that—could send out at us (click-click) *The Pruitts of Southampton* one moment, "Mark Twain Tonight!" (click-click) the next, and some 1937 Beulah Bondi movie (click-click-click) right afterward? Doubtless there are sound business reasons for all this. One damned well *knows*, in fact (one is a little naïve, but one struggles to keep up), that there are sound business reasons for all this. Just the same, Mark Twain is there before us on the screen. One can make contact with Mark Twain —at least a sort of distant contact. But who put him there? Producers, directors, yes. But who put them there, put the whole thing there? Who came in that morning at a quarter past five, turned on the great master switch, kicked the generator just a little to get it going, and announced to four hundred and sixty million homes, "All right, you poor benighted heathen, these are some of the things *I* like, or care about, am interested in, or . . ." I guess not. (Plant, equipment, stockholders, earnings per share—too big, too big.) "Mark Twain Tonight!" was good, though. Not quite as vibrant as it was onstage, but so what? A number of things on TV are good. Oh, I know one's intellectual-stockbroker friends are always saying, "TV? Yeah? Has there been anything worth seeing since the Army-McCarthy hearings?" (One's intellectual-stockbroker friends spend *their* evenings drinking Japanese beer and reading aloud the gutsy passages in *Ramparts* to their wives.) But TV comes up with some pretty fine stuff—at least here and there. Lately, for instance, Laurence Olivier and Michael Redgrave in *Uncle Vanya*. Or Theodore H. White's excellent ninety-minute Illustrated History of China from then to now. Or those three first-rate documentaries that Ted Yates did on Southeast Asia for NBC. Or a lot of the ABC sports coverage. Or CBS's documentary on homosexuality. Or the new *NBC Experiment in Television*. This last is a good program—a series of one-hour shows that NBC has stuck in at four o'clock on Sunday afternoon, which isn't exactly prime time but is a good deal better than eleven o'clock Sunday morning, which is when CBS pridefully presents *its* most intelligent regular show, *Camera Three*. The first of the "experiments" was an original teleplay called "Losers Weepers," by one Harry Dolan, a member of Budd Schulberg's writers' workshop in Watts, which was a very simple, strong, from-the-inside look at the frustrations and impotence of a Negro family's life in an urban ghetto. I know that sounds mighty gray and documentarish when you put it down on paper that way, but the play was very good. Very moving. Very straight. Full of life. And it showed some things, in passing, about the oppressive, destructive possibilities of the Negro slum matriarchy that I haven't seen handled—at any rate, not so forthrightly and effectively—this side of the Moynihan Report. The two other "experiments" I saw weren't as strong as Harry Dolan's play; one was built around a selection of Lawrence Ferlinghetti poems, which were read, sung, danced to, etc., by some University of Southern California theater students, and the other was a television adaptation of an Off Broadway play called *Good Day*—but both were solid and interesting and had some ideas stashed away in there. The Ferlinghetti actually seemed a bit old-timey in hippy '67 ("I am waiting for Ole Man River to just stop rolling along past the country club . . ."), but it was a USC student's idea to do it, so who knows? Maybe the hippyness gap isn't so wide after all. Anyway, the thing that NBC has going for it so far in its *Experiment* is that it's risking being just a little intelligent, and it's not pushing too hard on the culture button—and although this doesn't exactly indicate that we're on the threshold of another Golden Age of Television (how many Golden Ages of Television can a grateful nation take?), it's nice to have it around while it lasts. By the way, neither the *NBC Experiment* nor the CBS program on homosexuality (which was very good) was able to get a sponsor. I guess the moral to that one is: Don't count on your Age of Business Enlightenment until it's hatched.

MARSHALL MC LUHAN & THE
TECHNOLOGICAL EMBRACE

Marshall McLuhan, who, as just about everybody ought to know by now, is the Canadian agricultural expert and author of *The Romance of Wheat*— No. I am mistaken. Marshall McLuhan, who, as just about everybody ought to know by now, is the Canadian communications whizbang and author of a number of books about media, was on TV the other Sunday afternoon, on one of the new *NBC Experiment in Television* programs, and although McLuhan didn't say anything he hasn't said before (actually, he almost never says anything he hasn't said before, although sometimes he says it differently, and very reassuring is this note of constancy in a world gone mad), it was a mighty hippy, moderny, zim-zam-zap performance all the same, complete with the full Pop ritual of flashy, splashy lighting, electronic sound, fancy cutting, zooms, lots of stop action—in fact, the whole art-director's kit of exciting-visual-effects: go-go girls zazzing away but as if the film ran sidewise (why do they never show go-go girls dancing straight up, the way their mothers would want them to?), and, toward the end, a cute little bit of I-can-be-as-cool-as-you-are-buddy contemporary graphics showing an H-bomb exploding in the shape of an exclamation point as the narrator intoned, "The hydrogen bomb is history's exclamation point." (Once, I remember, McLuhan was pleased to describe a hydrogen-bomb explosion as "information," which goes to show you the sort of pressure the dictionary-revision people have to work under.) It was a snappy show, really. Interesting. But, for all its snap and flash, it was awfully reverential in tone—reverential toward McLuhan and reverential, more especially, toward the whole idea of modernism and technology. I don't know that it was supposed to work out that way. I don't know that McLuhanism is supposed to work out that way. Now and then, McLuhan will waft out to us a sentence ("There is absolutely no inevitability as long as there is a willingness to contemplate what is happening") that gives the impression, or maybe gives *him* the impression, that he is making some sort of evaluative confrontation of the onrush of technology. But a sentence like that doesn't ever appear to be connected to anything else, to any other thought—to any other sentence, even—and when you get right down to cases, it seems to me, the confrontation turns out to be largely illusory, turns out to be instead an almost bland embrace. The NBC program provided a fairly broad embrace, as these things go. "The electric age is having a profound effect on us," intoned the narrator, paraphrasing McLuhan. "We are in a period of fantastic change . . . that is coming about at fantastic speed. Your life is changing dramatically! You are numb to it!" And: "The walls of your rooms are coming down. It is becoming a simple matter to wire and pick out of your homes your private, once solely personal life and record it. Bugging is the new means for gathering information." And: "The family circle has widened, Mom and Dad! The world-pool of information constantly pouring in on your closely knit family is influencing them a lot more than you think." Well, okay. But it all sounds rather too much like the revival preacher, who doesn't really tell you anything about hellfire you didn't know before but who tells it to you more forcefully, with all the right, meliorative vogue words ("fantastic change . . . fantastic speed . . . dramatically . . . numb"), and so makes you feel appropriately important and guilty in the process. In this instance, McLuhan tells us, the fire next time will be technological and lit by an electric circuit, but, having told us that, the preacher seems content to take up the collection and walk out of the church, leaving us with happy, flagellated expressions and a vague sense of having been in touch with an important truth—if we could only remember what it was.

For myself, I'm not so sure about McLuhan's truths. He has this Big Idea, which he pushes, about the effects on Western man of the alphabet, movable type, print—how this visual-mental dependence on little letters all in a row, lines of type, *lines,* one word right after another, has created in man a linear response to the world, has created specialization, compartmentalization, civilization even, mass production, and sundry other evils. It's an interesting idea, all right, and there's a lot of substance to it, but, in the first place, it seems plain foolish to try to rest the full breadth and weight of man's linear sense of order on a single factor even as large as the alphabet and print. Art, after all, imitates life, and life is surely, among other things, intrinsically geometric. Nature is geometric. Trees, tides, plants, planets don't move psychedelically, they move geometrically, and as long as nature exists in any recognizable form the paths of force and tension and, consequently, the order that man intuitively responds to will in the main be linear too. In the second place, it seems worse than plain foolish to be so modernistically airy about man's sense of logic. McLuhan seems to have the idea that man's dependence on print has been constricting and unnatural and has resulted in an imbalance of the senses, and that, with the disappearance of print and the concomitant rise of electronic information-feeding technology, man will once again come into a fuller life of the senses. "Television . . . reintegrates the human senses, thereby making books obsolete" is one of the ways he put it that afternoon. Oh, boy, some life of the senses is my thought for the week, with Brother and Sis upstairs in the kids' communication room watching "Uncle Don's Visit to the Fulton Fish Market," which they can't smell, and Mom and Dad curled up on Acrilan grass in Dad's windowless information center, holding hands and watching a twenty-four-hour weather program. In any case, just because an electronic circuit looks circular, or sounds circular, and just because the hippy teen-agers that McLuhan admires so much (by gosh, fellows, I admire them, too) go floating about absorbing sense impressions and otherwise having a fine old time, doesn't seem to me much of a reason for supposing that we're going to start wanting to do without logic—intuitive, deductive, analytical, linear, call it what you will. After all, logic, brains, intellect, sustained formal thought are how we splendid, wonderful people got to be so splendid and wonderful in the first place, and when a philosopher-king like McLuhan starts saying things like, "The way you react to them [television and computers] is what is important, not what is in them or on them," it's hard to forget that the first thing that boring old Gutenberg printed was the Bible and the first thing television gave us was Uncle Miltie—and, on present evidence, there doesn't seem to be any very pressing basis for tossing out the first because of the second. McLuhan is so cheery and accommodating to the hard bewilderments of technology. I don't know, maybe he worries like hell about them, but he comes on cheery and accommodating. ("There is nothing sterile about television, except in the eye of the beholder.") I guess if you live here and now, you might as well enjoy it. Still, there's an appalling inevitability to this onrush of technology, and since much of it is likely to bring secondary effects that will just as inevitably diminish the possibilities of natural human life, I don't really see that you're doing much of anything when you toss up a line like "The new electronic interdependence re-creates the world in the image of a global village," or "We have begun again to structure the primordial feeling," or "Our new environment compels commitment and participation," and leave it hanging. I don't really see that you're doing much of anything except, possibly, trying to ride with the winners.

It seems a pity, because McLuhan is an original man. A lot of people, I know, are down on him these days, because he's been so much in the public eye (all those cover stories; even *Family Circle* had something on him this month, in which it referred to McLuhan as "the most sought-after dinner guest of our time in New York") and because, they say, he's inconsistent, which he is, and often wrong, which he is, and unfunny, which he certainly is, and even (they say) unoriginal. The thing is, about fifteen years ago, when McLuhan—then, as now, a teacher of undergraduate English courses—began writing about print and communications and media, he didn't claim to be entirely original. Most of these notions about print and type and Western man had been written about for a number of years by a number of people (even though the editors of *Life* may not have been reading them then). What McLuhan did that *was* original was to put them together in a new way and add a sort of twist of his own that gave them relevance—and expansiveness. One got a feeling, in reading those earlier books, of rooms being opened up. But that was a while ago. These days, I get the feeling, especially watching McLuhan on something like the NBC show, which was content to present his views pretty much at face value (as, indeed, most of the mass magazines have been), that, for all his talk about how he's mainly an investigator, a prober, how he's interested in getting people to think about their environment, the principal result of what he writes and speaks—partly because of what he says, partly because of how he says it—has been to diminish discussion. When he touches something ("The technology of the railway created the myth of a green-pasture world of innocence." "Pop Art simply tells you the only art form left for you today is your own natural environment"), he seems to do it in such a way that although there's often substance or interest in his thought, the effect is somehow to close the subject off, to leave it in the end (despite the aphoristic crackle) more dead than alive. At least, it's odd that for all the talk of controversy surrounding his work, most people trying to come to grips with it, in conversation or in print, rarely ever seem to do much more than helplessly paraphrase what he's already said. On the NBC program that afternoon, he appeared sometimes in darkness, sometimes in light, sometimes with a red light flickering on his face. He appeared, disappeared. Sentences hung in the air. Print. Electronics. Technology. The alphabet. Western man. Life. Death. Pop Art. The motorcar. The Beatles. Gutenberg. Civilization. Quite some time ago, Archimedes said, "Give me a lever long enough, and a place to stand, and I will move the world." McLuhan seems to be intent on moving the world, all right, and thinks he has found the lever—"the clash between print and electric technologies." But the lever keeps bending, and it's hard to find a place to stand. At least, he hasn't found one yet, which is perhaps why he keeps skittering all over the place. Maybe, one day, he'll settle for something less.

These are heady times we live in, all right. Goodnight David out on strike. Goodnight Chet not out on strike. Johnny Carson huddling with network biggies. Arnold Zenker filling in for Walter Cronkite. Arnold Zenker? Well, anyway. In the process, people have been discovering Great Truths about television, such as that the evening news as read by Mr. Zenker (who is twenty-eight years old and was an executive of CBS News before being called to higher duty) sounds pretty much the same as the evening news as read by Walter Cronkite (you all know who Walter Cronkite is), the main differences being that Cronkite's voice is lower and that Zenker gives the impression of being about to fall out of his chair at any moment.

This is probably as good a time as any to say that although television news is often maddeningly bad (inept, bland, secondhand, simplistic—a dozen cautions rolled into one), it can at times be very good indeed, as was a sixty-minute report called "Morley Safer's Vietnam," which CBS News presented last week. Safer's hour struck me, quite simply, as one of the best pieces of journalism to come out of the Vietnam war in any medium, and a large measure of its success seemed to be due to the fact that Safer (who has been a CBS correspondent in Vietnam for the past few years) was permitted to put the film together in his own way, with his own explicit point of view, with his own apparently strong sense of irony (you certainly don't see much of that on network news), and to be as personal as he wanted to be. The key word is "personal." There just hasn't been much personal reporting out of Vietnam by the networks (or the newspapers or the big magazines); it's as if it were all too large and important for one man to hoist aloft with an individual point of view— which is a pity, since although there are plenty of situations in which so-called factual, objective reporting makes sense, gives you something useful, there are a lot of other situations in which no useful facts are given, or in which many of the facts are somehow irrelevant (U.S. FORCES KILL 55 VIETCONG IN RAID), answering little and leaving the important questions (and answers) out there hidden in the fog. What Safer did was to grab off small handfuls of Vietnam—the people, the soldiers, the countryside, the dead, the living—and say, "This is who *I* am, this is how it looks and feels to *me*," and the result was as moving and as tough and as sensitive and as deeply felt a commentary on the war as I've run into.

It's nearly impossible, I know, to describe something like Safer's program in print with any success, especially since so much of this particular film's impact was in the sound of the dialogue and in the editing and cutting. For example, there was a sequence beginning with General Westmoreland visiting some troops in the field—the General, tall, strange, remote, looking down upon some young kid standing at attention out there in a Vietnamese clearing, his young face half hidden by a helmet liner, and asking him the kind of questions that, in other times and places, are supposed to connect people but that in this time and place seem only to confirm an unbelievable, nonhuman apartness:

WESTMORELAND: How's your morale?
GI: Pretty good, sir.
WESTMORELAND: How's your food?
GI: Real good, sir.
WESTMORELAND: Son, what state are you from?
GI: Texas, sir.
WESTMORELAND: What part?
GI: Southwest. Shullerville. . .

> WESTMORELAND: How old are you, son?
> GI: Twenty years old, sir.
> WESTMORELAND: Twenty years. Where did you get your basic training?
> GI: Fort Polk, Louisiana, sir.

It was absolutely dreamlike, and could have been out of an old movie. (Has there ever been a general since Alexander the Great who didn't stand sternly before his young soldiers, his own eyes staring through their heads and out beyond to India or Hanoi, and ask them, in flat, abstracted tones, where they took their basic training?) Safer then cut to another GI, a nice-looking young kid standing silhouetted against a line of trees and speaking in an easy-going, modest voice:

> GI: I don't like my job.
> SAFER: How's that?
> GI: I'd rather be back home.
> SAFER: What don't you like about it?
> GI: Just—I don't like riding the people's gardens down. And just, I'd rather be back home.

Then back to Westmoreland, interviewing an officer whose company has just been under fire:

> WESTMORELAND: Was he killed?
> OFFICER: Yes, sir, he was literally blown apart.

Then back to Safer, talking to another GI:

> SAFER: How about the brass?
> GI: They're not bad over here. . . . They don't worry you.
> SAFER: Just that Army life doesn't agree with you?
> GI: No, I'd rather be a civilian. I'm a civilian at heart.

Then a final glimpse of Westmoreland, giving a speech to the men he's been visiting:

> It's a matter of great pride to me to see the high morale that has obtained with the troops—well, for the last year and a half, when we've had a substantial number of troops here. I attribute this to many things. First, they believe that they are

performing an important mission. They take pride in doing a good job. They find this a very exciting experience. The food is good. The mail service is excellent, although from time to time there are delays—but these are exceptional.

I guess it's fair to say that Morley Safer isn't exactly happy about the Vietnam war, and since I'm not, either (as who is?), I may be guilty of admiring my own prejudices in what he showed us. But what I like to think I admire a whole lot more is his ability (and, for that matter, CBS's willingness) to risk an explicitly personal statement, and to bring a strong sense of irony to bear upon the war—although I can't see how it's really possible anywhere, any time, to report a war without irony. There was a whole lot of plain feeling, too, for the rigors of combat, for the strange languid rhythms of Army life, the softball playing, the waiting, the sleeping, the waiting, the writing letters home (only now they record them on tape), and especially for the particular time and place, our Army *there* and what *there* is—the people, the countryside, Saigon, the tanks, the peasants, the tanks *and* peasants. And a lot of toughness. I'm thinking, for example, of a scene outside an Army hospital in which a bunch of wounded men were watching a girl—as it happened, Nancy Sinatra—a real miniskirted babe in a Hollywood cowboy outfit and blue suède boots, prancing about on the grass and belting out a rock number, "These Boots Are Made for Walking," and, of course (or not of course), dozens of the men watching her, from beds or from wheelchairs, had bandages around their legs, or no legs, or no feet. This is one of the more familiar ironies of war (I guess), but it was damned real and brutal, with the camera cutting back and forth between Nancy Sinatra, in her blue boots, and all those wounded men, who were obviously enjoying themselves—taking pictures of Nancy Sinatra with their cameras. Nancy Sinatra looked like such a doll. The sun was shining. The band was loud. The song was great.

There were other strong moments. A scene of Madame Ky, along with other highborn or at least high-placed Vietnamese ladies and remnants of the French colony (all beautifully gussied up in 1938 Deauville dresses), attending the annual garden show in Saigon. A scene in which a burly Negro soldier was washing the head of a little Vietnamese kid and muttering gruffly about the bad "hygiene habits" of the South Vietnamese. A remarkable dialogue in a service club, where Safer was interviewing the crew of an attack helicopter recently returned from a mission, the men smiling, relaxed, milling around with their beer cans—all nice boys. Safer asked them, "How do you feel when you make a kill like that?"

> PILOT: I feel sort of detached from the whole thing. It's not personal. . . .
> CAPTAIN: I feel real good when we do it. It's kind of a feeling of accomplishment. It's the only way you're going to win, I guess, is to kill 'em.
> THIRD PILOT: I just feel like it's just another target. You know, like in the States you shot at dummies, over here you shoot at Vietnamese. Vietnamese Cong.
> ANOTHER PILOT'S VOICE (*interrupting*): Cong. You shoot at Cong. You don't shoot at Vietnamese.
> THIRD PILOT (*laughing*): All right. You shoot at Cong. Anyway, when you come out on the run and then you see them, and they come into your sights, it's just like a wooden dummy or something there, you just thumb off a couple pair of rockets. Like they weren't people at all.

Or when Safer was interviewing a young soldier, one of those fair-haired, blue-eyed soldiers with seemingly untouched farmboy faces, and was asking him what he felt about the war. The boy started out with what one imagines is the usual sort of mechanical response—"I'd be lying if I said I was glad to be here, but since I am here I'm glad to be doing what I'm doing"—and then, in one of those sudden moments when everything comes alive in a gesture, a look in the eye, he glanced around him, his face for one instant full of surprised affection. "The country's so *beautiful*, fertile, and everything . . ." he said.

It was an excellent film. The cameraman who shot much of it, by the way, was Ha Thuc Can, a Vietnamese.

THE BODILESS TACKLE,
THE SECOND-HAND THUD

Jack Whitaker, the gray eagle of CBS sportscasting, jaunty as a Hudson riverboat gambler in his Balliol Old Boy's blazer, held himself gracefully upright in the empty press box of Baltimore's Memorial Stadium the other Sunday, the camera alternating fondly between Whitaker, the near-empty stands around him, and the spectacle of a dozen or so soccer players (all those shorts and knobby knees—nothing totalitarian about *that* uniform) milling about on the baseball field below, and observed that we were shortly to become witnesses to history. He may have said hostages, but I think it was witnesses. The history, in any case, referred to the approaching début in this country of the National Professional Soccer League, a hastily assembled federation of ten teams (many of which are owned by the owners of baseball teams) and the only sports organization I know of that seems to have been put together expressly for the purpose of making a potful of money out of television—the baseball (now soccer) owners expecting to make their potful by television contracts and by having a few people come out to the parks on non-ballplaying days, and the TV people expecting to make theirs by buying rights to televise soccer games on the cheap, promoting the game into a big TV attraction, and then selling the commercial spots at a profit. Who is to knock People's Capitalism these days? The only drawbacks to this glorious plan, or plot, seem to be that there may not be an awful lot of people in this country right now who think they want to watch soccer, and that since the International Soccer Federation has refused its sanction to the CBS-sponsored league, with the result that only young unknowns or old-timers (the word usually favored is "veterans") are willing to play in it, the soccer played isn't likely to be especially brilliant. But who knows? Soccer is a good sport—in fact, as knowledgeable people are forever eager enough to remind one, it is the most popular sport in the world this side of South African Frog Rolling (perhaps that side of South African Frog Rolling)—being fast-moving, fluid, and televisable in a way that baseball, for example, isn't, and maybe eventually it will catch on here. Televisable seems to be the key word. Baseball still has a big TV audience, all right, and a good team still draws people out to the ball park, but the audience seems to be mostly a kind of holdover audience—baseball doesn't *pull* people (the way football now does), because the game just doesn't come across really well on television. Television distills baseball down to moments of action, but in baseball the heart of the game isn't so much in the isolated instances of action (the hit, the catch, the put-out) as in the number of moves that may be taking place at a given time: the runner leading off base, the pitcher in his windup; the ball hit, fielded, thrown; the flight of the ball and the flight of the runner, and the measurement of both. Much of what baseball is about is centered on this awareness of measurement, and television usually can't cover it—can't look in many directions at once, can't really see the game as well as someone in the stands can see it. The other thing that baseball is about, of course, is the feel of being out there at a ball game, and although it's easy to sound like a retread Lake Poet burbling on about bleachers and hot dogs and dust blowing in across the infield and the sharp, sweet crackle of Dolph Camilli's windbreaker, the fact is that these things are real, this appeal to the senses is real (as real, certainly, as the rhythms of the premotorized American summer that gave shape to it)—and not only is it real but it provides a substance to the game that, so to speak, fills out all the intervals of inaction, and gives the intervals meaning. Football appeals to the senses, too, but less than baseball. (The action distilled through the camera eye in a football game is a much larger natural part of the game than it is in a baseball game.) What seems to account for football's immense rise in popularity in recent years isn't so much this fact of its being an action sport (although that has a lot to do with it) as this simpler, or at least more technical, fact of the television viewer's finding the game much more intelligible on his set than from the stands; by this I mean that the key to understanding, and therefore liking, football is in the play—what goes on after the ball is snapped—and that now, with imaginative camera positions and stop-action, you can follow the moves in a way that you simply can't from Row Q on the twenty-yard line, or even the fifty-yard line.

There's no doubt, really, that television has to some degree affected just about every sport of consequence that is being played in this country. In fact, the only sports I can think of that it hasn't affected are the ones, such as yachting and bridge, that are virtually TV-proof. In a relatively short time, it has turned minor sports into major sports—golf, say, and, for heaven's sake, bowling. It's true that the present mass popularity of golf derives in good measure from the natural consequences of "the new leisure" and "disposable income"—from the whole trend toward the proletarianizing of sport. But it's just as true that this popularity was polarized and accelerated by television, with its showering of prize money into the game, its dramatization of the money glamour as well as of the actual drama (all those Arnold Palmer clutch finishes a couple of years ago), and also—you notice this especially on color TV—of the real beauty of some of the great courses, such as Pebble Beach and Augusta. In the same relatively short time, it has practically destroyed other sports, such as boxing, which doesn't seem to have recovered at all from TV's greedy insistence, in its early days, on presenting three or four big fights a week, with the predictable, and predicted, result that the fights ran out of fighters, and so new fighters were rushed up from the club level to the big time, where they had no business being (I'm reminded of an amiable left-handed welterweight from Michigan State who bumbled along for a while until one night he was more or less literally chopped to pieces by Kid Gavilan—a lousy business), and so gradually the club fights disappeared (people could watch supposedly big-league stuff on TV, so why should they go to a club fight?), and finally there was no place for boxers to develop. And TV has placed baseball, the National Pastime, in a precarious position, forcing it into an ever closer alliance with the entertainment business (Judge Hofheinz's Astrodome in Houston seems a long, long journey from Commerce, Oklahoma) and requiring the all-too-willing owners to constantly alter the structure of the sport by such essentially TV-pleasing gestures as the introduction of peppier, more hittable baseballs, the lengthening of schedules (from 154 games to 162), and the expansion of the leagues (from eight teams apiece to ten)—as if baseball, like any good sport, didn't depend on a carefully evolved, carefully balanced arrangement of internal rules, tensions, dynamics that simply can't be fiddled around with like a boxful of building blocks if the game is to not so much "stay alive" as continue to have meaning to itself. In 1911, for example, Home Run Baker set the year's record for home runs with nine. In 1927, Ruth hit sixty, with a peppier ball. Yet the remarkable thing about Ruth's feat wasn't merely the number but the fact that in those days there were mighty few players who could just plain hit the ball so far. Nowadays, since people like to see home runs, and since, as a result, the ball has become still lighter and faster, there are mighty few shortstops so thin-wristed that they can't, and don't, hit a handful of homers each season. So, although it's true that sports should and do evolve, like anything else, it's also true that the evolution of most American sports is now being effected, for the most part, heedlessly and meretriciously from the outside—from television—and that a sport like baseball, which, whether one is bored by it or not, has such a strong, deep connection with many of the fundamental rhythms of American life, is gradually being gimmicked into becoming something quite different, a sort of neo-baseball, whose connections are largely with show business. In a way, of course, for all the increase these days in the numbers of people watching sports, for all the increase in the numbers of people supposedly engaging in sports, it's hard to see, really, how even the concept of sport is going to survive into this eerie and unphysical era of technology and technocracy. Right now, we stay at home and watch Notre Dame play Michigan State and still manage to inform the disconnected photographic image of the game (itself an image) with an animating nostalgia—a nostalgia that seems to go deeper than the more conscious "Wouldn't it be nice if life were still so simple and beautiful that one could care half a damn for Notre Dame and Rockne and the Gipper?" It's a nostalgia, probably, for a time when physical conflict between teams, players, athletes, men, meant more, because the physical quality of life meant more. In football, the brute, uncomplicated nineteenth-century flying wedge (those masses of mustached, open-countenanced Protestant boys mashing into each other) gave way to individual blocking; then came the introduction of the detached, more cerebral and technical forward pass; and now the game is so solidly given over to passing that a line-plunging runner like Jim Taylor seems almost an anachronism. Life evolves, sport evolves, each becoming more technical, drawing further away from nature; and, in the case of sport, which drew its original meaning from natural sources, the disconnection seems to be abetted by an audience that now observes sport largely through a machine that filters out the senses, that somehow makes all baseballs travel at the same speed, that silences, and so renders nearly meaningless, the thud of hockey players against the boards, and that places us finally in the position of watching, with a peculiarly modern sort of bland, detached excitement, the leaps and strain and prowess of modern athletes as if from the other side of a pane of glass. Athletes evolve too. Babe Ruth, who, in answer to a question from a radio interviewer about the speed of Walter Johnson's fast ball, slammed his fist into his leather windbreaker, then blurted, "Jesus Christ, I bust the goddam cigars," gives way to Maury Wills, articulate, grammatical, natty (not too natty), talking smoothly in a post-game interview about his off-season business career. At any rate, where once people went, almost instinctively, to sporting events (perhaps in the same sort of way that other peoples once went to the drama) because both the facts and the sensory appeal of these conflicts corresponded to their own view of the world, now, it seems, they go to them, or watch them on TV, in part because of "excitement" but mostly, as a guess, out of memory, as if looking at a Colts-Packers game on TV, with all its stylized confrontations, with its lack of smells and touch and heat and cold, with its lack of any sense of what a forty-two-yard pass feels like to throw or catch, with its lack of any sense, really (except for the disconnected clack of shoulder pads), of bodies touching one another—as if even this distilled, unsensual experience could somehow take one back, back to a time when life was more densely centered on human bodies and on nature, and when men acted out things that were important to them, rushing at each other across open fields and meadows, rowing on rivers, and skating upon frozen lakes.

Oh, yes. The soccer game between Atlanta and Baltimore. It was pretty ragged—I think that's the word—but it wasn't too bad. A large player from Trinidad called Guy St. Vil scored the only goal of the game (for Baltimore) on the only good pass. The Atlanta goalie was Sven Lindberg, presumably also new to the South.

THE TELLY

London

The thing about English television is that it's really so very, very *English*—which isn't (he said hopefully) such a simple-minded statement as all that when you consider that French television, say, which is run by the government and is the most boring thing in Europe this side of Bulgarian religious drama, isn't particularly French, and that even American television, which is indeed owned not by the government but by the simple stockholders of the farms and prairies (laughter), for the most part succeeds in reflecting back to us a slick and greedy and mentally undemanding world that's surely just a fraction of what actually exists. English television seems somehow to be different from most other television—certainly in its ability to take the country fairly much the way it is and then play it back straight. To be sure, the country is fairly straight to start with, so things often get rather quiet on the telly as a result. This morning, for example, which is Sunday, at around noon (and I mean *around* noon—most programs here begin at something like 12:08, which is known elsewhere as the Oriental sense of time) we had a nice half-hour show called "Forming Metals" ("After each operation, the scale is blown away from the die and the lubricant is applied") on the BBC, and on the Independent channel a pleasant program called "First Steps in Physics," which sounded pretty much ("Conduction occurs mainly in solids") the way ("Describe the vacuum flask") you'd think it would sound. One could even go so far as to say that things are quiet on the telly rather a lot of the time, to the point that sometimes, for whole stretches of the day, it doesn't seem to be broadcasting at all. Last week, for instance, on a random day, the BBC kicked off smartly at 9:38 a.m. with a broadcast for schools and colleges, stopped for twenty-five minutes, then went into "Watch with Mother" at 10:45, then disappeared promptly at eleven, to be replaced by a test pattern and peculiar "light music" until 1:23, at which time there was suddenly eight minutes of news; then it faded out again until 4:40, at which moment the afternoon children's programs began (including *Top Cat*, who is known hereabouts as *The Boss Cat*), and then prime-time programs, and then off-the-air for the night with a fine "God Save the Queen" at 11:45. Actually, 11:48.

This is probably as good a place as any to explain that right now there are what one could describe as two and a half channels being used for TV broadcasting in England. There's BBC, now known as BBC-1. There is also the twelve-year-old Independent television channel, otherwise known as the ITV, which is controlled by the Independent Television Authority, and is, like the BBC, a public corporation, but one that appoints private producing companies such as Granada and Rediffusion to produce shows, rather than producing them itself. The private companies are allowed to include commercials. And for the last couple of years there's been BBC-2, which is UHF, which still isn't received into too many homes, and which broadcasts for only four or five hours a day but then usually presents high-quality special stuff. It was BBC-2, for example, that, a few evenings ago when I looked in, was carrying *La Traviata* live from Covent Garden—a three-hour performance that was excellent. The relationship of the ITV to the BBC seems fairly simple. The ITV is commercial, was set up because people started grumping about the increasingly Establishment tone of the BBC (all those coronation-voice announcers, like the late Richard Dimbleby), and attracts about half the audience. What is "commercial" in London, though, isn't yet the sort of thing that an American network manager would probably look on too fondly as a model of unbridled free enterprise. The ITV has ads, all right, but it runs them only between programs, or, occasionally, at "natural breaks" during long programs—after *Batman*, for instance, a current ITV favorite, you get about seven or eight quick spot commercials jammed into a space of two minutes, and you get no commercials at all during the program. Before *Batman*, by the way, in one of those endearing, slightly sticky English touches, a voice comes on to admonish the Youth of Britain: "Please remember that Batman possesses all sorts of special skills and equipment that enable him to perform his various tricks. Do not try to be Batman." Ah, well. The ITV also limits itself in the number of imported programs it will show to fourteen per cent of its schedule, as does the BBC, although right now neither channel seems to be showing much over ten per cent.

As for the BBC—well, the BBC is a story unto itself. The BBC has been broadcasting television for a long time now—since 1936, in fact. (John L. Baird, who was the first man to produce television pictures, was British.) It has indeed been guilty for much of its TV history of sounding excessively pompous and like the Voice of Government, and clearly one of the best things that ever happened to it was the advent of the ITV, which made it get on the stick and think about becoming competitive, think about using its immense resources of talent. The crucial thing to remember about the BBC, though, is that it isn't government-owned and is certainly not government-run. The rest of the world's television seems to be divided pretty much between straight government operations, such as in France and East Germany, and straight commercial operations, such as in the United States and, to some degree, in Japan. The BBC exists on its own—a public corporation like no other public corporation, a sort of cross between the TVA and the Federal Reserve Board but without the political dependency of the TVA and without the political vulnerability of the Fed. The BBC itself exists, legally and politically, as a completely independent institution, deriving its moneys, which are considerable, from the annual licensing of television sets (£5 per set)—somebody once called the BBC the only living, breathing example of pay TV—and deriving its talent, which is now also considerable, from the fact that the dozens of repertory companies all over England still turn out a greater quantity of soundly trained theater people than anywhere else one can think of, and that the BBC itself has gained such a reputation for letting creative young cameramen, directors, and writers have their heads that young men here who want to do things in the communications world instinctively turn to it. To be sure, it's not always quite that rosy. The BBC still squashes things from time to time. It let Peter Watkins do the film *The War Game* and then wouldn't show it; however, as a BBC man recently said, "Since the top people don't necessarily understand what they're going to get, they sometimes have to step in at the last moment. But at least young men with ideas here usually get to do the thing in the first place." And, also to be sure, there are not that many other creative communications places for people to work in here. Still, the BBC has somehow managed to avoid the usual bureaucratic hangups, to keep the Director-General at Broadcasting House in central London and the producing staff in Shepherd's Bush, several miles way, and at other locations outside of London, with the result that in Shepherd's Bush now, the aseptic, neo-Bauhaus corridors seem full of young men with great mops of scruffy hair and dark green shirts and corduroy trousers who are twenty-six years old and directing, writing, and producing major programs—young men, for example, like John Speight or Tony Palmer or Peter Watkins or the ubiquitous Jonathan Miller, all of whom intelligent people in London talk about and regard and mix with in a way that you certainly don't see taking place in New York between the *New York Review of Books* crowd and the *CBS Playhouse* people.

Speaking of John Speight, who's one of the best of the current young BBC writers, I saw reruns of some of the programs in a comedy series called *Till Death Us Do Part* that he'd done earlier in the year—about this marvelously horrid Typical British Family: Father, who is an unabashed jingo, constantly sounding off about wogs and lascars and the glories of the monarchy; Mum, who's an old fool; and the son and daughter, who go about in seedy Mod clothing and spend a lot of their time arguing with their parents on vaguely liberal subjects (the son wants to turn England into a republic) that they don't know much about and aren't really interested in anyway. One installment I especially remember, which had been shown to twenty million people on Boxing Day (the day after Christmas), showed the family seated around the table at the traditional Christmas dinner, having a filthy time, and arguing with each other periodically on such subjects as the Queen's class problems with Harold Wilson ("You don't suppose someone like *'er* would have anything to say to somebody like *'im*. Vulgar is what I mean. . . . Of course, you don't have to be very bright to be Prime Minister these days"), Christianity ("God made everybody Christian at the beginning. I mean, everybody was Christian for years and years. Then Jesus Christ came down, and those *other people* killed 'im"), and the delicate nuances of the British race issue ("In the old days," says Father angrily, "when them coons came over here, people in charge of things gave them instructions on what to do. They were instructed to take themselves back home. Oh, I tell you, Old Winnie would have told those lascars where to get off. Now look at Suez"). This probably sounds rather aimless and nasty in print, and out of context, but the thing is, of course—it *is* nasty. It isn't Dick Van Dyke, but it's very funny (closer, really, to W. C. Fields' view of family life than anything I've seen in either country for quite some time)—very strong, askew, and full of that free-floating, intelligent British gift for bad-taste humor that may yet keep the Goths away from the door.

Obviously, not everything on English TV hits quite as high as *Till Death Us Do Part* and live *La Traviata* broadcasts, but even the more routinely presented dramas seem of good quality. On a single evening last week there were two originals—one a very vivid, gripping, sensitive piece about the man who assassinated Trotsky, which was full of interesting documentary-style techniques but was mostly full of good writing and good acting, and the other, part of a series of originals called *The Wednesday Play*, about three different couples who are getting ready to go to a symbolic party, which had the usual problems that plays about couples getting ready to go to symbolic parties seem to have, except that it was alive. It wasn't a great, or even a particularly good, play, but it was alive. One of the couples was Negro;

another was homosexual. (The Negro couple at one point did a wonderfully savage, funny minstrel-show parody.) You had the feeling—so rare on network TV, with its warmed-over classics; so rare on NET, with its undercooked Off-Broadway—that the world one lives in was, to at least some degree, talking back.

In some ways it's probably hard for Americans, who seem to like things to be more consistent, to understand how a nation can happily exist with one segment of the population bobbing and curtsying and falling all over its feet in order to say "thenkew" before you've even asked for something, and another, admittedly smaller, segment of the population wheeling about in leathery Bentleys with beautiful girls, dropping fifteen hundred quid at Crockford's, and quite prepared to walk right through you unless they know you rather well—and what would one be doing there anyway, with a seventeen-year-old towheaded duke standing pleasantly on one's shoes, unless one was indeed, ah, *known?* British television doesn't do too much business on the far extremes of this frontier, but it occupies most of the wide spaces in between. It connects with the Mum-and-Dad world in programs like *Coronation Street*, which has been an ITV mainstay for several years—a never-ending, rather ughgy series about a half-dozen typical smiling-but-miserable families who live on Coronation Street in a Midland town—and which, if you ask me, could stand a bit more sex and violence. And, of course, it does the same in sports, which both channels, especially the BBC, broadcast a great deal of. Last Saturday afternoon, for instance, huge quantities of soccer, rugger, cricket, horseracing, and swimming came over the BBC's *Grandstand*—generally very well presented, too, with none of this siss-boom-bah announcer business of trying to make every left-field double into an individual Greek drama. And, although the intelligent middle-class people (or whatever it is that all those people who aren't towheaded dukes are) don't exactly go rushing about the streets exclaiming over *their* favorite programs, the fact is (or seems to be) that the serious things—the drama, the news, the public-affairs shows (which usually take the form of "magazines," such as Monday night's *Panorama*)—are all generally done with an intelligence and a consistency and a sort of humorous coolness that make them seem attractive and worthwhile to watch and listen to. Just by chance the other day I came upon a BBC program about Expo 67 (in part coming in live from Montreal), which isn't normally the sort of thing that causes the heart to leap, and on the screen were all those fancy buildings in the background, which is what one expects, but in the foreground was this fellow from the BBC, in a floppy old sweater and no tie, talking to us very easily and humorously about all this stuff in Montreal. It was lovely. He wandered about a bit and showed us things (not too many), and even managed to get in a few casually phrased but quite tough swipes at the fair for presenting a largely unreal, euphemistic view of the world, which may or may not be the case but probably is, and you could see he really meant it. English expertise with humor, however, still seems to have its limits. Right now, for instance, one of the most popular entertainment shows in England is *The Frost Report*, a weekly satire-and-interview show presided over by David Frost, a *That Was the Week That Was* alumnus who seems to have become, as a result, the most popular TV personality in England. A few days ago, to give you an idea, one of Frost's earlier programs won something called a Golden Rose at a TV festival in Montreux, Switzerland, and the papers here had him all over the headlines. I mean, the *headlines*. The English, you have to remember, are very realistic, worldly-wise Old Europeans, who don't ever go in for that impulsive, lovable, but brainless stuff that some other nations I might mention get caught at every so often. (The day before the Frost feat, as I remember, the evening headlines were all about the price of detergents being reduced, so I guess there's always the possibility that they really *are* realistic, worldly-wise Old Europeans but have just been having a lot of headline trouble lately.) Anyway, I watched *The Frost Report*, this one being on the general theme of advertising, and although you'd have to be a pretty rotten, mean critic not to say that it had its moments ("*The Frost Report* . . . has . . . its moments!"), most of the moments didn't seem too many cuts above the *Yale Record*, which is to say that Frost comes on and makes some comment about, for example, encyclopedia salesmen, and then there's a little skit about an encyclopedia salesman, which involves a lot of books dropping to the floor at one point, and then you go on to something else. The encyclopedia joke was fairly funny as a standup routine (and who's to sneeze at standup routines?), but it simply took attitudes that everybody already knew by heart and then more or less drew a funny picture about them. What Frost really seems to have going for him is a nearly classless voice and an ability to give an abrasive, satiric edge to it, regardless, it often seems, of what he's talking about. Speaking of advertising, though, or rather of its absence, that's the one thing that all the television people here have going for them—even on the ITV, where the sandwiching of ads between programs makes them, at any rate, seem brief and not very noticeable, and on the BBC, of course, where they don't exist at all. So partly because it's England, and partly because it's England and there are no ads, life on the whole seems very cozy around the telly. The telly is very calm. It doesn't raise its voice—or rarely. It can be as boring as anything. It can be sharp and bright and funny. Mostly, it seems fairly intelligent, and, I should imagine, useful to the nation (in that it mirrors the breadth as well as the intellectual capacities of the nation back to it in a unique way), and easy to live with, which last is no small potatoes. Cliff Michelmore, for example, who does the late, late, *late* news for the BBC (meaning around 10:30 p.m.), came on the other evening, a solid, plain-spoken, plain-looking, fiftyish man. "There's been a bit of a row today in Paris," he said, "about an exchange of letters between Jean-Paul Sartre and General de Gaulle. I thought we'd ask our Paris man about it." We did, too—Michelmore and the BBC Paris man talking for about fifteen minutes about de Gaulle and Sartre and their varying views about political power and justice and so forth. It was a fine sort of journalism to listen to, easeful and intelligent—and, after all, something had meant enough to those two men to have caused them to write those letters. And the audience seems to survive it all pretty well.

TELEVISION'S WAR

Summertime now, or very nearly. Kids already gabbling about the last day of school. Women walking down East Eighty-sixth Street in those jouncy cotton dresses. Connecticut suntans. Air-conditioning in Schrafft's. *Daktari* reruns on the television. *Lassie* reruns. *Gilligan's Island* reruns. *Star Trek* reruns. Lots of baseball. (Not much doing on television in the good old, mythic old American summertime.) The other Saturday, just back from a trip, and for some reason conscious more pointlessly than ever of that miserable war, I made a mental note to watch, at five o'clock that afternoon, an NBC program called *Vietnam Weekly Review* for whatever it might have to offer, and went outside (it was a nice day—warm, sunny, full of the first hints of summer's dust and laziness, of all those hammocks one will never swing in), toward Fifth Avenue and the park, past which close to one hundred thousand men, women, and children were marching as part of a "Support Our Boys in Vietnam" parade. Lots of people in the streets. Lots of American Legion posts. Lots of those Catholic high-school bands. A flatbed truck went by full of teamsters, many of them holding aloft placards reading, "It's Your Country! Love It Or Leave It!" The Putnam County John Birch Society went by, singing "America the Beautiful." An American Legionnaire went by in a wheelchair, carrying a placard reading, "Victory over Atheistic Communism." The crowd applauded. Somewhere up toward Ninety-sixth Street a band was playing "The Yellow

Rose of Texas." Children all around me clutched American flags and looked the way children usually do, with or without flags.

I went back home at ten to five, got out a beer, turned on the TV set. There was a baseball game in progress on NBC. (No *Vietnam Review* that week.) Not a bad game, either. Clendenon hit a long ball in the tenth and wrapped it up for Pittsburgh. I forget who was playing Pittsburgh, but you could look it up. From Fifth Avenue, two blocks away (you could hear it through the open window), a band was finishing up "The Marine Corps Hymn," then started "Sister Kate." Sometimes I wonder what it is that the people who run television think about the war. I'm sure they think about it. Everybody thinks about it. I'm sure they care a lot. (At times, I even picture them sitting around in the Communications Club after hours, brows furrowed in meditation, their tumblers of brandy and Perrier water barely sipped at. Finally a voice is raised. "Well, hang it, Fred. I think Tom Hayden speaks for all of us . . .") Perhaps one is unfair. Perhaps not. In any case, there are good men who work for television trying to tell us about the war. For example, the other Monday night, a little after seven, Walter Cronkite peered out at us pleasantly from the TV screen, said, "Today's Vietnam story in a moment," and then there we were, via film that had been taken twenty-six hours earlier, eighteen miles south of the DMZ, watching a Marine scout detail that had been sent out to look for North Vietnamese encampments. The film began routinely, with the CO briefing his patrol leaders (a sequence that always seems to be staged, although it probably isn't), and then we were watching a small group of men on their way up a thickly wooded hill ("They went up to investigate the distant voices," said the on-the-scene correspondent), and heard the sound of faraway small-arms fire, and suddenly men were running here and there in front of the camera, the small-arms fire became louder and more intense, and once again—in our living room, or was it at the Yale Club bar, or lying on the deck of the grand yacht *Fatima* with a Sony portable TV upon our belly?—we were watching, a bit numbly perhaps (we have watched it so often), real men get shot at, real men (our surrogates, in fact) get killed and wounded. At one point in the film, a mortar round fell near the cameraman, and for a couple of seconds the film spun crazily until it (and he) got straightened out again, and then we were looking, through the camera, at a young man—a boy, surely no more than nineteen or twenty—square-jawed, handsome, All-American, poised there on the side of the hill, rifle held in close to him, waiting on the side of the hill for the signal to move up to where the shooting was, and afraid. In the background, you could hear machine guns firing and the voice of the platoon sergeant, a deep-voiced Negro, calling, "Git on up there! Git! Git!" And the boy stayed there for several moments in the camera's eye, his own eyes staring straight ahead, his face so full of youth, fear, bravery, whatever else, until he finally moved up. One thinks of how one's memories of those other wars (wars one didn't fight in) exist for the most part frozen in the still photographs of the great war photographers—Robert Capa's picture of the Spanish Loyalist falling on the Catalonian hillside, Eugene Smith's Marine face down on the beach at Tarawa, Margaret Bourke-White's St. Paul's Cathedral against the blitz, David Duncan's Marines advancing through the Korean mud. Vietnam is different, to be sure. Not quite so "exciting." Not quite so photogenic. But it seems to me that Kurt Volkert, the man who held and worked that camera, who caught the meaning of that face, is one of the best journalists of the war, and one could probably say the same for many of the other cameramen covering Vietnam for the American networks.

Another afternoon not long ago, I watched a routine film clip, this one taken by Vo Huynh, a Vietnamese who works for NBC, about a military engagement in the South: scenes of men moving in to attack, and attacking—scenes, in fact, of men living close to death and killing—with one heart-rending sequence of a young soldier being carried out, his leg apparently smashed, screaming to his comrades, "It hurts! It hurts!" The special qualities of courage, energy, and strange, tough sensitivity that made men like Robert Capa so good at what they did—so good because so useful, so useful because they went in there (Capa's great pictures of the second wave at Omaha Beach were so blurred that you could barely make out the faces) and tried to show us what it was really like—are qualities that don't exist to any lesser degree in men like Kurt Volkert and Vo Huynh. They too seem to be trying to show us what it's like—at least, what the small, small corner allotted to them is like—and Lord knows there are mighty few other people on television who seem to be trying.

Vietnam is often referred to as "television's war," in the sense that this is the first war that has been brought to the people preponderantly by television. People indeed look at television. They really look at it. They look at Dick Van Dyke and become his friend. They look at a new Pontiac in a commercial and go out and buy it. They look at thoughtful Chet Huntley and find him thoughtful, and at witty David Brinkley and find him witty. They look at Vietnam. They look at Vietnam, it seems, as a child kneeling in the corridor, his eye to the keyhole, looks at two grownups arguing in a locked room—the aperture of the keyhole small; the figures shadowy, mostly out of sight; the voices indistinct, isolated threats without meaning; isolated glimpses, part of an elbow, a man's jacket (who is the man?), part of a face, a woman's face. Ah, she is crying. One sees the tears. (The voices continue indistinctly.) One counts the tears. Two tears. Three tears. Two bombing raids. Four seek-and-destroy missions. Six administration pronouncements. Such a fine-looking woman. One searches in vain for the other grownup, but, ah, the keyhole is so small, he is somehow never in the line of sight. Look! There is General Ky. Look! There are some planes returning safely to the *Ticonderoga*. I wonder (sometimes) what it is that the people who run television think about the war, because *they* have given us this keyhole view; we have given them the airwaves, and now, at this critical time, they have given back to us this keyhole view—and I wonder if they truly think that those isolated glimpses of elbow, face, a swirl of dress (who *is* that other person, anyway?) are all we children can really stand to see of what is going on inside that room.

Vo Huynh, admittedly, will show us as much of the larger

truth of a small battle and of a wounded soldier as he is able to, and CBS, as it did some nights ago, will show us a half-hour special interview with Marine Corps General Walt, which is nice of CBS, but there are other things, it seems, that make up the Vietnam war, that intelligent men *know* make up the Vietnam war—factors of doubt, politics, propaganda, truth, untruth, of what we actually do and actually don't do, that aren't in most ways tangible, or certifiably right or wrong, or easily reducible to simple mathematics, but that, even so (and even now), exist as parts of this equation that we're all supposedly trying so hard to solve—and almost none of them get mentioned. It seems almost never to get mentioned, for example, that there's considerable doubt as to the effectiveness of the search-and-destroy missions we watch so frequently on television. (The enemy casualty figures seem to be arbitrarily rigged, and the ground we take isn't anything we usually plan to keep.) It seems almost never to get mentioned, for example, that there's considerable doubt as to the actual efficacy of many of the highly publicized (on TV, as elsewhere) sweeps into territory that, if you read the fine print, you realize the enemy has often already left, and presumably will come back to when we, in turn, have gone. It seems rarely to get mentioned that there has been considerable doubt as to the effectiveness of our bombing, or that an air force that can't always hit the right village certainly can't avoid killing civilians when it bombs power plants in Hanoi. It doesn't seem to get mentioned, for example, that we are using "anti-personnel" weapons such as the Guava and the Pineapple more than the military appears to want to admit, or that any people who drop their tortures from planes flying at five thousand feet are likely to be regarded as no less accomplices than if they had stood in person in some village square and driven little slivers of metal, at high velocity, into the flesh of other human beings. It doesn't seem to get mentioned, for example, that "anti-personnel," "delivering hardware," "pacification mission," and "nation building" are phrases, along with "better dead than Red," that only a people out of touch with the meaning of language could use with any seriousness. It doesn't seem to get mentioned, for example, that when a senior member of the administration states that he sees no reason for thinking we will have to send more troops to Vietnam this year he is probably not telling the truth, and that the fact of his probably not telling the truth is now more important than the fact of the troops. It doesn't seem to get mentioned— Well, enough of that. It is summertime now, or nearly. My kids were squabbling over bathing suits this morning, and who will learn to sail and who to ride. In summertime we cook outdoors a lot, play coronary tennis, drink, watch pretty sunsets out across the water. This summer, I will almost certainly perfect my backhand, write something beautiful (or very nearly), read *Finnegans Wake,* or something like it. This summer —already the streets outside seem quieter, more humane. A car rolls softly over a manhole cover—a small clank. All those quiet streets, all those brave middle-class apartments—and what lies beneath those manhole covers? Wires? Cables? Dying soldiers? Dying children? Sounds of gunfire? Screaming? Madness? My television set plays on, talking to itself—another baseball game, in fact. Juan Marichal is pitching to Ron Hunt. Hunt shifts his stance. Marichal winds up. The count is three and two.

A DAY IN THE LIFE

One Thursday morning recently, very early—about six o'clock—but with the sun already up and the air already sticky and warm, John Laurence, who is twenty-seven years old and a correspondent with CBS News, pulled himself out of bed at the slick but not notably comfortable Marine-built press center at Danang, put on his green combat fatigues, filled up his two canteens with purified water in the kitchen, and together with his cameraman, a twenty-five-year-old named Keith Kay, and his sound man, a thirty-one-year-old Vietnamese named Pham Tan Dan, headed off in the direction of Con Thien, a Marine artillery outpost three-quarters of a mile south of the Demilitarized Zone. Con Thien isn't very far from Danang—about a hundred miles—but it is hard to get to nowadays. Laurence and his crew took one of the big C-130 transports that make regular thirty-minute flights to the Marine base at Dong Ha, then boarded a truck in a convoy that leaves Dong Ha each morning on the westerly route along what's still called Route 9, toward the village of Cam Lo. There were about twelve vehicles in the convoy, mostly trucks, and mostly carrying ammunition, food, water, mail, and some Marines who had been on leave or in hospitals and were being returned to duty at the artillery batteries. Laurence rode in an open truck with a dozen Marines, his sound man, Dan, nearby, and Kay, the cameraman, perched on the cab, half-leaning against a machine gun mounted there. The young Marines read the comics from last Sunday's paper and talked easily among themselves. One asked Laurence what he was doing there, and he said he was going out to do a show about Con Thien.

"When's it going to be on?" the Marine asked.

"With any luck, in two or three days," Laurence said.

A couple of them joked about that. It can take between seven and ten days for letters to go from a soldier in the field in Vietnam to the States, and one man had wanted to write his family and tell them there was going to be a TV show about his base.

"Anyhow, you can't be sure," said Laurence. "You never know what's going to get on."

Another asked him, "What kind of film are you using?"

"Sixteen-millimeter color," said Laurence.

The Marine thought for a moment. "If you're shooting color, you really ought to go down to Khe Sanh, because of the beautiful greens and browns," he said. "You know, they have six different shades of green down there."

After about a forty-minute drive, the convoy stopped at Cam Lo, which was once a village but is now just another Marine artillery battery. The road from Dong Ha to Cam Lo is reasonably safe these days (except at night), but the road from Cam Lo north to Con Thien hasn't been so successfully pacified as yet. There had been two ambushes within the last ten days—some Marines had been killed in the first one—so the convoy waited for two tanks and two Ontos (an Ontos is a track vehicle a little smaller than a tank, mounting a cluster of six 106-millimeter rifles, six 50-caliber spotting rifles, and one 30-caliber machine gun) to come up and join it. During the ride from Dong Ha, Laurence had noticed a seemingly introspective young Marine sitting toward the front of the truck, who had something written on the back of his flak jacket, and while they were stopped he asked him about it. The Marine—Corporal Edward Broderick—said it was a poem he'd written a few months before. Laurence asked him if he would recite it on camera. The corporal nodded. Kay clambered down from the cab of the truck, Dan adjusted his sound equipment, and Laurence held the mike.

"I don't know that I can remember it right off," the corporal said, looking at Laurence's mike.

"Well, try it once on your own," said Laurence.

The corporal took off his flak jacket, read the poem, then put the flak jacket back on again. "Okay," he said.

Kay's camera started whirring. The Marine stared straight ahead and recited. "When youth was a soldier," he began, his voice low and flat, "and I fought across the sea,/We were young and cold hearts, of bloody savagery,/Born of indignation, children of our times,/We were orphans of creation, and dying in our prime." Everyone in the truck was very silent.

Kay was shooting back through Laurence and the corporal to the other trucks in the convoy.

"What made you write that poem?" Laurence asked.

"Well, just the way things are," the corporal said. He then went on to say some things about how it was better anyway to be in the front lines at Con Thien than back at some base camp like Danang.

Laurence asked him what his overriding feeling about the war was right now.

The corporal thought for a moment. "Better to be fighting the Communists here than fighting them back in San Diego," he said.

Two tanks appeared, rumbling down the road from Cam Lo, and Laurence called to Kay that he was going to try to do an "open" (meaning an opening for the film piece) before the convoy got under way.

"We don't have much time," Kay said.

"I'll ad-lib it," Laurence said. He moved to the seat in the truck that was nearest the tailgate. Kay once again took up his station near the cab and started up his camera. Laurence, still holding the mike, stared at the floor for a moment. "The convoy for Con Thien goes once a day, and it does not stay long. It is the only source of supply for the Marine outpost on the Demilitarized Zone; it rides the only road that goes there," he began. "The convoy carries food, water, and ammunition, and returns the few men who have been lucky enough to get away for a few days. . . ."

When the convoy started up again, the Marines seemed to be in a changed mood. Some went back to reading comics, but the road was really too bumpy, and for the most part they just sat in silence and stared out at the muddy, reddish-brown dirt on either side of the road, the dry-looking scrub, the rolling dark green hills extending into the distance. Shortly, one by one, they started inserting ammunition clips in their M-16s and putting them on safe. Laurence nodded at Kay, and Kay's camera began whirring. Twenty minutes farther on, at a place called Charlie Two, near the entrance to a Marine battery, the convoy passed the burned hulk of a light tank, lying abandoned twenty feet off the road. One of the Marines took hold of Laurence's arm and started telling him about the ambush ten days before (he'd been one of its victims), pointing to where it had happened, describing how the tank had been hit, telling him in an intense, informative way what a serious fight it had been. The men had now stopped every other activity and were looking out on either side of the road with peering, impassive faces. The convoy bumped along. The sun grew hotter. For the first time some of the men began to sweat a little.

Around noon the trucks reached Con Thien—the end of the road. The road points directly toward the camp, then stops at the base of a slight hill. The convoy stopped, and there was a good deal of discussion among the drivers as to how far the trucks should go up toward the camp, because of the accuracy of the enemy artillery across the DMZ, and because of the mud, and because many of the trucks were carrying ammunition. "Hell, let's take 'em right up," the driver of Laurence's truck said, and the trucks roared up the hill.

Everybody quickly clambered out. Beyond the hill is a shallow valley, and in the valley sit the gun emplacements, just the barrels of the guns showing, the rest hidden behind sandbags, and everything in view—sandbags, terrain (there are no trees, no vegetation, just sandbags, guns, empty shell cases, and boxes of ammunition)—light brown, the color of dry dirt. Laurence and his crew walked down the hill, each man wearing a pack, and Kay and Dan carrying their equipment besides. Laurence asked someone which was the command bunker (since most of the men were either naked to the waist or wearing olive-colored T-shirts, it was hard to tell rank), and the man pointed to the largest bunker in the camp, built right into the side of the hill. The executive officer came out to greet them—a Marine major in his mid-thirties, who seemed a bit tense.

"Hi," said Laurence. "I'm Jack Laurence of CBS News. We've come up to take pictures of you winning the war up here."

"How long are you planning to stay?" the major asked.

"Oh, just as long as we need to get some action," said Laurence. "A day, a week."

"You really want to spend the night up *here*?" the major said. "We haven't had any press around in about three weeks."

Laurence and his crew threw their packs off outside the bunker and followed the major in. Inside, it was very dark; a few men were sitting silent at tables, with candles for light. Four military-band field radios were squawking. There was a large map standing upright in the center of the bunker, about eight feet high and divided into three panels, like a screen.

"What about something to eat?" Kay whispered to Laurence. "I haven't had anything all morning."

The major walked over. "Come on," he said, "I'll give you a briefing."

Laurence and Kay and Dan stood in front of the big map, and the major pointed out the various places where the battalion's companies were now operating.

A soldier came hurrying in with a message for the major.

"Kilo Company is in contact with snipers," the major said, and showed them where Kilo Company was on the map.

The major finished the briefing at last, and Laurence, Kay, and Dan (whose Vietnamese face had been stared at suspiciously by some of the officers in the bunker) stumbled out into the sun, where the sergeant major came over and handed them each a can of C rations—in this case, something described on the label as "turkey loaf."

A man in a green T-shirt who had a bright red mustache came over and introduced himself as Captain Jansen and began to tell Laurence about how to take cover during an artillery barrage. "Above all, don't follow me when you see me running down the side of the hill," Jansen said. "I like to be off by myself when the shells come in. I have this feeling that the round that has your number on it shouldn't kill anyone else—and I certainly don't want to get someone else's round. Actually, the best thing for *you* to do is watch the other guys. When they start running, hurry after them." Jansen went off to sit on the ground nearby and read *Stars & Stripes*.

Everything seemed relaxed. Laurence took out his pocket compass and fooled around with it. A soldier came up to him and said that Lieutenant Colonel Lee R. Bendel, the battery commander, was still tied up but would be available shortly. Laurence wandered off to take a look around, walking away from the command bunker up toward the top of the hill, and stepping over cast-off shell cases and the ruins of the colonel's shower, which had been destroyed by an incoming round. At the top he stood for a moment trying to figure out from his compass where true north was. From a bunker nearby a voice was saying, "I swear I got the actual word. We're going in four days. Colonel's orders." Other voices chimed in from other bunkers. "Hey, we're getting out. We're getting out of here."

A corporal came up and asked Laurence to come down the hill a bit and see the new infrared radar beam—a large green machine, on the order of a searchlight, that was mounted on a jeep. The corporal explained in a proud manner how the infrared beam worked—you turn it on at night and wear infrared goggles, and then you can see the VC when they move across the ground in the dark. Suddenly, in midsentence, the corporal's head turned toward the north. He quickly got down on his knees and seemed to be looking at the ground. He glanced up at Laurence. "Hell, no sense staying out here," he said. "Let's get in a bunker." Laurence and the corporal started walking quickly, then ran. From somewhere a voice yelled, "Incoming!" There was a large explosion quite far away. Laurence and the corporal tumbled into a bunker where there were about twelve other men. Everyone else seemed very casual.

"I'm Jack Laurence from CBS News," said Laurence.

"Have a beer," said one of the men.

Some of them were talking about the war, and Laurence took out a small tape recorder and turned it on. "What do you think of the enemy?" he asked.

A big Southern corporal leaned forward. "When we first came up here we used to call the enemy Victor Charlie," he said. "But now we call him Charles. Mister Charles."

"Lord Charles," somebody else said, and laughed.

The men talked on—with Laurence recording their words— about their frustrating efforts to get at the enemy artillery. "Our shelling don't seem to have much effect, because those enemy guns keep hitting the camp every day," said one. "Often we get about a hundred rounds a day."

"Why are you crazy enough to come up to Con Thien?" one man asked Laurence.

"You're here," said Laurence. "We might as well tell the people back home how well you're doing."

After about twenty minutes, in which there was no more shelling, the corporal in charge of the infrared radar machine told Laurence it was okay to leave. "I'll show you the observation post," he said. They walked toward it—the sun now very hot, everything hot and dry. A voice again yelled, "Incoming!" and Laurence and the corporal ran forward and tumbled into a small open bunker with a telescopelike object, a field radio, and two young soldiers all lying on the bottom. This turned out to be the observation post. There was another big explosion, also far away. The two soldiers didn't seem to be frightened, but they both had their heads flat to the ground. A voice came over the field radio.

"Do you see where those rounds are coming from?" One of the soldiers raised his head sufficiently to reply to the radio. "No, sir. Don't see a thing," he said, and he grinned at Laurence. "Every time we get incoming, that lieutenant calls on the radio and asks us if we see where it's coming from, and every time we say, 'No, sir, we don't see a thing.' The fact is, those damned guns of theirs are firing from the back slopes in the DMZ, and they're too far away and too well camouflaged for us to do much about them."

After ten minutes or so, when the shelling again seemed to have stopped, Laurence got out of the observation post and ran back to the command bunker to look for Kay and Dan. Colonel Bendel was there. Kay was seated on the floor inside the bunker, reloading his camera, and when he had finished plugging it into the battery pack over his shoulder, Laurence and his crew went outside again, quickly following the colonel, who had muttered something about wanting to get a "better vantage point" from which to see his two companies. The better vantage point turned out to be on the rim of the same hill Laurence had been standing on earlier, only on the far side, in the direction of the road, away from the camp and out of sight of it. It was a lonely-seeming spot, which had obviously not been much used—at least, not by Americans. Near where they were standing, Laurence spotted five small foxholes dug into the side of the hill. The shelling now seemed to have stopped completely. The colonel was standing on a small, jutting piece of ground, peering below him through binoculars. "You can see Kilo Company moving down there," the colonel said. "Look—three fingers to the right of this tree." He pointed. "See them?"

Laurence, who wears glasses, peered below him and, about three-quarters of a mile away, saw a line of Marines walking in the open across a field. Just at that moment, there was a loud, sharp pop, pop, pop-pop-pop, pop, and a few seconds later a string of mortar rounds exploded in a line across the field, in the midst of the Marines. There was a moment of absolute silence.

"Are you sure those are *our* troops?" Laurence asked the colonel incredulously. "Aren't *we* shelling *them*?"

Some of the Marines in the field could now be seen to run forward, and a few seconds later another barrage of shells exploded, this time making a much deeper sound. Laurence heard Kay's camera whirring and turned back to him to ask, "How much of that can we get?"

"Just the smoke," Kay said. "The damned lens isn't long enough."

"Well, get a little of the smoke out there," Laurence said. "Perhaps it can be used."

"Okay," said Kay. "But it's not going to be very clear."

Captain Jansen came up with a field radio on his back and stood beside the colonel. The colonel alternately listened to chatter coming out of the radio and peered down through his binoculars at the again silent field. Laurence dropped on one knee to get out of Kay's picture and extended his mike toward the colonel.

"Every time we move, we take heavy fire," a man's voice said over the radio.

"Okay, it looks like we've got the grid on the one that's getting —that you're getting the incoming from," the colonel replied. "Hold your present positions. I hope you're in holes there as best you can."

Two jets suddenly appeared above the Marines in the field— narrow, pointed F-4Cs, circling at about five thousand feet. Kay aimed his camera toward them. One of the jets went into a dive, came in very low—no more than a couple of hundred feet above the ground—passed over the field, and then climbed again.

"A dud," said Captain Jansen.

The second jet came in and made the same pass, and suddenly the far edge of the field exploded with a black and orange flash, and a bright sheet of fire rushed forward very fast.

"Maybe that will show up," said Kay. "But don't count on it."

The radio was now very active, with several excited voices talking back and forth. "We're in very heavy contact here," one man's voice was saying tensely.

The colonel, speaking calmly, asked the man to tell him which way he was facing and where his platoons were.

"Tell him to make his strafing runs one hundred meters in another direction!" a second voice called.

"We're *still* in very heavy contact!" the first voice called.

The colonel put down his binoculars and held the radio. "Okay, Bill," he said, speaking in a fatherly tone. "Just try to pull your people together and get them linked up to Mike Company. This is still your show."

There was silence for a moment. Then the voice came back: "I think we may have to have help. We might get overrun."

"All right, Bill," the colonel said, still in a fatherly voice. "I'm going to try to bring Mike Company up to you. I'm positioning tanks to fire in your support. But I *have* to have your coordinates —your position."

Just then somebody yelled, "Incoming!" and Laurence, who until that instant had been kneeling on the ground beside the colonel, trying to tape the dialogue, jumped into one of the foxholes, and so did Kay and Dan. Kay's camera was still whirring, although he was holding it to cover his face. A shell exploded somewhere on the other side of the hill. Laurence looked over the edge of the foxhole and saw the colonel and his staff all flattened out on the ground, the radio chattering but none of the Marines talking—just olive-green backs on the ground.

"We've *got* to get some of this," Laurence said to Kay.

Kay raised his head from the foxhole and pointed his camera at the colonel and his staff. At that moment Captain Jansen turned his head and saw Kay, and then immediately the staff jumped to its feet as several shells burst with great thumping noises. The captain organized the staff into separate foxholes. Laurence moved forward into the foxhole now occupied by the colonel and Captain Jansen and motioned to Kay to continue taking pictures. The artillery barrage was coming in steadily, with two or three very loud, ground-shaking explosions at a time. The staff was all crouched low in the foxholes, except for the colonel, who was standing up, with one foot on the edge of the hole, and leaning forward. Laurence huddled low over his microphone and spoke in a soft voice: "You don't spend long in Con Thien before the action starts. Some time ago two companies from the battalion defending this outpost ran into enemy contact, and it has become increasingly heavy. Colonel Bendel is watching the action less than a mile away and moving his troops into position."

"Okay, look," the colonel was saying to an officer who had come up. "Do you see where that smoke is?"

"Yes, sir."

"That far, where the shells landed, is about three hundred meters," the colonel was saying. "Right where that big tree is out there, three hundred to four hundred meters southeast."

The noise from the battlefield now became very intense as the air strikes continued: a loud roaring of jet engines, sounds of gunfire and machine-gun fire, the constant explosions of the shells, and then some strange little buzzing sounds, which, Jansen explained to Laurence, were made by bullets going by very close. The colonel, who was on the radio again, trying to get Mike Company to move around toward Kilo Company, also appeared a little mystified and irritated by the buzzing. "Don't worry about them," said Jansen. "They're almost spent."

In the middle of the shelling a major appeared, running across the hill. "I've got to have those coordinates!" he yelled. "I can't fire if I don't have those coordinates!"

The colonel repeated the request over the radio, and a voice came back apologetically. "I didn't have my map, but I have it now. I'm trying to figure where we are."

The major turned to go back, caught his foot on the wire running between Laurence's mike and Dan's sound box, and sent the mike spinning out of Laurence's hand and across the ground. "Goddam wire!" he said.

The colonel turned. "Look, some of you people just move on back."

"You're all right where you are," Jansen said to Laurence.

Kay, in the meantime, had run back to the command bunker to get some more equipment and was now crouched in his foxhole, trying to change film inside his changing bag—a black cloth affair with two sleeves in which he had inserted his arms. It took about five minutes, and he finished just as a fresh barrage hit, apparently right inside the camp.

More and more bullets were now buzzing by. The colonel continued to stand with one foot on the edge of the foxhole. Jansen was seated on the edge. Laurence got up beside Jansen, and, with Kay's camera on the three of them, again spoke softly into the mike. "That whistling sound you hear is incoming artillery fire," he said. "You may actually be able to see it landing."

Kay somehow overheard him and quickly panned his camera from right to left, and just at that point four artillery rounds burst, with great crashes, inside the camp. The colonel looked around. "Let's make sure we spread out here," he said.

"That one landed about one hundred and fifty yards away," Laurence said into his microphone, and then glanced back and saw that Kay was furiously taking his camera case apart.

"Goddam camera won't work!" Kay yelled to Laurence. In a moment he had it working again.

Two helicopters came into view and landed beside the camp, their engines roaring, the dust blowing up around them. Soldiers appeared from within the camp carrying men on stretchers—men who had been wounded by the artillery bombardment. Kay's camera was rolling on them; then once again he stopped and began to pull his camera apart. This time it wouldn't start up again. Kay was cursing and muttering as he and Dan crouched in their foxhole, pieces of Arriflex littered around them.

"What is it?" Laurence called.

"It's the battery pack," said Dan. "It's out of power."

Kay and Dan continued to fiddle with the camera. More shells landed nearby. Captain Jansen remained seated on the edge of the foxhole. One shell landed very close by, shattering the ground and sending off shock waves. Laurence, with nothing to do and suddenly edgy, tumbled back into the hole. "It's okay," Jansen said to him. "It's not close enough to hurt you, and the next shell won't be in on top."

Kay called to Laurence that the camera was really dead.

"Are you sure?" Laurence asked.

"I'm sure," said Kay.

"If you want to get out of here, you can go back with the convoy," Jansen said.

Laurence considered for a moment. "Okay," he said. "I guess we will."

The three CBS men got their gear together, while the colonel went on directing Mike Company up to a position on Kilo Company's flank. "Now, if you'll just get everyone linked up . . ." the colonel was saying into the radio. Jansen formed Laurence, Kay, and Dan into a line, spaced about ten feet apart, and walked them down the side of the hill toward the road. The colonel looked at them over his shoulder. "That's a real fine squad you got there, Jansen," he said. Jansen, seeming embarrassed, waved at him. Just as they neared the foot of the hill another incoming round came in, and they all dived into a tiny three-foot-deep pit, sprawling on their backs on top of each other—except for Jansen, who sat on the edge, remarking, "I'll know when it's going to hit us." An incredibly loud explosion burst nearby, making the ground shake, and they all looked up, to see that a fire had started in the midst of a stack of wooden crates containing 105-milli-meter ammunition.

A sergeant appeared, running. It was the convoy sergeant, who had just brought the ammunition up. "If that stuff blows, we're dead," he said.

A lieutenant also appeared, on the run. "Get back! Get back!" he yelled. "It's going to blow!"

A number of men rushed out of the nearby bunkers and ran away from the fire. No one had told Laurence what to do, and he stood transfixed beside Jansen, who continued to sit still, watching. A Marine with a small hand-held fire extinguisher appeared briefly, made some dancing motions toward the fire, and then sped off.

A captain appeared a little distance away, yelled, "Everybody in the hole!" and disappeared.

The fire continued to blaze.

"For Chrissake!" the convoy sergeant said. "*Somebody's* got to put it out!"

"Incoming!" a voice yelled, and this time Laurence and Jansen both dived into the tiny hole with the others. When they stuck their heads up again, the convoy sergeant was walking back across the ground toward them, holding an empty five-gallon water can. "Fire's out," he said. He dropped the can on the ground. "If you're all coming with me," he said, "let's get the hell out of here." He pointed to a jeep about fifty yards away and started to run toward it.

Laurence, Dan, and Kay chased after him, their packs bouncing on their backs. The sergeant clambered into the jeep, which was a small one, and the others began to fall in after him.

A voice in the distance yelled, "Incoming!"

"Everybody in?" the sergeant called, starting to pull away as Laurence dived into the back, his legs sticking out behind the tailgate. A couple of shells landed nearby—great crunches. The sergeant had his foot all the way down on the accelerator and was tearing across the terrain—skidding, turning, with all four wheels sometimes leaving the ground as they hit a bump—muttering incessantly, "Don't worry. We're going to make it." A huge explosion hit just behind, shaking the jeep. "Goddammit, they're trying to get us," he said, and added excitedly, "But they're gonna have to catch us!" He pushed the accelerator to the floor again and, reaching down between the legs of the man beside him—it was Kay—picked up a submachine gun and handed it back to Laurence, saying, "Hey, kid, know how to use this?"

Laurence took the gun, looked at it in bewilderment, and passed it to one of the soldiers, who put it on the floor beside him. Two more loud explosions hit, off to one side of the jeep.

The sergeant was driving at top speed, the jeep screeching around the curves of the hill. In a couple of minutes he reached the rest of the convoy—a line of trucks parked at the edge of the road, with Marines standing beside them.

"Everybody onto the trucks!" the sergeant yelled. "Let's get the hell outa here!"

Laurence, Kay, and Dan climbed onto a truck with six or seven Marines, and in a second all the trucks were moving, with Marines hanging on to the backs and sides and being hauled inside by friends. The convoy hurtled south along the road to Cam Lo.

About halfway to Cam Lo, gunfire started from the right side of the road, its source invisible—sharp cracks and pings, a few at first, and then more and more. The Marines fired back as they sped by. One truck was hit and caught on fire. The rest of the convoy reached Cam Lo in forty minutes and stopped. The sergeant came around the truck to see Laurence. His eyes were very bright, and his right hand was bleeding. "I've had enough today," he said. "I'm not going any farther." He glanced abstractedly at his hand. "Come on and stay with us tonight," he said. "I'll buy you boys a beer." It was about six o'clock.

Laurence went into one of the tents, took off his pack, sat down on a bed, and started to write in a small notebook. The sergeant brought him a can of beer, which Laurence placed on the floor beside him, and when he had finished writing he called to Dan, who was just outside the tent, setting up his sound equipment, that he was now ready to do the "voice-over," meaning a tape of his voice to be used with various filmed sequences of action. Laurence thereupon took a pillow from one of the beds, put it in the center of the bed, put his microphone on the pillow, and sat down on the edge of the bed.

"Level," called Dan from outside the tent.

"The enemy is one hazard, nature another, . . ." Laurence said.

"Okay," said Dan.

Laurence took a breath. "Convoy to Con Thien," he said into the microphone. "Narration. Cameraman, Kay. Sound man, Dan." He paused. "The enemy is one hazard, nature another," he began, glancing at the notebook, which was on the bed beside him. "Two days of rain have nearly washed out the soft dirt road. It will be impassable within a month, with the coming of the fall monsoon. The convoy arrives safely, unloads quickly, and turns around, because the camp is continually under artillery attack." He paused again for a moment. "Every few minutes, and sometimes every few seconds, the guns go off, their guns and our guns, whistling and pounding with the incessant, methodical efficiency of a carpenter hammering nails. In the battle outside the camp, at least twenty men are killed on both sides, perhaps a hundred wounded, as each recovers its casualties quickly and prepares for the night of shelling, and the following day of fighting."

The convoy spent Thursday night in Cam Lo, and the next day it went back to Dong Ha, running into a company of Marines along the way—in a field a few hundred feet off to the side of the road—who were being shelled by rockets. Kay's camera was working again (he had had it recharged with a generator in Cam Lo), and, crouching with Laurence and Dan in a hole by the side of the road, he photographed some of the action—tanks racing out of range, soldiers running—for the few minutes that the shelling lasted. The convoy reached Danang an hour or so later.

Laurence called Edward Fouhy, the CBS bureau chief in Saigon, who asked him to ship the film down to him right away, in the hope of getting it home in time for the Saturday-evening news. Then Laurence ran back inside the CBS hut in the Danang press center and quickly scribbled out a "voice-over close," and, with his mike on the bed, as at Cam Lo, and Dan outside the door with his equipment, recited it in a measured voice: "The next day, on the road to Con Thien, another American company is shelled in an open field a hundred yards ahead, again with amazing accuracy, this time with rockets. One tank is hit, a tread knocked apart, and the rest of the tanks, vulnerable to rockets, pull back out of range. They carry away some of the casualties from the rocket attack—some of the young men the corporal wrote his poem about." He paused, then added, "John Laurence, CBS News, on the road to Con Thien."

After that, Laurence packed the cans of film and tape in a big yellow net bag and took them to the Danang air base, where he put them aboard an Air Force flight to Saigon. A CBS man in Saigon rushed them onto the Pan American flight to San Francisco, where they were put aboard a United Airlines flight to New York. The film didn't arrive in time for the Saturday news, so it was shown on Monday night, when it ran for four minutes and prompted a congratulatory telegram to Laurence, Kay, and Dan from Walter Cronkite.

TELEVISION AND THE PRESS IN VIETNAM; OR, YES, I CAN HEAR YOU VERY WELL—JUST WHAT WAS IT YOU WERE SAYING?

Saigon

There's still rubber, of course—the rubber that finds its way from the large French plantations in the south and in the Central Highlands into Michelin and other Free World tires—but, aside from that, probably the largest and most valued single export item from South Vietnam these days is American journalism. The stuff pours out of Saigon each day in a torrent of television film, still photographs, and words—the film and the photographs heading east toward relay stations in Tokyo or San Francisco on the now daily jet flights out of Tan Son Nhut Airport, and the words rushing along the new cable that links Saigon, Guam, Honolulu, and the West Coast and that makes a phone conversation between Saigon and Chicago infinitely clearer than anything that can usually be managed between one Saigon hotel room and another. General William Westmoreland has a telephone in his quarters that enables him to speak instantly with the Commander-in-Chief in Washington. Simmons Fentress, of *Time-Life*, has a telephone that enables *him* to communicate instantly with the *Time-Life* news bureau in Rockefeller Center. Most bureaus are not quite that up-to-the-minute; in fact, many bureaus, the *Times* among them, borrow the Reuters lease line, the *Times* men trudging up to their small office on Tu-Do Street after dinner in order to file their three or four daily stories by one or two in the morning, which is one or two in the afternoon (the previous afternoon) in New York, and thus get them there in time for the next morning's edition. All the same, there is a staggering amount of communication going on in Vietnam: the military, with all its field radios and private telephones and teletype machines, communicating within the military; the embassy and the CIA and USAID and so forth communicating within "the mission"; all of them communicating, when they choose to, with the journalists; the journalists communicating with their editors, and the editors with the public—hundreds of teletypes and Telexes clackety-clacking away all over the bloody country, roughly five-hundred working journalists (and working pretty hard for the most part, too), and where it all ends up, where it all ends up is Fred leans forward in his chair at eleven-thirty in the evening, stares briefly and intensely at the floor, sticks his chin out a bit, adopts a thoughtful look, and, speaking somewhere in the direction of his left shoe, declares, "Well, it's certainly, um, you have to say, ah . . . a very . . . *complex* situation."

After even a little time in Vietnam, a couple of things seem fairly clear. One is that although in a certain sense one can hardly avoid calling the situation in Vietnam "complex" (for that matter, the cell structure of the Arizona tree frog is complex), on a number of possibly more useful levels (for instance, the level of operable communication, of what can be sent out and what can be received) it isn't so complex after all. (The word "complex" tends to be one of our contemporary talismans; whatever you touch with it becomes somehow embalmed and unreachable, and the "complexity" itself is likely to become more interesting or important than the subject it is supposed to enfold.) The situation in Vietnam is obviously composed of many different parts—parts involving such seemingly disparate elements as power politics, South Vietnamese peasant life, the United States Congress, military firepower and tactics, local politics, and corruption—but the parts themselves are relatively simple, or, at any rate, relatively comprehensible. One will never know everything there is to know about politics in the United States. One will never know everything there is to know about politics in Vietnam. Still, if one had the time, or took the trouble, to get in touch with a certain number of reliable Vietnamese political authorities and ask them what was actually happening as a result of such-and-such a power alignment, or what might happen if such-and-such a Cabinet change was effected, they could probably tell one enough so that one could put together a fairly concrete, useful analysis of the subject, so that, for example, in the aftermath of the recent Vietnamese elections, with the Buddhists marching and the students getting beaten up and the Assembly threatening to throw out the vote, one wouldn't get stuck, as most of the American television stations and newspapers got stuck, with trying hastily to explain to the public at the end of September what it was that had been going on for more than a month and had been pointing in the direction of such an outburst (and for the most part not even trying to explain, just giving the bare facts or running around trying to illustrate them), and with the public, responding to yet another overquick, undercooked explanation, once again nodding its head and muttering, "I told you so. Another mixed-up South American republic."

Vietnam may be the Number 1 story, but journalists don't have that smooth a time covering it. Virtually none of them speaks Vietnamese. Most newspapermen and TV men are here nowadays on only six-month tours of duty, which is hardly enough time to find out the name of the province chief in Binh Dinh, let alone ask him how the corruption situation is coming along—and, in any case, most of the six months is usually spent in chasing Vietnamese fire engines for the New York desk. When somebody gets on to a story, as CBS did with Con Thien early in September, then everyone goes chasing after it—wire services, newspapers, rival networks—the Saigon bureau chiefs receiving "rockets" from New York to get competitive (not really much different from the way the papers and TV cover a fast-breaking news event back home). The trouble is, Vietnam isn't a fast-breaking news event most of the time. The papers back home have their deadlines; the TV stations have their scheduled news broadcasts. The journalists here try to feed the stuff back—there's usually some kind of stuff to feed back, some of it technically useful, and now and then it's good (R. W. Apple had a fine long piece in the *Times* this August on the "stalemate" in the war); sometimes it's ridiculous (as are the solemn transmissions of enemy casualty figures that are often obtained by a pilot looking down from a spotter plane a couple of thousand feet in the air)—and a lot of chatter comes out of the newspapers and picture tubes, but sometimes nothing really happens. Or, when it does happen, it happens in a time and space that often isn't very meaningfully evoked in terms of standard hard-news copy. People have this feeling that they're not getting the "true picture" of Vietnam from daily journalism. (Just about the first thing anyone asks a returning visitor from Vietnam is "What's *really* going on there?") People are, on the whole, right, and what makes the failure of the press to communicate the reality of the Vietnam war something well worth looking into is that the Vietnam war isn't such an isolated phenomenon as many people seem to think it is. "Not like the Second Wor'd War," people say. Indeed it isn't: no formal front lines, no supportive religious illusions about a Holy War, no happy embrace of propaganda ("We're all in this together, Fred. Hang the Kaiser. Down with Tojo. Here's a toast to Winnie, Uncle Joe, and Madame Chiang"). A different world now, a different war. The Detroit riots of 1967 are qualitatively, not just chronologically, different from the Detroit riots of 1943. The waves of energy emanating from the hippies in California are qualitatively different from those that emanated from the Lindy Hoppers that short while ago. It isn't, perhaps, that the world is deeper in chaos than it used to be, but that the element of chaos which has always been there in life, which really *is* life (after all, there were minority groups and emerging nations in the eleventh century too), is now coming more and more out from under wraps: Father has left the house, and the children have some new toys and are threatening to knock the house to pieces, and that would be all right, it would be manageable, if we could somehow get inside the house and really find out what was going on, could sit down and try to understand the children, listen to them, at any rate if we could confront what it was that they were doing (let alone thinking about), but, as things are, we make this big thing about how we know everything that's going on—*nothing* escapes us, because we too have new toys, which tell us things—but what really happens is that we sit outside the house and every now and then a maid comes out onto the porch and stamps one foot lightly for attention and then reads us a brief announcement, and we sit there looking thoughtful or impatient and listening to the sounds of breaking furniture from somewhere on the second story. We have this great arrogance about communications. We've given up much of our capacity for first-hand experience—certainly for first-hand sensory experience—cheerfully sitting at home shrouded in plastic, film, magnetic tape, peering out at the world through lenses, electronic tubes, photographs, lines of type. And we've also, at a time when the ability of a people to order and enhance its existence depends increasingly on its ability to know what is really going on (no more just getting the word from Father or the King; no more milling around in front of White-hall to find out what really gives with Kitchener in the Sudan)—we've also given up the ideal of knowing first hand about our-selves and the world in favor of receiving sometimes arbitrary and often nearly stenographic reports through a machine system we call "communications," which for the most part neither rec-ognizes the element of chaos in the world for what it is nor is able to make contact with it except on a single narrow-beam wavelength.

It's ironic, maybe, that, among the methods men have devised for usefully reflecting the world back to themselves, only those methods that the population at large doesn't really take very seriously—one thinks especially of the novel and the film—have made any significant attempt to cope with the evolving human experience. Not so long ago, in the nineteenth century, when the world was held in place by nuts and bolts, when the doors to all the upstairs rooms were locked up tight, when Father was home and brooked no nonsense—in those days, because it seemed relevant and interesting to find out about the things in people's lives, what work they did, what trolley car they took from where to where, and whom they married, novelists wrote book after book after book that covered these things in an orderly way, and that often appeared to describe the universe largely in terms of stationary articles of furniture. Nowadays it seems more relevant to write about the inside of people's heads (or at least the writers' heads) and about how they really live—about how life doesn't always go in a straight line from here to there but moves forward, backward, upside down, inside the head, and outside. The nervier writers—the Mailers, the Pynchons, the Updikes—go reaching out and grabbing at how things seem to be right now. A book by Mailer, or a film by Antonioni, may not define the world, and you may not like it, but, taken all in all, the novels and films being turned out to-day seem to attempt to reflect more of the shifting dynamism of present-day life than does even the best of daily journalism (both press and television), which we take *very* seriously and defer to for most of our public and private impressions of the world and, one imagines, of ourselves. Daily journalism, in fact, seems to have changed very little over the last few decades—as if nobody quite knew what to do with it (except for adding more white space, syndicating Clayton Fritchey, and "livening up" the women's page), as if its conventions were somehow eternal. The *Times*, which has editors and reporters with sufficient imagination and sense of history to recognize that there is more to be reflected upon in our evolving experience in Vietnam than the daily bombing reports, continues for the most part to treat the war as an accounting exercise—and "treat" is right, for the hurly-burly of the world emerges in the pages of the *Times* somehow ordered and dignified, a bit the way a man's ridiculous life emerges as so splendidly established (all those "estate"s and "issue"s and so forth) when he listens to the lawyer read him out his will. Television, with all its technical resources, with all the possibilities of film and film-editing for revealing fluid motion, continues for the most part to report the war as a long, long narrative broken into two-minute, three-minute, or four-minute stretches of visual incident. Now, it's obvious that there are plenty of events in the war, or anywhere, that ought to be treated in an accountant's manner, and also that there are plenty of incidents that are inherently visual and can most accurately be revealed on film. If there's an important battle, it ought to be put down, covered—just that. The thing is, though, that it doesn't take one very long in Vietnam to realize—perhaps "feel" would be closer than "realize"—that there is a crucial difference between what seems to be *here* and what is reflected of it back home on television and in newspapers. It isn't so much a matter of the press distorting the picture (one of the favorite themes of our embassy in Saigon), because, although there's a certain amount of that—a certain amount of deferring to official pronouncements that one knows are biased, a certain amount of translating battles in which we lost a cruel number of men into gallant actions that were "gallant" because we took so many losses—somehow the concept of press distortion implies a demonology that for the most part just doesn't exist. What really seems to be standing in the way of an accurate reflection of Vietnam right now isn't that the press is "lying" or not telling all it knows. It's partly that much of the press, especially the wire services and television, just doesn't have either the time or the inclination to investigate the various parts of the Vietnam picture—what's the true military situation, what's being done with new technology, what can't be done, how solid is the government's hold on the villages, how solid is the government, how good or bad is the ARVN, and so on. And, more important, when they do get hold of one of these parts, neither most of the newspapers nor most of television seems to be able to do anything more with it than to treat it as an isolated piece of detail—maybe an important piece of detail, maybe unimportant, but isolated in any case, cut off by the rigors and conventions of journalism from the events and forces that brought it into being, cut off, too, from the events and forces that it will in turn animate. The other week, as a small example, a crew from ABC flew in here to do an interview with Ambassador Ellsworth Bunker. The ambassador sat behind his desk and, in response to questions gently shoved at him by ABC's John Scali, discoursed at length on such matters as the "new stability" that would, he said, result from the Thieu-Ky election, and on the fine prospects for Thieu and Ky to work well together in the new government ("They have worked together very well in the last two years"). The program was presented a few days later in the United States—presented, naturally, at face value. At the end of the next week, Buddhists were marching in the streets here, students were getting clubbed by the police, reporters and TV crews (including ABC's) were tearing around Saigon trying to cover a situation that was, after all, a fairly predictable result of the unpopularity of the recent elections, of the fact that the "new stability" we are so hopefully committed to in many instances seems to depend largely on the ability of General Loan to hold down the lid on the kettle, even of the fact that Thieu and Ky have trouble staying in the same room with each other, let alone in the same government. The point isn't that Mr. Bunker shouldn't have said what he said, or that journalists shouldn't have been chasing after riot coverage, but that in life, after all, events don't sit stiffly, separately upon a page, don't take place in terms of three-minute narrative slices of film; they push and jostle and flow and mix against one another, and the process of this mixing is often a more important and revelatory part of what is really going on (this continuing reality that we so proudly call history when it has gone past us) than the isolated announcements that we usually have to make do with. It's obviously not fair—or, at any rate, not realistic—to expect a consistent resourcefulness in writing, political analysis, and so forth from a profession (journalism) that has traditionally been longer on energy than on anything else. But it seems true to say that most journalists here convey a more firmly realized picture of Vietnam in a couple of hours of conversation in the evening (with all those elisions made, the separate parts connected) than they've achieved sometimes (in complicity with their editors and their public) in six months of filing detached, hard-news reports. And it seems even truer to say that one of the notable results of all this has been the almost tangible inability of people back home to pay any very rigorous attention to Vietnam. It obsesses people, certainly, but more as a neurosis (which it's become, it often seems, largely as a result of this inability to confront it) than as a very real, evolving attempt of a large, important nation to relate outward to a large, important sector of the world, which, whether one finds the attempt good or bad, moral or immoral, useful or useless, is what it's all about.

People often refer to television's coverage of Vietnam as "television's war" (as one could probably describe television's coverage of civil rights as "television's civil war"), and although it seems fair to say that in general television has done very well strictly in terms of what it has set out to report about Vietnam—in terms of those usually combat-oriented film clips that appear on the morning and evening news programs—it also seems fair to say that for the most part television in Vietnam has operated on a level not much more perceptive than that of a sort of illustrated wire service, with the television crews racketing around the countryside seeking to illustrate the various stories that are chalked on the assignment boards in Saigon ("4th Div. Opn.," "Chopper story," "Hobo Woods Opn.," "Buddhist march"), constantly under pressure to feed the New York news programs new stories (ideally, combat stories), moving in here, moving out, moving in there the next day. Recently, the major effort of the military war has been taking place up north in the I Corps area, and, as a result, many of the television and newspaper correspondents are now working out of the Danang press center. Ordinarily, though, much of the work is done almost in bankerish fashion from Saigon, and one says "bankerish" not to disparage the factor of risk-taking in their covering of various operations (a factor that ranges from slight to very considerable), but as an indication of how difficult it is to get close to a strange war in an unfamiliar country by a process that more often than not consists in your having breakfast at the Hotel Caravelle at seven-thirty, driving out to a helicopter base, going by chopper to where some military operation is occurring (say, a search of an area where a Vietcong ammunition dump supposedly exists, the possible picture value being in the blowing up of the ammo dump), wandering around in the woods taking pictures until three-thirty, maybe getting shot at a bit and maybe not, then taking the chopper back, doing all your paperwork and film-shipment arrangements, and meeting friends in the Continental bar at seven o'clock. The correspondents tend to have mixed feelings about all this themselves. Many of them, to be sure, are older men with families and are not crazy about spending more time than necessary out in the field, and, doubtless like journalists everywhere, they complain of not having enough time to cover the "right stories," and of the pressure from New York to provide combat coverage. Of the newspapermen and magazine correspondents, in fact, except for a couple of people like Peter Arnett and Henri Huet of the AP, and David Greenway of *Time*, and Dana Stone of UPI, virtually none are doing the combat work that television is now doing almost on a routine basis (a seemingly routine basis, anyway). And although it's true that the Vietnam story is more than the story of men shooting at one another (the television people themselves refer to it as "bang-bang" coverage, and have a healthy respect for what goes into the getting of it), it's also true that American men (and Vietnamese men) are indeed getting shot and killed, and are shooting and killing others, and one would have to be a pretty self-indulgent pacifist to say that it wasn't somebody's job to record and witness something of that. The trouble is that television doesn't do much more than that. It doesn't try. There are the highly structured news programs, with correspondents from around the world coming on for a few minutes at a time. And then, as a way of circumventing this limitation, there are the "news specials," which up to now have generally been done with the same hasty, unfeeling, technically skillful professionalism that (more justifiably) characterizes the shorter film clips. For the most part, "television's war" is a prisoner of its own structure, a prisoner of such facts as that although television is the chief source of news and information for the majority of the people, the News & Information act is still just another aspect of the world's greatest continuous floating variety show; that the scope and cost of television news require an immense weight of administrative managing from above; that for TV the newsworthiness of daily events is still so restrictively determined by visual criteria. For example, people watching an evening news show about an ammo dump being blown up in the Hobo Woods might reasonably conclude, on a day, say, when a nationwide strike was averted in San Diego, when a rebel army was captured in Nigeria, when the Pope fell sick, and when Indonesia broke relations with Red China, that there was some special significance to the blowing up of this particular ammo dump, or not even anything special about it, just some significance —that its presentation on the screen in front of one said something useful about the war. In all too many cases, though, what the blowing up of the ammo dump says is that when you blow up an ammo dump it goes boom-boom-boom and there is a lot of smoke, and that is about it. Daily journalism in general seems to be virtually rooted in its traditional single-minded way of presenting the actuality of daily life, as if some invisible sacred bond existed between the conventional structures of daily journalism and the conventional attitudes of so many of the people whom daily journalism serves. This has been increasingly noticeable in journalism's severely conventional covering of most of the major matters of our time—covering civil rights, for instance, with its technically proficient battle-action accounts of rioting, and its distracted, uncomprehending, essentially uninterested sliding over of the dark silences that fill the empty spaces in between the riots. It is now especially evident, and damaging, in Vietnam, where, for the most part, American journalism has practically surrendered itself to a consecutive, activist, piecemeal, the-next-day-the-First-Army-forged-onward-toward-Aachen approach to a war that even the journalists covering it know to be non-consecutive, non-activist, a war of silences, strange motions, where a bang on the table gets you nothing and an inadvertent blink causes things to happen in rooms you haven't even looked into yet, where there is no Aachen, and "onward" is a word that doesn't seem to translate very well into the local language. The journalists reorder the actuality of Vietnam into these isolated hard-news incidents for the benefit of their editors. The editors say that that's what the public wants, and, to a great extent, the editors are right about that. The public does indeed want and need hard news, something concrete amid the chaos, something you can reach out to over the morning coffee and almost touch— a hill number, for example. Hill 63. Hill 881. It's a truism, especially among wire-service reporters in Vietnam, that if you can somehow get a hill number attached to a military operation (most operations start at one latitude-longitude point and move to another), regardless of the number of casualties, regardless, especially, of the relevance of this operation to the rest of the war, the story will run on for days, particularly in the pages of the small-to-medium-circulation newspapers that buy most of the wire-service copy. The public also presumably wants and needs a sense of progress, and since this is a public that tends to measure progress numerically—so many yards gained rushing, so many villages pacified, earnings per share up, body counts down, carloadings steady—there is a tendency on the part of the dispensers of information, the military and the government, to scour Vietnam for positive statistics and dole them out to newsmen, who are always under pressure to supply copy, and who know that there is nearly always a market back home for these firm-sounding stories that seem to be about numbers, which in turn seem to mean something, but in fact are often just about the numbers. One of the better *Catch-22* effects over here is to pick up the daily *Stars & Stripes* and read the wire-service lead, datelined Saigon—"Hurtling out of an overcast sky, warplanes of the United States Seventh Fleet delivered another massive air strike against the port city of Haiphong," and so on—and try to recall the atmosphere and the phrasing when the source information was delivered in the course of the daily briefing, the famous "five-o'clock follies" held each day at the Mission Press Center. A couple of dozen correspondents are slouched in chairs in the briefing room, a bored Air Force major is reading aloud in a flat, uninflected voice the summary of the various air strikes conducted that morning and earlier that afternoon: "Airplanes of the United States Seventh Fleet flew 267 missions against targets in the south. . . . Airplanes of the 12th Tactical Fighter Wing flew 245 missions and 62 sorties against selected targets, including the warehouse system outside Hanoi and bridges in the Loc Binh area. . . ." Everybody has been dozing along, except that now someone asks, "Say, Major, isn't that Loc Binh just five miles from the Chinese border?" The major will acknowledge that it is. "Say, Major, isn't that the closest we've yet come to the Chinese border?" The major will acknowledge that it is. "Major," another voice will ask, "wouldn't you say that was a 'first'—I mean in proximity terms?" The major looks thoughtful for a moment. "In proximity terms," he will reply, "I would say 'affirmative.'"

Television correspondents try to get around the limitations, not of their medium but of what they are structurally required to cover (at least, the more political and thoughtful among them do), by inserting some sort of verbal point of view in the taped narrative they send off with their brief film reports, as though to say, Okay, fellows, here's your bang-bang footage, but if I put a little edge in my voice maybe it will come out a bit closer to the way things were. Morley Safer used to do this with a vengeance on CBS, and CBS's David Schoumacher and NBC's Dean Brelis do it to a certain degree now, and in some ways it's effective—it sharpens a point of view, if there should be one to begin with, and it allows for a slight intrusion of irony into a war that most news organizations are attempting to report without irony. (Trying to report a war without irony is a bit like trying to keep sex out of a discussion of the relations between men and women.) The fact is, though, that if you show some film of, say, half a dozen helicopters whirring in onto the ground, our men rushing out with rifles at the ready amid sounds of gunfire here and there, a platoon commander on the radio, men running by with stretchers amid more gunfire, what you are really doing is adding another centimeter or millimeter to what is often no more than an illusion of American military progress (our boys rushing forward, those roaring helicopters, the authoritative voice of the captain). And to stand up there afterward, microphone in hand, and say, with all the edge in your voice you can muster, as Safer used to do, "Another typical engagement in Vietnam. . . . A couple of battalions of the Army went into these woods looking for the enemy. The enemy was gone. There was a little sniper fire at one moment; three of our men were hit, but not seriously. It was pretty much the way it usually goes," doesn't pull the picture back quite straight—or perhaps, to be a bit more accurate, it focuses one's eyes on a picture that may not really have any useful connection with the situation it claims to be communicating about. Communications. One is so terribly serious about some things. One has a direct circuit installed between Rockefeller Center and the Hotel Caravelle. One can whoosh eight cans of 16-millimeter film two-thirds of the way around the world in less than twenty hours. For around seventy-five hundred bucks, one can buy thirty minutes' worth of satellite time and relay the film in from Tokyo. The television people work like hell in Vietnam —Saturdays, Sundays, all the time, really. Many of the journalists there work like hell—able men, responsible men, pasting detail upon detail into some sort of continuing scrapbook of stories about bombing raids, and pacification programs, and bombing raids, and about the Buddhist march, and the new infrared searchlight, and bombing raids, and about the fact that forty thousand Vietcong defected in the last six months. And the detail accretes, day in, day out; paragraphs clatter out over the cable, film by the bagload heads home for processing, detail, detail, detail, and people back home, who have been fed more words and pictures on Vietnam than on any other event in the last twenty years, have the vague, unhappy feeling that they still haven't been told it straight. And, of course, it's true. When President Johnson stands behind the podium in the East Room, looks into the cameras, and declares that he has "read all the reports" and that the reports tell him "progress is being made," it isn't that he's lying. He doesn't need to lie for the situation to be potentially disastrous; all he needs to do is defer to the authority of a reportorial system (one is thinking especially of the government's) that, in terms of the sensitivities, the writing skill, and the general bias of the reporters, is unlikely to be automatically accurate, or anywhere near it. Patriotism doesn't have much to do with it, any more than inaccuracy or distortion has much to do with whatever it is that gives old Fred—after three years in which he has read 725,000 words about Vietnam—the feeling that he couldn't write three intelligible sentences about the subject on a postcard to his mother.

There are a couple of things one could probably do to improve the situation. In television, the most likely would be to loosen up and expand the evening news programs so that the correspondents could handle larger themes, and then be less restrictively visual about the assignments. (The networks might also get some correspondents whose interest in daily events wasn't entirely confined to hustling 450 feet of film into a can.) In newspapers (the best of which are far less limited, obviously, than television), one might conceivably do the same sort of thing—loosen the paper up, get some new writers, encourage them to at least allow themselves the possibility of breaking through the barriers of the orthodox good-newspaper-writing declarative sentence ("McCormick Place, the huge exposition center that draws more than a million visitors a year to Chicago, was ravaged by fire today. Damage was estimated at $100 million" is the way *The New York Times* sings it). In television, again—although this, admittedly, isn't very likely, at least in this Golden Age—it might even happen that a network official would someday have the nerve and imagination to call on a few of the really inventive movie-makers, like Godard, Antonioni, and Richardson, or, since they might be a bit hard to get, on some of the young inventive movie-makers like Stan Vanderbeek, Shirley Clarke, Donn Pennebaker, and say, "How about you and you and you going in there for a while, to Vietnam, Harlem, Texas, and bringing back some film of what you think is going on?" After all, there *are* these really inventive movie-makers, and one of the reasons they're in movies, and not TV, is that TV tends to remain so consistently nerveless and conventional in its use of film. And both the papers and TV could stand being a great deal more investigative, because if the emperor doesn't have any clothes on you're surely not doing the empire much of a favor by saying he does. Right now, for example, there's a big public-relations push going on among the military and the embassy people here to get across the idea that the ARVN is a fine, competent, reliable modern army, which it certainly isn't—partly because we spent three years (between 1959 and 1961) training it to be an old-fashioned army, and partly for reasons having to do with corruption and such matters. With the exception of Peter Arnett of the AP, and Merton Perry of *Newsweek*, and a very few others, however, nobody has really gone into the ARVN story, which isn't to say that everyone has been praising the ARVN; even *Time* qualifies its statements about it to the extent of acknowledging that the ARVN hasn't yet fully "found itself." Still, it's an important story to do (many of the things you find out about the ARVN are inextricably connected with the rest of Vietnamese life), and it's here, it's here all the time (maybe a bit the way Negro slums are there all the time back home), and nobody really looks into it until something happens—a victory, a defeat, a campaign. Or, when somebody does, he does it the way ABC looked into the ARVN the other day, which was to run a three-minute film clip on one of its few decent battalions receiving a Presidential citation from General Westmoreland, concluding with a few well-chosen words from the general on the great improvement he had lately detected in the South Vietnamese Army—all presented absolutely straight. The thing is, one takes note of these various deficiencies, inabilities, disinclinations; one dutifully nudges forward one's little "constructive suggestions"—but they're no more than that. We're all prisoners of the same landscape, and it hardly seems realistic to expect that we'll ever derive a truly intelligent, accurate, sensitive reflection of actuality from a free-market communications system that is manned and operated by people like us, and that will, inevitably, tell us for the most part what we want to know. In Vietnam recently the war has shifted—superficially, maybe, but shifted anyway—up into the I Corps area, where, just below the DMZ, we have some batteries of Marine artillery, which were placed there last February in an aggressive move to fire upon the enemy infiltration routes, and which have now become exposed, potentially isolated, and subjected to extremely heavy shelling from the enemy's guns, these being in the main well camouflaged, dug in behind the hills within the DMZ, and hard to hit. The other day, after a month-long period in which Con Thien in particular had taken as many as a thousand rounds of artillery fire in a single day, the military headquarters in Saigon (four hundred miles to the south) suddenly announced that the enemy had pulled back from his positions, that we had in fact won at Con Thien, had punished him too severely with our artillery and bombers, and instantly there was a great outpouring of cables and messages back home. U.S. GUNS BATTER REDS AT CON THIEN, headlined the *New York Post*. REDS FLEE GUN POSTS; CON THIEN SIEGE ENDS, said the *Denver Post*. The AP put a big story on the wire which began, "Massive American firepower has broken the back of the Communists' month-long artillery siege of Con Thien," and went on to quote General Westmoreland as having said, "We made it a Dien Bien Phu in reverse." One of the few exceptions was Charles Mohr of the *Times*, who had recently been up there and who filed a long piece to his paper two days later to the effect that Con Thien was still extremely exposed, that "aerial photos confirmed a limited withdrawal but did not necessarily prove that the bulk of the gun pits—most of which have never been located—were hit by B-52 bombing raids and United States artillery," and that "few sources believe that more than a respite has been gained." There is disagreement among journalists here as to the real likelihood of our suffering a military defeat in I Corps, at a place, say, such as Con Thien. There are those who point out that two weeks ago eighteen inches of rain fell on Con Thien in two days, that air strikes could not get in, that trucks could not supply the base with ammunition, or even with water, that it is not totally implausible, considering the fact that the enemy has superior forces in the area, for a combination of circumstances to occur in which the enemy might indeed overrun Con Thien, destroy the guns, raise hell, get out—and then you really would have a sort of mini-Dien Bien Phu disaster. There are also those—the majority—who regard a successful enemy attack on Con Thien as very unlikely, who think that Con Thien could never get that exposed, and who cite as evidence the fact that the enemy is as impeded by monsoon weather as we are. The majority view is probably right. ("The United States Command disclosed today that about 4000 men of the First Air Cavalry Division had been moved north to within 20 miles of Danang," the AP filed a few days later, forgetting perhaps to disclose that Danang is the central staging area for I Corps and the outposts near the DMZ, or that the reinforcement of the Marine Corps by the Army is not yet an everyday occurrence in Vietnam or anywhere else.) But, in either case, most journalists who have been up north (some of the same men, indeed, who seem to have so blithely passed along those "Victory at Con Thien" announcements) recognize that the shifting situation in I Corps, and notably around Con Thien (where for the first time Vietnam has turned into a conventional war; in fact, not just a conventional war—a small-scale replica of the First World War), not only says a great deal about the military possibilities in Vietnam right now but, even more important, raises a good many questions about the limits of technology as a cure-all in every modern military situation, about the hazards of trying to fight what appears increasingly to be a ground war with insufficient troops, about the possibilities of negotiating a peace settlement with an enemy who seems to be able to effectively increase his infantry capabilities more than we can. ("Long-range Communist artillery and Red mortars opened up again yesterday and today on U.S. Marine positions south of the Demilitarized Zone," the AP dispatch began on October 11, as if the previous ones had never existed.) Con Thien—lately, anyway—raises these sorts of questions, but, with few exceptions, such as Mohr, and Lee Lescaze of the *Washington Post*, nobody seems to even hear the questions, let alone try to pass them on. (Television, it should be pointed out, first broke the Con Thien story, first took note of the fact that the situation had shifted from an aggressive gun emplacement last February to a defensive battery holding on for dear life in the fall, but, in terms of the three-minute film clips on the evening news, it hasn't done much beyond showing what the place is like—no mean trick itself.) Back home now, one gathers, the tide of impatience and unhappiness with the war keeps growing. Governor Reagan, one reads, advises that we should use the "full technological resources of the United States" to win the war. An eminent Midwestern senator visiting Saigon the other day slammed his thick hand upon the table and declared in anguish and frustration (the special anguish and frustration of eminent people) that he could see "no alternatives remaining" except that we "step up the bombing" or "pack up and leave." A journalist was talking here recently, a young man who works for television and who has been up to Con Thien. "The real hazard about Con Thien," he was saying, "is that we'll get so frustrated trying to win a ground war without enough troops that we'll indeed step up the technology, whatever that means. I hate to think what that means." There are so many real and possible tragedies connected with Vietnam—the tragedies of men and women dead, of men and women dying, of nations dying. (Perhaps there's no worse tragedy than people dying.) But sometimes, listening to the note of anger and impatience that arises above the towns and cities in our country, that hovers over daily life, feeling the growing swell of semi-automatic hawkishness and doveishness that pushes so many people nowadays, and seems to say less for what they rigorously, intelligently believe is right than for the inability of many persons to stand in uncertainty much longer when there are firm choices to be seen on either side, sometimes one has the sense that maybe as great a tragedy as any other will be that we will indeed *do* something shortly (this nation of men and women that always has to be doing something to keep sane), distracted, numbed, isolated by detail that seemed to have been information but was only detail, isolated by a journalism that too often told us only what we thought we wanted to hear, isolated, in fact, by communications—expressing pieties, firmness, regrets, what you will, citizens patting each other on the back ("We did the right thing, Fred"), and not know what we did. Or why. And, once again, will have learned nothing.

WALDO

"Frankly, we tried to capture some of the honest-to-Christ *ten-dresse* that still exists in the world, in the form of a boy's love for his pet" is the way veteran producer Harry J. Frost describes his new outdoor-adventure series, *Waldo*, the story of what happens when a towheaded nine-year-old boy called Biff Magowan saves an anopheles mosquito (Waldo) from drowning in a bowl of won-ton soup and then is unable to "give him up," despite the good-natured remonstrances of Biff's mother that Waldo is a "wild thing" who ought to be "making his family with other wild things," and the good-natured reminders of Biff's father, Biff Magowan, Sr., deputy insect-control warden for the area, that one nip from Waldo nets you about fifteen and a half months of 109-degree fever, plus a long, lingering recovery, and "other attendant side effects." In an episode last week, Biff, Waldo, and his mother have been left alone in the house, when they are suddenly set upon by a Killer Gnat. Thereupon ensues what veteran producer Frost has described as "one of the most dramatic semi-authentic fights-to-the-finish between an anopheles mosquito and a Killer Gnat ever filmed." Biff, Sr., returns several days later, in time to put a comradely arm around Waldo and deliver a brief lecture on the various pros and cons of forest fires.

NORTH FROM COS COB

"We like to think of this as a railroading story with a difference," says Hodding Hodding, star of *North from Cos Cob*, the new series that tells the epic history of the building of the New Haven Railroad—the "Iron Mouse" that thundered its way across the flatlands of the untamed Connecticut Valley in the latter years of the nineteenth century and, in the words of Grenville Tobermory, writer-producer of the show, "made possible the Bridgeport we all know today." Hodding Hodding plays Major Lem Wassoon, the impetuous young Army officer who staked his future on the hunch that "if you laid enough track north from Cos Cob and kept most of it out of the water, sooner or later you'd hit Providence or something." Manfred LeRoy plays W. Rutherford Gallant, the irascible old man who first envisioned the possibilities of "changing at Springfield." The initial episode dramatizes the early efforts of Cyrus (Jeph) Martingale, chief engineer of the line, to get the mail through to Hartford twenty-two minutes faster by jettisoning the passengers along the roadbed.

BLAKE

Blake is the personal story of Gil Blake, tough, dedicated, and hard-driving, one of the "new breed" of investigative dentists who have been shaking up the whole dynamics of the dental profession in recent years. Blake's offices are in a sleek little building in the fashionable Trumpington Hills section of Los Angeles, where, with a couple of old drills, a few X-rays, and his associate, Wally Sheinbaum (played by Negro actor Henry Woodlawn), he appears to be running a comfortable society practice. Inwardly, though, Blake is seething. "Filling! Polishing! It's not enough!" he seethes. "When I see a pair of upper canines walk in here, I want to know: What made those upper canines the way they are? A lousy, no-good marriage? A crummy, stinking childhood? A couple of rotten pieces of gravel?" In a recent episode,

"The Tides in the Sargasso Run Deep," Blake is trapped in his office by a homicidal maniac and is forced to give him a free gum massage. Later, Blake remembers a "peculiar discoloration" on a lower left molar, and sets off on a search for the young killer that takes him through eight Western states, Canada, Mexico, Greece, and Mexico again, and ends up in a chase through the back corridors of the Vandivert Tooth Sanitarium in Lausanne.

THE ARNOLD NEWQUIST SPECIAL

Arnold Newquist, chief electrician at CBS for the past thirty-six years, patiently waited his turn for his own Special, and the result, which was shown live and in color last Tuesday night, was a relaxed, understated, deceptively casual performance that amply demonstrated Mr. Newquist's instinctive grasp of the new medium. In the first part of the show Mr. Newquist, informally attired in an old sweater and some underwear, sang a number of Indiana U. fraternity songs, hummed a little from Gilbert and Sullivan, and participated in a comedy skit with special guest star Mimmsey Mommeier (Cindy Paragon in *Annabelle Rattoon*) about defrosting ice trays. In the second part Mr. Newquist reappeared, more relaxed than ever, in bathrobe and pajamas, and did imitations of Warner Baxter, Millard Fillmore, and somebody he thought might be Count Ciano or might not be, and then sang "Stardust" several times. A musical dance number based on the Repeal of the Corn Laws was superbly executed by the Julian Grigsby Dancers.

LUNDIGAN'S DISEASE

"Lundigan's Disease" is never precisely named, or even seen, but the implication is clear that when it comes on, young Gregory Lundigan (Fuzz Clinton) becomes something of a mess—hives, nasty rashes, falling down a lot in public. The premise behind this series is that in order to get away from his disease, handsome, independently wealthy young Lundigan will do just about anything—except, ironically, see a doctor. In a notable installment several weeks ago, "Who Is Sylvia . . . What Is She?" Lundigan is indulging in his favorite independently wealthy occupation, single-sculling down the Ragatawanda River, when he is set upon by a homicidal maniac and forced to enter the Eastern Collegiate Sprint Championships, which are taking place a couple of miles upstream. Lundigan is half a boat length ahead of the University of California when small-arms and machine-gun fire from state troopers on the shore causes him to "catch a crab" and capsize. As the beautiful daughter of a prominent East Coast industrialist watches anxiously from the shore, Lundigan is compelled to make a dramatic choice between a stranger's life, justice, religious liberty, home rule for Ireland, and his boat.

CLUB 122

Club 122 is a series based on the real-life exploits of Sergeant Grover Greengrove, of the Los Angeles Riot Control Department—the owner of Club 122, a small wooden object that dangles unassumingly from his belt. Greengrove, in the words of director Luke Esterhazy, is "dedicated primarily to upholding law and order wherever he can find it," but is also quick to recognize that "kids" and "some other people" have their rights, too. In a recent episode, Greengrove (Matt Matlock) and his wisecracking assistant, Sean O'Malley (played by the Negro actor Douglas David), are assigned to riot-control an explosive situation in the Mendocino Avenue shopping center, where a gang of elderly retired realtors from Santa Barbara has shown up for the express purpose of "beating hell" out of some teen-agers. Greengrove rushes down to the corner with his club, and tear gas, and grenades, and small tactical demolition charges, only to discover that his daughter Tracy, whom he hasn't seen for seven years, is one of the teen-agers, and that the tight-lipped old gentleman gunning down toward her on the bright pink Harley-Davidson is Walter Carslake.

POMFRET

"You just couldn't have made a show like this eleven or twenty-three years ago," says W. Loring Brickhouse, executive producer of *Pomfret*, the daring new series that attempts to deal head on with the "racial crisis." Henderson Pomfret, a Negro, is a brilliant young assistant professor of history at Hanford University, a Rhodes Scholar, a squash champion, beautifully mannered, not really too dark, who finds one day that his path to the chairmanship of the department is being blocked by the undisguised animosity of elderly Professor Jocko Lee. Professor Lee claims that his disapproval of Pomfret (played with great sensitivity by Toshira Okada) is based on nothing more than that Pomfret is only twenty-three years old, has published only one book—a personal attack on Dred Scott—and "looks a little funny, or something, although I can't quite put my finger on it." Pomfret, however, suspects that Lee "knows" he is a Negro and is out to get him. In a recent episode, "I Dreamt I Dwelt in Marble Halls," Lee accuses Pomfret of cheating at squash.

NEWS SPECIAL: "THE LAPP IMMIGRANT"

This courageous documentary took a year and a half to make and ran for three hours last Saturday night, when, with the aid of newsreel clips, slides, 55,000 feet of film, and 47 correspondents, the plight of the 37 Lapp immigrants to this country was searchingly examined as it had never been before. Correspondents visited Lapp immigrants all over the country, showing them as they really are, in their hovels and apartment houses (a previously undisclosed fact: 22 per cent of all Lapp immigrants own their own apartment houses), and drawing an unhesitatingly tiresome picture of what associate task-force producer Donn Marley yesterday described as "the realities of Lapp immigration." The program included shots of the famous O'Hare Street riots of 1897, scenes of the never-before-filmed Falling Through the Ice Dance at the annual Lapp Festival in Spent Bullet, Wyoming, and concluded with a panel discussion between Professor Andrew Kerr-Rutledge, Norman Mailer, General William C. Binton, and popular sportscaster Buzz Joplin on the "relative merits" or "demerits" of the Lapp experience.

DISGUSTING WIFE

"Frankly, what with Vietnam and the pill and everything, I think the public is ready for something a little more sophisticated and contemporary in its comedy shows," says Pia Paxton, the vivacious, serious young actress who plays Millie Wentworth, the "disgusting wife" in the new adult-comedy series of that name, which studio executives describe as a "sort of hippie, up-to-the-minute, fun treatment of the way young adults really live today." In the first episode of the show, Millie's husband, W. Gardner Wentworth (Bruno Ilg), a handsome, hip young rent-a-car executive, goes down to the corner for a pack of Gauloises and, when he returns, finds Millie upstairs in the broom closet with Farraday Cleveland, the raffish young student activist from nearby Densher College. Cleveland hastily explains that he came over to ask Gardner's advice about a new ad-hoc committee on double parking and just "bumped into" Millie in the broom closet, but Gardner is too much of a swinger to be jealous, and laughingly suggests that they all go downstairs and sniff glue. To make Gardner mad, Millie threatens to adopt a couple of children.

COWBOY IN SPACE

Cowboy in Space is about a cowboy in space. The cowboy's name is Victor Verdun (Lamar Cragshaw). In the first episode, Verdun (Cragshaw) discovers that King Ott II, mad ruler of the planet Throg, is planning to get rid of 550 head of cattle at 25 per cent above markup, and threatens to expose him to the Intergalactic Cattle Council. King Ott retaliates by threatening to use his much feared "peace ray" on Sanji Singh, Verdun's (Cragshaw's) wily Indian sidekick (played by Negro actor F. W. Taprock). Verdun says okay.

P B L

I see by the *Times* (TV LABORATORY'S FIRST VENTURE GETS LARGELY ADVERSE REACTION) that Fred Friendly, TV consultant to the Ford Foundation, regards last Sunday's first appearance of the Ford Foundation-backed Public Broadcast Laboratory's two-and-a-half-hour news program as "disappointing." ("It was disappointing," said Mr. Friendly in the article, in case you think I would kid around about a thing like that.) It seems like only yesteryear that Mr. Friendly was being disappointed by the Columbia Broadcasting System, in whole or in part, and here he is not entirely satisfied with the début of PBL, and right now I don't know what there is for any of us to do except just get back to study hall and work a whole lot harder for the rest of the term. For my part, I thought that PBL's first show was pretty damned good. Oh, *good?* I mean, what's good? *King Lear* is great. *The Merchant of Venice* is good. So where does that leave Raoul Dufy, Edward R. Murrow, and the Budapest String Quartet? People, who for the most part don't do anything more definite in their own lives than hold a job and inadvertently have a couple of children, insist on being so *definite* about whether the things that come in and touch them from the world are "good enough" or not. My friend Grigsby, the intellectual stockbroker (observed last Tuesday carrying *Death Kit* onto the Lexington Avenue express), keeps moaning on about how Broadway is destroying itself with its insistence that every single play be a hit, and so what do we have of a certain evening but Grigsby the playgoer ambling out of *The Birthday Party* and saying with great seriousness (his beautiful Racquet Club face glowing with the truth and beauty of his discrimination), "Of course, it's *not* Shakespeare, but"—and here a brave little smile—"it had some interesting moments." The day after the PBL début, in fact, I saw that a television critic had begun his column saying, "The première last night of the Public Broadcast Laboratory was not the second coming of Marconi." Well, that's all right, I guess. Marconi is different things to different men is my motto. Even so, it seems that journalism everywhere, but especially broadcast journalism, is in such a state of disrepair that anything even half as good as that first PBL show ought to be treated with great care, and—I suppose it is a sappy thing to say—with some affection. Oh, yes, I grant you that one ought to preserve one's critical detachment ("critical function," I think it's also called), and that if something isn't up to snuff one ought to say so, and not go mousing along about how those wonderful kids in the chorus line worked so hard in Philadelphia, and so on. The thing is that, despite the complaints of one's more politically sexy friends that PBL didn't go far enough (and, of course, the complaints of various Educational-TV stations that it went too far), there just isn't anything around on American TV that gives any sign of being able to do what this outfit can do, and, especially, could do if it had the steady money, and independence, and sense of ease and mission with which to develop both a really good staff and —well, not so much a point of view as maybe a firm, independent grip on what the hell is going on around us.

On the first Sunday's show—the source of Mr. Friendly's disappointment—sure, there were some things that didn't work. A whole lot of that opening section on the political races in Gary, Cleveland, and Boston seemed like second-best network-TV coverage: announcers standing in front of the camera to "define" the story and to presumably provide that viewer identification with a nice-looking, baritone reporter that networks regard as an integral part of serious television journalism; the camera showing often irrelevant but "visual" events, such as a bunch of old biddies dancing around a street in Boston, while a voice-over narrator delivered captionlike observations about Mrs. Hicks and the backlash situation; another voice-over narrator saying on at least two occasions that the striking thing about the beginning of Stokes's campaign had been his attempt to run as a non-racial candidate, and also showing a seemingly significant film clip of a Stokes speech in which none of that came through; and what seemed like just a lot of rather bumbly newsreel camerawork, as if the cameramen were somehow determined not to be "commercial" and had read somewhere about *cinéma vérité* being a desirable intellectualish alternative and thought they would give it a good try. Well, okay. It must have made the hearts sing over at the big networks to see the "nonprofit" people at PBL try to do the same things they do (and especially after all those ads about "we promise" and "we intend" and "we are going to show you") and then not even do as well. But there were a couple of other things in those two and a half hours that ought to make people, if not exactly amok with enthusiasm, at least a little more modest about the point and the effect of adding their gleaming, shining, so, so valuable (for heaven's sakes, let's not lower our critical standards) weight of disappointment on top of an enterprise that needs just about all the unweighted freedom of movement it can get. The first was that section in Chicago, where PBL had piled a whole bunch of people into what looked like a prize ring but was really only the studios of the Educational-TV station in Chicago, and had got them talking and haranguing and now and then yelling at each other about black and white. It was just very good, although maybe you and I and the Bishop of Brompton would have done it a bit differently—I mean, there was that second-string Black Power guru, Russ Meeks, who kept grinding on and on and on and on, standing up there eyeball to eyeball with all those sweet little liberal old ladies and just blasting them to pieces with what at times seemed like an unnecessary amount of heavy artillery, and that vague, do-gooding Negro minister who seemed to be part of some other program, and those two wise Negro kids in the back who kept giving sass to all the poor white liberals, which would have been okay except it was second-hand sass, and so forth and so forth. I mean, the "dialogue" was out of kilter—it really wasn't a dialogue at all. It wasn't balanced. Why should it be balanced? It was just very good, it unfolded, showed people expressing things they thought about this issue; and if I knew anywhere else on the airwaves that you found this sort of thing I'd maybe be a little more offhand about what PBL did that night, but then I don't.

The same thing goes for the supposedly controversial play "Day of Absence," by Douglas Turner Ward, which took up the rest of the program, and which many of the Educational-TV stations in the South seem to have found so tough to handle, and which Mr. Friendly (there goes Mr. Friendly again; I'm sorry, Mr. Friendly) found tedious. I guess it was a bit tedious, after all. It had a lot of mannerisms it didn't really seem to need—that scene at the beginning with those two old guys drowsing on the front stoop—and then about five minutes before the actual end it seemed about to end but didn't, which was a pity, and when the ending did come you felt the playwright had fished into a hat containing fifteen possible endings and just closed his eyes and pulled one out. I think it's fair to say that Ward's play was on the long side, but I think it's also fair to say that there are probably only three and a half people in this country right now who can be counted on to know the difference between editing and the sort of technical censorship described as "cutting" ("Awful sorry, Mr. Strindberg, but the choreographer says we'll have to lose a couple of speeches in the second act . . ."), and, it seems to me, if you happen to somehow stumble onto a genuine individual talent such as Mr. Ward's, maybe the best thing is to show a little nerve and go along with him—bit of tedium and all. Tedium, admittedly, is pretty grim, but maybe the only worse thing than feeling it is never being given the chance to find out whose tedium it really is. I don't think Ward's play is going to set Parnassus, or even Marconi, on fire—why should it?—but if there's been a more interesting piece of imaginative work on television about the racial question than "Day of Absence," I don't know what it is, or where it's been. It certainly wasn't last season's ricky-tick offering by *CBS Playhouse* ("The Final War of Olly Winter") about a Negro GI in Vietnam.

In short, I think there were some genuinely special things about that first PBL show, which you just don't get on network TV and which you haven't up to now had on Educational TV: the aforementioned "dialogue" in Chicago, and Ward's play, and (as a smaller sample) a section of film, preceding the Chicago dialogue, that had been filmed and narrated by Mr. Meeks without "any interference or censorship" by PBL—and the fact that it's useful and relevant for people like PBL to make that sort of disclaimer may be an indication of where things still are in the world's largest non-state-operated, non-authoritarian, free-market broadcast system. In short, maybe people might relax their critical instincts just a little—at least to the point of not getting quite so anxious about their own individual artistic or journalistic purities being deflowered or otherwise impaired by some not absolutely first-rate ("Well, it's not II Isaiah, but . . .") piece of work—and then perhaps an enterprise like PBL will have the chance to develop into something really useful. One thing that certainly seems more likely than not, anyway, is that, relax or not, within either the medium term or the short term, commercial TV will split most of its prime-time programing between movies (which it's nearly already done) and large-scale news-and-information shows (which, with the apparent suicide of the new series shows, and the relative success of CBS's four-part Warren Report study, ABC's four-hour "special" on Africa, and the expanded Huntley-Brinkley format, seems a trend now dimly under way), and although I think it will be a fine thing if the networks turn themselves into *Life* Magazines of the Air—a finer thing, anyway, than their current incarnations as Pulp Fiction Magazines of the Air—there damned well ought to be a *New Republic* Magazine of the Air somewhere on the horizon, or we will pretty soon all sink, singing bravely, into the mud.

Oh, yes. One small note: It seems to me the PBL people could get along without those fake commercials. I mean, do a serious takeout on cigarettes or cigarette commercials, or hire some smart young kid from the *Yale Record* and do a funny one. There was something so maddeningly heavy and pious about that young lady breaking the long cigarette in two and then delivering a little sermon (sermonette?) on the evils thereof—it made one want to light up at least six cigarettes at once in self-defense.

PRESIDENT JOHNSON MODELS THE
NEW MICROPHONE, THE GOVERNOR
OF MICHIGAN BRANDISHES AN
ISSUE, THE SHIP OF STATE SAILS
ON, & OTHER MELODIES OF
THE NINETEEN-SIXTIES

In 1669, according to the story, Dr. Barrow, then holding the famous Lucasian Chair of Mathematics at Cambridge, called in one of his students, Isaac Newton, and declared that since Newton was so much brighter than he was, he was handing over the job to him, and did so, and then moved on to other things and lived happily ever after. Unfortunately, this excellent method of handling the succession to high office seems to have started and stopped with the Lucasian Chair of Mathematics at Cambridge in 1669, and so last Friday morning in Washington, D.C., the President of the United States held one of his infrequent press conferences in the East Room of the White House and more or less officially opened the 1968 campaign. It was a pretty effective performance, as these things go. The President disdained the usual business of standing behind the lectern and delivering homilies in his celebrated Pedernales Slowspeech manner, in favor of wearing a microphone hidden under his suit jacket and ambling up and down in front of the lectern, alternately gesticulating, waving his arms, scowling, smiling, drawing imaginary figures in the air, and, in general, doing just about everything a man walking around loose with a microphone under his coat could do except award prizes to the audience. Followers of the Presidential image were quick to remark on the President's new manner—or, rather, on his new old manner. It was "pretty darned effective," a Republican congressman said to The New York Times, thereupon asking that his name not be used, doubtless aware that when a congressman says "darned" the *Times* will not hesitate to print it. Others, mostly non-Republicans, seemed to feel that "the real Johnson" was finally coming through. The great thing about a television press conference, of course, is that the President, even if he can't control most of the questions, can control the rhythm of the questions and answers (certainly the answers), and in so doing can in effect conduct a sort of personal essay, an exercise in style, under the guise of a discussion of issues. For example, when the President, in answer to a question about "your present assessment of our progress and prospects in Vietnam," replies, "First, I think every American heart should swell with pride at the competence and capacity of our leadership in Vietnam," he obviously isn't trying to tell anyone about the war or its prospects or its progress; he's trying to advertise himself as the kind of man whose heart swells with pride. And then, in case one should think that while his heart was swelling his brain was shrinking, he quickly goes on to advertise his Grasp of the Realities. "I have spent—I've had three meetings with Ambassador Bunker and three with General Westmoreland. I had coffee with him at length this morning just before I came here. Our American people, when we get in a contest of any kind, whether it's in a war or in an election or in a football game or what it is—they want it decided and decided quickly, and get in or get out, and they like for that curve to rise like this [much arm-waving here] and for the opposition to go down like this [more arm-waving]. Now, that's not the kind of war we're fighting in Vietnam. . . . We don't march out and have a big battle each day in a guerrilla war. It's a new kind of war for us, so it doesn't move that fast. . . ." Which is all marvelous stuff, from the coffee with General Westmoreland ("at length," too), with its implication of the two old pros having a little man-talk around the corral, and all that business about the curve rising like this and the opposition going down like this (which must have been the first time anyone in Grover's Corners had thought to think about it *that* way), to the information that the war isn't moving so fast because it's a guerrilla war, which is true enough, except that, as General Westmoreland might have remarked over an additional prune Danish, maybe the more interesting point is that only one of the sides is fighting it as a guerrilla war—not, unfortunately, ours. Oh, well. Politics. Style. The art of the possible, and so forth.

People nowadays have this funny thing about style in politics. They throw the word around a lot in a wishfully modernist sort of way, but with this great wariness—as if all of us were really terribly serious people, whose minds were constantly struggling toward a rigorous, deeply meaningful exploration of some wal- nutty objective substance known as the "issues," only to be peri- odically distracted, against our better judgment, by such super- ficial and shady considerations as personality (which is what it was called twenty years ago), or style. Of course, politics is such an attractive thing these days. Everyone is serious about politics. Brave young Wall Street lawyers—the kind who, if they play their cards right, can look forward to becoming partners any time within the next eighty-two years—get off into corners of expensively furnished living rooms and announce, with hopeful sexiness, that their "real interest is politics; I mean, it's the only thing." And yet, actually, perhaps one of the larger ironies of the time is that at the very same moment everyone is so bravely talk- ing about the seriousness of politics the world seems to be moving into an area where the public actions of individual men are less and less able to affect the things they are supposed to affect. The racial problem in America, for example, is certainly in need of laws and programs and organization and, in general, all the structuring and restructuring that go under the name of political action, but— what is more important, and more obvious—it also appears to be far above, below, or beyond the reach of politics; politics touches such a small part of the life of a modern nation, and surely one of the main reasons for President Kennedy's enduring grip on the people of this country is that, for all the talk about the Irish Mafia and political activism, his appeal was so minimally political.

Television has got wound increasingly into politics of late, be- cause it's obviously the best (or easiest) way of both showing and seeing a candidate, and because people seem to have this feeling that TV exerts a mysterious power over politicians and electorates, as if there were some sort of magic aura connected with TV exposure—as opposed to "real" exposure—as if, with the right TV consultant and a smooth speech and an attractive smile, even a movie actor could be elected President. I guess there's some truth in that. TV (plus a lot of money) does give you a great deal of exposure, and if you have any cash left over you can indeed hire a TV consultant who will tell you what shirt to wear, which side of your face looks less alarming, and so forth. But it's hard to see, really, that TV as a mechanical device has any particular style-evoking magic to it. If people were really more concerned with issues than with the personality of public figures, TV would as blandly transmit the issues, the facts, the statistics, the heart-of-the-matter, the meat around the bone—the crop reports and so forth, as it does on East German TV, and which no one even there can stand to look at. But people nowadays, for whatever reasons, seem to want so terribly to touch and be reassured by personality—not just by its presence but by its implications (the hope, for example, that one attaches in one's own feelings to a leader, and that is still so much a realer thing than any issue), and TV simply happens to be the best way to effect that—certainly the best way for the politician to reveal himself, because to such a considerable degree he can control the revelation. TV, in other words, will reveal whatever it is you want to have revealed, and these days (I don't know what it was in Bryan's time) it is style —the reality or the appearance of personal qualities, it doesn't seem to much matter which. It's hard to believe that it was the issues that defeated Goldwater in 1964, although I admit he was pushing them pretty far. It's hard to see how the "issues" are going to be what really elect or defeat anyone in 1968. The Vietnam war, in fact, provides an almost classic example of the relative unimportance to people of the issues of a given situation. There are plenty of issues on all sides—enough for a great many speeches—but most of the political candidates, whether they're pro-war or anti-war, seem to handle them rather distractedly, as if the man standing up there in the big auditorium holding an issue carefully in his hands ("corruption," "losing the war," "winning the war") knew that in fact he was performing a sort of ritual, the ritual of holding the issue aloft so that the congregation could look upon it and pretend to worship it, whereas actually he and they understand that all the time the congregation is gazing adoringly at the man, though none of them can stand to admit it, and neither can anyone else. President Johnson appears to know this perfectly well—that people are going to reelect him or not because of his style, because of the *way* he went about things in Vietnam, rather than because of what he actually did or didn't do. Governor Romney ("of Michigan," as the *Times* would say) was on TV too the other day—on a Sunday-afternoon *Face the Nation*—and it's hard to know what the Governor really thinks about style, and so on, except that his seems better suited to still photographs than to moving, talking pictures. You get that great Coeur-de-Lion face on a full-page spread in *Life,* for instance, with maybe a little caption beneath it about the Governor launching into a full-scale attack on this or that, and you have something quite beautiful. On TV, though, that day, Romney kept worrying around for issues, which is okay (you have to talk about something), but the effort seemed to show rather much. "The President of the United States made a colossal mistake," declared the Governor, in the manner of a man announcing that the sky has fallen, "in the campaign of 1964," and then went into some business about how Lyndon Johnson's campaign statements at that time had had the effect of persuading the North Vietnamese to intensify the war. "I want to submit," said the Governor, "that it's entirely possible that those statements made in the 1964 campaign had an effect on Vietnam, and what we've had to do there, and what the South Vietnamese have had to face." Yes. Well. Gosh. But.

Speaking of style and issues, at the same hour that CBS had Governor Romney blowing the lid off the 1964 campaign, NBC had Ambassador Bunker and General Westmoreland together on *Meet the Press,* and I am here to tell you they were two smooth

old boys; oh, they both sat up there behind that table—the ambassador, who is seventy-three years old, and the general, who is
not seventy-three years old (the general was the one with all the
medals)—and just told it to us like it was. The general told us
about how the North Vietnamese Army was falling apart ("Well,
as I said, they are having manpower problems. They had hoped to
send leadership from the north and recruit their troops in the
south. This they have been unable to do because the South Vietnamese youngster does not in general want to join the Vietcong,
and, second, there has been considerable attrition on his guerrilla
ranks. . . . He is going to the young age and older group. He
has been very hungry for a victory. He has tried desperately to
get one, and each time he has initiated a big operation it has
rebounded in his disfavor"). The ambassador put the "corruption" issue in its proper perspective ("Obviously there is corruption there. . . . I imagine there is some corruption in this country too. I don't pretend that it is going to be completely eradi-
cated there any more than it is here, or elsewhere. But steps are
being taken to do something about it. In the first place, Vice-
President Ky says . . ."). The swell thing about the Bunker-
Westmoreland routine was that it was so beautifully controlled.
The four newsmen asking them questions were perfectly able,
the questions were okay (not at all too deferential, some of them
quite tough), but the answers were all based on revealed scrip-
ture, the answers had all been brought down from the Mount,
and none of the newsmen had apparently been up there recently.
I imagine there will be a good deal more of that sort of thing
before the next twelve months are out—some Iowa Republican
dressed up in the latest modish anti-administration manner, with
shaggy hair, pink glasses, and an exploding shirt, standing on his
chair and saying indignantly, "Well, what about land reform?"
and the sweet little old lady, who has sixteen grandchildren in the
101st Airborne and is at that moment representing the administration, standing on the podium, wearing spurs and an American
flag, and replying sweetly but firmly, "The past government that
just went out of power distributed some a hundred and twenty-

eight thousand titles" (as Ambassador Bunker replied last Sunday). As if anyone knew how many were available for distribution. As if anyone knew who it was they were being distributed to. As if (come on, now, really) anyone cared that much about land reform.

PROPAGANDA

Journalism is in a state of change, like everything else these days, in part shaping its audience, its readers—the people who call it into being; mostly, one suspects (despite modern genuflections to the religious power of media), being in fact *shaped* by the forces already at work within the people, and one of the more striking directions it seems to have been heading in over the past few years is toward an increasing, almost casual acceptance of propaganda as the most effective and natural vehicle for communicating about matters of recognized importance. Propaganda admittedly means different things to different people—usually pejorative, usually carrying with it some misty image of Dr. Goebbels speaking benignly into a microphone about the occupation of the Sudetenland. But if that's propaganda (which it is), so also is President Johnson's press conference, and so, too, is Senator Fulbright's press conference, and so are most speeches or writings by most people in public life, which aren't strictly journalism but which, transcribed at face value by the press, become journalism, and which now in turn seem to be breeding a growing counterpropaganda, as apparently (or so say the counterpropagandists) the only method of setting the picture straight. *Time*'s recent stories about the war in Vietnam seem to be mainly propaganda. Mary McCarthy's articles on Vietnam in the *New York Review of Books* seem also to be propaganda. *Life*'s "reporting" on runaway kids in the East Village seems to be propaganda, as does an informative article in *Ramparts* on the drug scene in San Francisco. In fact, it's hard right now to find many sources of journalism where propaganda is consistently absent; mostly, propaganda isn't only there but is the fluid that just about everything else seems to be swimming in. To be sure, larger and larger areas of the press more or less have to print it—the *Times*, for example, which is required by its information-happy readers to carry Secretary So-and-So's recent address about the poverty program but can't really get around to examining it, to connecting it to reality, until a later date, or, at best, in somebody else's story on some other page. Or TV news, which is also required by its audience to eye-witness public history, and thus, since public history is mostly propaganda, gets stuck most of the time with just passing along everybody else's propaganda: Hubert Humphrey's in Vietnam, Norman Mailer's in Washington—you name it. But what seems to be happening more and more these days is that even in those areas in which propaganda isn't so structurally required (in the general magazines, especially in the intellectual magazines, and to a now considerable degree in TV news-and-information programs), propaganda appears to be the vocabulary that people have simply come to feel is best suited to the times—as if in considering an actual situation today (for example, Negro rioting in Newark or the burning of a village in Vietnam) one had made some sort of explicit decision that although the actuality of the situation was real and important, what was more real and more important was what the people you were communicating with could be brought to feel about it. The substance at the center is not the actuality but the feelings around it. The main thing is not the event, and the need to describe it, but to describe it in such a way that people will feel the way you would like them to feel about it. *Fortune* handles information to make its readers feel "right" about AT&T. The *Nation* handles information to make its readers feel "right" about the Bolivian guerrilla movement. *Look* handles information to make its readers feel "right" about the hippies. Even in entertainment journalism, the new-school, "interpretive-journalist" approach to, say, a jazz musician or a movie star certainly isn't the actuality—what the movie star said is no longer important for having actually been *said*, and thus is no longer transcribed with that in mind, or later read with that in mind. What's important is the feel of it all, the feelings the writer hopes he can evoke in the reader about the movie star (and usually, in these cases, about himself as well), and when these feelings run counter to the spoken word, the observed act, the word and the act are usually bent—and nobody much seems to mind. If writers write differently now, maybe it's because people read differently; it's hard to tell.

Speaking of such matters, a couple of Fridays ago NBC put on a much-publicized news special about the Negro soldier in Vietnam, called "Same Mud, Same Blood," which seemed to have little reason for existence at all except as propaganda—and such damned casual, good-guy, racist propaganda, too. Frank McGee, who has generally been reasonably intelligent and straight about these matters, apparently went to Vietnam last fall and spent a number of weeks with an American platoon (which was a good thing to do) and then came back and put together sixty minutes of film, consisting almost entirely of McGee (off camera) and various white and black soldiers patting each other on the back about what a great thing it is to be a Negro in the United States Army, where a man is but a man & so forth: what a great thing it is for the Negro (who is now presumably extended the possibility of achieving manhood and death in the same instant—certainly a classical, if not an entirely forward, step), and what a great redemptive thing, by implication, it is for all of us poor benighted heathen back here in our segregated clubs and ice-cream parlors.

McGee: For this report, the fact that Larry [Sergeant Lewis Larry] is a Negro is of paramount importance. To the officers and men he serves with, it's a matter of total irrelevance. . . .

Specialist 4th Class Hawkins: He just doesn't come up and tell you to do something he wouldn't do himself. He'll sort of ask you to do something, where in a sense he's asking you to do it and telling you to do it and making you want to do it. . . .

McGee: In civilian life, it is still rare for whites to take orders from Negroes, particularly in the South. . . .

Captain Mavroudis: There are lots of Southern boys in Sergeant Larry's platoon that possibly in civilian life would resent working for a Negro, but when we're out in the field, which is almost all the time, people go beyond the color barrier.

Private Faircloth: It doesn't seem to bother anyone to take orders from him. Nobody in the field—they don't think nothing about it. I've never heard a sling thrown at him because he is of the Negro race.

Well, this isn't exactly (or necessarily) rubbish. But it surely isn't news, either, that the Army gives a fair shake to the Negro —although there are doubtless a small number of grown people in this country who keep insisting that the Negro is the victim of some gigantic military-sociological plot to shanghai him out of his ghetto, stuff him into an olive-drab uniform, and pack him off below decks to Samarkand or Southeast Asia to die for White America. For a number of years it hasn't been exactly a secret that the American military is a pretty good way station for the American Negro—at one point, I think, Daniel Patrick Moynihan Himself was saying that one ought to *encourage* the Negro to go into the military—but then, for much the same sort of reasons, so is the backfield of the Detroit Lions, and one would think that the implications of *that* sort of Manhood syndrome would be a good deal more to the point than any self-comforting talk about how, white or black, it's all the sweet same at the bottom of the pile-up.

McGee: Until now, there's been a belief Negro soldiers lacked courage. . . .

Lieutenant Unger: On the subject of the courage of the Negro soldier, there's been a lot written that they did not measure up to the courage commonly found in the white soldier. . . . A man is a man and each one has his own fears . . . and I think you get just as many white cowards as you get black cowards. And you get just as many black heroes as you get white heroes.

MᴄGᴇᴇ: The officers above Larry and the men beneath him have seen him under fire. There is no more severe test of a man. At such times, buried racial antagonisms might surface. . . .

Pʀɪᴠᴀᴛᴇ Fᴀɪʀᴄʟᴏᴛʜ: You look at 'em . . . and, well, they're just another guy out there, a guy you can bum a cigarette off of if you're out, or get a drink of water if you're out, or a can of food. Everything is share and share alike.

MᴄGᴇᴇ: Arkansas [Faircloth] grew up where Negroes must drink from separate fountains. Today he drinks from the same canteen cup. I wondered how the folks back home would feel about that.

Pʀɪᴠᴀᴛᴇ Fᴀɪʀᴄʟᴏᴛʜ: Most of them would think it was the most terrible thing in the world, you know. They come over here and spend a couple of months, they'd learn it, too. . . .

Sᴘᴇᴄɪᴀʟɪsᴛ 4ᴛʜ Cʟᴀss Hᴀᴡᴋɪɴs: After you're with them so long, you're not looking at a man's color. You're looking at his intentions and his job and what he's doing.

What made much of this (and there was a lot of it) so appalling was that on its own terms it wasn't wrong; if a white soldier says that when he's out on patrol he doesn't worry about the color of a man's skin, not only is it probably true but it isn't even really worth saying. Out there in an open lifeboat in the North Atlantic, your average Guelph probably doesn't get fussed too much by your average Ghibelline, either. It's when the wind dies down, the sea grows calm, and everybody comes ashore that all hell breaks loose. Negroes and whites make it in combat because of what combat is, and this says more about the inability of most people to hold more than one strong idea in their heads at a given time than it does about anyone's great sense of humanity, brotherhood, or whatever. In Germany, for example, where there are a number of American troops but no combat, the racial situation in the Army settles back into something approximating what it is back home; the Army in Germany is technically desegregated, and the Negro has his fair shake there too, but blacks and whites keep mostly to themselves—tend to frequent different bars off base, and so forth—and at times express the predictable hostilities. The thing is, I guess, that the Army doesn't teach you much about anything except the Army, or maybe another army. The Army is a very bare room with men in it, only men, and a few objects, and although it's true that now and then men will rush at one another's throats because of theories generated entirely inside their minds, it seems more generally true that people are intrinsically passive about life, and if you take away for a moment the mother weeping, the bishop preaching, the neighbor arguing, the editor editorializing—if you take away most of the hundreds of tiny things that push or pull men one way or the other—you tend to end up with someone who is pretty well content to go along, and get through the day, and share his canteen. Man in the Army isn't man in life, and when you bring back the forces of life—the bishop, the wife, the welfare clerk, the Black Power leader—whatever susceptibilities were there before are usually still there, and the ball game goes on.

Toward the end of the program there was a brief sequence showing the men in Sergeant Larry's platoon under fire, and a small scene of a memorial service for the dead—which might have been more moving if the program, to begin with, had been about men instead of dialectics—and then McGee's voice came on again:

McGee: Some may feel that our society, through the war in Vietnam, is making a terrible demand on the Negro in exchange for accepting him as a man, a human being. But Sergeant Larry feels a debt to the Army.

Sergeant Larry: I feel that I have too much of military experience to get out. I think I'd be wasting it. I think I would hurt the Army. I think they can use my experience. The younger people that are going to come are going to need somebody to help them.

McGee: Our history books have taken little notice of the Negro soldier. How do the troops of this war, black and white, want its history written?

CAPTAIN MAVROUDIS: You can't divide them as a group. It's the man, not the color, and as far as I'm concerned the credit for anything that happens in this war, no matter what the outcome, belongs to both the white and Negro.

MCGEE: Wilkinson, the young Negro officer, told how he would want a child of his to question him about the war.

LIEUTENANT WILKINSON: I would want my child to ask me the role of the American soldier in Vietnam. But as to breaking it down, to, say, "Well, we have a total of good deeds by colored soldiers this high, and we have a stack of good deeds by white soldiers this high"—I mean no, I won't have it come out that way. . . .

It went on a bit longer like that, and then the program stopped, and it all seemed so strange—I couldn't figure out why. And then later I realized that not only had the documentary-makers all the time been casually employing the best of modern propaganda techniques upon their subjects, but the subjects had been just as casually and blandly employing different propaganda techniques upon themselves. There had been actual people speaking actual words in an actual place—and none of it had been real. Except maybe that since propaganda has become such a large part of our lives, the propaganda itself is now reality. And there you have it.

SOMETHING LIVE

I was trying to figure out, the other day, how many people were watching PBL on Sunday evenings, and called the press office there to find out if they had any idea. No, they said, they didn't have any idea at all. PBL didn't have enough money to go spending it on rating services, they said, in a tone that implied that if they had the money they certainly wouldn't be spending it on anything as crass and worldly as trying to find out how many and what sort of people they were talking to. *TV Guide* that week was a bit more helpful. It reported that "a few commercial networkers" had figured out that since there hadn't been much doing on Educational TV on Sunday nights before PBL came along, the people now watching PBL were people who had previously been watching the network shows, and so they had simply made some additions and some subtractions and had come up with a hypothetical Nielsen of roughly 0.9 per cent for PBL (compared to a recent Sunday evening Nielsen rating of 27.2 for Ed Sullivan and 24.3 for the Smothers Brothers). This seems a little hard on PBL, since you'd imagine that a good many of the people whom PBL is supposed to attract are people who wouldn't be watching Ed Sullivan anyway. All the same, whatever the statistic is worth, a Nielsen of 0.9 per cent adds up to roughly five hundred thousand families, which is peanuts, and if that's anything like the number of people who are actually watching PBL it's a damned shame besides, because ever since its start, a few weeks ago, PBL has been the most consistently interesting and substantial public-affairs program right now in American broadcasting. Granted, the stuff it does isn't always wonderful. Granted, it tends to tumble rather easily into pipe-and-corduroy liberal good-guyism—like uncorking a sixty-minute sage-and-student session with Walter Lippmann last month as if he were the Fisher King himself. But for the most part, it seems to me, the PBL people do very well by their mandate. They go after relevant subjects, and they go after them live wherever possible, and although it's true that doing something live doesn't automatically make it good, there's still the fact that live coverage, whether it's a President's funeral or a couple of people talking, or even one of those blessed football games, is the one moment in time when TV itself becomes alive—becomes more than a piece of furniture, or a dispensing machine for prefilmed entertainment or information.

On a recent Sunday, for example, PBL had the idea of getting some policemen and Negroes and sociologists and so forth together to talk about the role of the police in the community. There were a bunch of cops sitting on little chairs in a studio in Philadelphia, and some professors in New York, and various experts in places like St. Louis and Denver, and a whole churchful of black militants in Detroit, and Edward P. Morgan, PBL's moderator, would throw out a question to, say, a police official in Philadelphia, and then have somebody in the Detroit church comment on his answer—all of it live, and a lot of it noisy and boisterous, with some big cop steaming on about how the rabble-rousers "like King and Carmichael" were causing all the trouble to begin with, and this beautifully smooth, demagogic minister in Detroit cutting in to say a little something about how "Whitey's police" were interested only in "committing genocide on the black race," and the professors in New York sadly telling each other about how the "discussion" seemed to be becoming increasingly "polarized." And it was, at that. A whole lot of the discussion didn't add up to an awful lot, and wasn't always even a discussion, since the more militant cops and anti-cops were mostly talking to themselves, and seemed irretrievably embedded in their own prejudices. But, for all its blather and rhetoric, I thought the program was very good and useful, and I'm not saying that just because I want to pat PBL on the head for being so sweet and uncommercial. When you come right down to it, what is this neat-and-positive "something" that discussions are always supposed to add up to? At the end of the PBL show, I kept thinking of those people who, at two in the morning, after a really grand free-for-all, with everyone yelling or sulking or rolling around on the rug, go around cleaning up ashtrays and muttering about "Well, and I'd so hoped we were going to get a really constructive discussion going." What was good about PBL that night— even that night, which was one of its weaker programs—was that it really tried to pitch into a contemporary, highly relevant subject, and it did it live and straight, which means that it risked having the people on its program be boring or bigoted or "unconstructive" themselves, and didn't feel the need to be constantly protecting *us* from *them* by editing and analysis, by "Come in, Walter," and "How about that, Chet?"

Not that everything on TV would be better for being live, by any means. A couple of Tuesdays ago, at ten in the evening, CBS News slid across a *CBS Reports* called "What about Ronald Reagan?" which I think is quite simply one of the best TV documentaries I've seen, and one that could well stand as a model for straightforward, responsible, uncanted TV journalism. Harry Reasoner did the narration for the Reagan program, and I imagine a lot of the credit goes to him, not just because he wrote his own material (which he did, and which was intelligent and remarkably free of cliché and had a nice pace to it) but because I had the impression that he and the other CBS people had worked hard at getting a lot of substantial material about Reagan, and that they'd then put it all down as straight as possible, not taking the easy routes, and not getting hung up, either, on the sort of artificial balancing act that seems to afflict so many TV documentaries on difficult subjects. If there was a balance to the report, it was a balance that seemed to come out of the material, and not out of the network. They had a whole lot of interesting stuff from old Reagan home movies (Reagan as a lifeguard, etc.); scenes from Reagan's Hollywood movies, which were handled with a good touch; interviews with movie people who had known Reagan in the old Hollywood days; film clips of Reagan's speeches during his campaign for governor and as governor; and a couple of striking interviews with members of the California right wing, who seemed to be now disowning Reagan. "He's talking the conservative language, but practically everything he's doing is more liberal than the administration we had here under Pat Brown," said a conservative businessman called William Penn Patrick. "These are things the conservatives are concerned about, and they have a right to be. We have, in my opinion, been betrayed by Mr. Reagan." Reagan is such an easy target to be joky about, and though Reasoner & Co. were hardly engaged in deep knee bends of awe and wonder, they were at pains to point out that Reagan was now a genuine political figure, with immense general appeal, and that nobody recently had gained very much by not taking him seriously. By the end of the program, I felt that Reagan had emerged as a man, rather than as a cartoon, and one of the things I thought was especially good about it all was that, for the first time since I can remember, a TV news outfit had used film techniques both imaginatively and responsibly on a hard-news subject. In other words, they didn't waste a whole lot of time on Reagan galloping his horse just because it was "visual." They spent most of the time, really, on what Reagan said and what people were saying about Reagan—speeches and interviews, dull stuff. They did it filmically, though, cutting and panning, but cutting and panning in terms of the material, not in terms of what some art director thought was sexy, and the result was that it wasn't dull at all. It moved and was alive, and seemed honest.

Oh, yes. Speaking of honesty, or something. There was a mighty curious bit of business on CBS the other afternoon— "Airlift: Vietnam." The *Times* TV listing seemed to describe it as a documentary—and there was old Bob Considine in his combat greens, and there we were in Vietnam, with a lot of aircraft and helicopters, and Big Bob was interviewing soldiers about the "airlift."

"What do you think of the airlift, son?" Big Bob would say.

"Oh, I like it, sir," the GI would answer.

"Why do you like it, son?" Big Bob would ask.

"Because it brings us food and water and ammunition," the GI would say.

Dozens of interviews more or less like that. And General Westmoreland. And flags flying. And more aircraft. At the end of the program, a little note appeared on the screen: "Produced as a Public Service by American Airlines."

I called CBS later to ask them about it.

CBS didn't know anything; they said it belonged to WCBS-TV, their New York affiliate.

I called WCBS-TV.

"Oh, yes, the Considine show," a cheery voice answered.

I asked who had paid for it.

"Who paid for it?" There was a longish pause. "American Airlines paid for it."

Well, it's nice to know these things. I guess if there's no law that says McCann-Erickson can't produce its own entertainment series, there's no law that says American Airlines can't produce its own documentaries. But maybe somebody ought to start running one up the flagpole pretty soon.

When TV goes dead, it really goes dead—like one of those machines in Antonioni's *Red Desert*, which actually don't ever stop but keep on pumping and grinding, grinding and pumping, seemingly aimlessly, with no sign of life around them, no sign of life in them, no people visible, and all the time one looks at them and knows that machines don't yet exist for other machines, they exist for men, are made by men for other men, and if the machines are really like this, what then (one wonders) must the men be like? I suppose one can be too serious about these things. Mike Douglas opened his show the other afternoon singing "How Come You Do Me Like You Do Do Do?"—walking up and down the aisle of the studio with the microphone cord trailing behind him, and when it was over he stopped beside a middle-aged woman in the audience. "I had a feeling that was going to be just the right sort of song for today," he said, and patted the woman on the top of her head. The woman giggled. "I was right, wasn't I?" The woman giggled again. "Oh, I think we're going to have a whole lot of fun from here on in, a whole lot of fun," he said. The audience applauded, and Douglas went back onstage and introduced the film critic Judith Crist. ("You mean you actually get *paid* for going to the movies?" "Honestly, Mike, I wouldn't do anything else.") The other evening Jerry Lewis was standing onstage beside a horse. Lewis was wearing riding breeches, buck teeth, and rimless glasses, and was holding the horse by a rope. "You heard the old line," he was saying, "about how you can lead a horse to water but you can't make him drink." He grinned. "They must have been talking about Mexican horses." Small laughter. "Anyway, Mexican water." Loud laughter. Lewis ducked his head and peered out brightly. "They call them trotters." A great crash of laughter and applause. Over at CBS, Red Skelton was also standing onstage, without a horse, but wearing a long fur coat. "It's supposed to be mink," he said, "but I put it in the closet with my wife's fur coat that I bought last year, and when I opened the door the next day we had five coats." Laughter. "You can see that fur coats are made from rodents. That's right, a mink is just a rodent. A mink is nothing but a rat with a press agent." Laughter. "Oh, it's so cold here in California." Skelton pulled the coat tighter around him. More laughter. "You know, I don't want to complain about CBS." Laughter. "But their idea of heating this place is to have"—big grimace—"three hippies down here." Laughter. "Burning their draft cards." Tremendous laughter and applause. "I come from Indiana, and the winters back there, we used to have those Sophia Loren snows. You know, Sophia Loren snows. Forty inches." Big crash of laughter. "All right. I'm going to tell you about this spinster woman who went into the store to buy an electric blanket." Laughter. "The salesman said to her, 'Lady, do you want a single blanket or a double?'" Laughter. "*She* said, 'Well, if it was a double'"—grimace and helpless chuckle—"'do you think I'd be needing a blanket?'" Waves of laughter and handclapping. I called CBS a few days later to ask them how they dubbed the laughter on the Skelton show. They said they didn't. It was the audience. There wasn't much of an audience for Helen Gurley Brown's show, *Outrageous Opinions*. Helen Gurley Brown tried to interview the actor Dustin Hoffman about his love life. Dustin Hoffman wouldn't speak about his love life, but he spoke some about his career, the two of them sitting in those little moderny chairs, both, as far as one could see, sound asleep, except that their eyes seemed to be open and sentences would now and then languorously issue from their mouths. "I think the . . . reasons . . . for . . . my . . . success," said Hoffman, "are . . . um . . . luck . . . mostly luck . . . I would say . . . and then being the right . . . type . . . at . . . um . . . the . . . right . . . time." On the Jackie Gleason show, Gleason had Milton Berle for a guest. Berle and Gleason were onstage together, and they had this skit going in which Berle was supposed to play straight man to Gleason so that Gleason could get all the laughs. Gleason would begin one of his jokes, and Berle would go tearing offstage and reappear in a funny costume. At one point, Berle reappeared in a safari outfit—very short pants and some sort of funny safari hat. They both stood there for a moment, looking at each other, and then Gleason gave up what he was doing and came over to Berle and put his arms around him and just shook with laughter. On Channel 13 a Swedish journalist was talking, in UN English, about conditions in China eight months ago, and then Marya Mannes appeared, speaking very crossly about the tyranny of the younger generation. "I have never heard, incidentally," said Miss Mannes, "the phrase 'old talent.'" Everyone seems a bit unplugged these days, but maybe it's just the time of the year. On Channel 7 recently ABC scrambled together a ninety-minute spy-adventure thing called "It Takes a Thief," which starred Robert Wagner as a dashing young burglar who goes to work for the SIA to help it swipe back important documents that have fallen into wrong hands, and which I don't believe contained a single line or scene that hadn't been used, and used better, in some other place at some other time. "Do you think you could handle a woman?" the girl says to dashing Bob. "Oh, anything but people," he says airily. At least, that's what you assume it said in the script. ("HE [*airily*]: Oh, anything but people.") Where ABC was content to rummage through Universal Studios for the sort of discarded third-rate Cary Grant and Hitchcock type of footage that would have sunk the real Grant and Hitchcock years ago without a trace, *Run for Your Life*, the Ben Gazzara series on NBC, aims higher, and, on the night I saw it, did a fudged-over version of *In the Heat of the Night*, with most of the plot missing but with an impressive number of the details very nicely reproduced, right down to Bert Freed playing Rod Steiger playing a sheriff in a small, Neanderthal Southern town (tough, mean, feet on the desk, and everything), and Warren Oates, who played the weak, smiley, nice cop in the movie, this time playing a weak, smiley, mean cop. There was lots of fashionable menace and semi-sadism but, unfortunately, no sex, owing perhaps to the strange nature of the Gazzara character's terminal disease. I guess it's hard, all right, not to crib something if you have to turn out this stuff every week. The thing is that now a good many TV people don't bother cribbing plots, which, after all, can have a new life if they're done again in an individual way. They crib the acting, the stage business, the ambiance, the bloody individuality itself—as in *Mission: Impossible* the other week, where they had a nice scene, involving a spy-turned-fashion-photographer photographing a model, that seemed to have been lifted nearly frame by frame from *Blow-Up*, the only important difference, perhaps, being that the *Mission: Impossible* model had chunky knees and nothing like Veruschka's flare of the nostrils. It was a pretty good show, though, all the same, about this master agent from an unfriendly nation who is set on releasing deadly germs all over our country—a plot, now that I think of it, that was lifted more or less intact from the first *Mission: Impossible* show I saw, last year, also about a master agent from an unfriendly nation who is set on releasing deadly germs, etc. Actually, little similarities like this one on *Mission: Impossible* are all right with me, owing to this strange terminal weakness I seem to have for stories built around potential national catastrophe on an extremely large scale —people swiping cobalt bombs or monkeying around with death rays or threatening to melt the polar icecaps. (Laurence Olivier, as it happens, was in an excellent movie in the nineteen-thirties about a death ray, but I seem to be the only person to have seen it. Or who will admit to having seen it. The death ray was mounted on a ship in the middle of the English Channel, and made, as I remember, a terrifying noise when operated, very much like an electric shoe-polishing machine. I'll try not to say any more about it.) Back to the *Mission: Impossible* show.

What happens is that the master agent is living happily in Connecticut, in what appears to be Henry Luce's old house, posing as this successful fashion photographer (one of these days a master agent is going to get a case of the smarts and start posing as an *un*successful something or other), and is naturally discovered by the *Mission: Impossible* people, who start sneaking about his house in their impenetrable disguises (in this instance, of southern-California television actors posing as *Mission: Impossible* people posing as fashion photographers' models) and right into the master agent's bomb shelter, where he has been keeping all his office supplies, guns, stamps, envelopes, and what appears to be a desk calculating machine by which he regularly gets into contact with his hundreds of subagents all over the country, or maybe the world. The master agent's own country, one should say, is never precisely identified, except that it is small, unfriendly, and has one (1) atomic bomb. Israel, one might guess, although the master agent looks rather more Swedish or Swiss. Still, everything goes beautifully for a while. The master agent is dividing his time usefully and profitably between his fashion photographer's studio and his bomb shelter. The *Mission: Impossible* people are swarming all over the place in their impenetrable disguises, hiding large motor vehicles behind bushes on the master agent's property and jamming the master agent's desk-calculator transmitting apparatus with what appears to be an especially powerful portable dictating machine. Then two of the *Mission: Impossible* people get caught, and the master agent—realizing that his plan for releasing the deadly germs is going phffft—does the only sensible thing. He jogs on down to his bomb shelter and desk-calculates a message off to Sweden or Switzerland to go ahead and drop their one rotten bomb on New York. ("Why New York?" one of the captured *Mission: Impossible* people asks him. The master agent shrugs. Maybe the master agent is a New Yorker, after all.) Anyway, things start to get pretty tense and classic. The master agent stays down there in his bomb shelter with all his secret office supplies and code books, refusing to come out because of the imminent (he thinks) rearrangement of Manhattan, and becoming increasingly strange and moody, doubtless realizing how much he will miss the Pan Am Building and all those $1.40 *al fresco* lunches at the Museum of Modern Art next April. The *Mission: Impossible* people are out there on *top* of the bomb shelter, having cleverly jammed the master agent's desk-calculator request for an atomic bomb. Then *they* do the only sensible thing. They set off a fake atomic-bomb explosion—a wad of TNT or something—right there on the front lawn of Henry Luce's old house. Blam! The master agent goes *very* moody for about four seconds, then waits the appropriate minute and a half for such special effects as the fireball to go by, and then tears up aboveground, and—you guessed it! There is Henry Luce's old house standing just as it used to, and the birds are cheeping, and the grass is growing, and the *Mission: Impossible* people are milling around looking pleasant and helpful, and everyone feels pretty damn silly. I think I still prefer that Laurence Olivier movie, but maybe, with any luck, *Mission: Impossible* will get around to doing it someday.

WATCHMAN, WHAT OF THE NIGHT?

. . . OR, GOD BLESS OUR PUBLIC INTEREST: FURTHER FABLES FOR OUR TIME

Do you remember Walter Judd? Some seven and a half years ago Walter Judd stood upon a platform in the Chicago amphitheater, shrouded in smoke and flags and glare and those hot TV lights, and delivered the keynote address to the Republican Convention, which went on to nominate Richard Nixon. "We believe," said Representative Judd, jabbing his finger out into time and space, "that middle-of-the-road government is in the long run the best kind of government for everyone." And several other things. A little over two weeks ago Dr. Judd, who is retired from Congress now and lives in Washington, sent a letter to his friend Representative John Ashbrook, of the Seventeenth District in Ohio. "Dear Friend," the letter began, in a friendly fashion, and went on to say, "I hope you will read and sign the accompanying letter protesting the proposed showing on the Educational-TV network of Felix Greene's film on North Vietnam—presenting blatant propaganda on behalf of avowed enemies of our country and derogatory to our cause and our fighting men. . . . When American youth are giving their lives in a war against a ruthless enemy, surely we have an obligation to protect their families and the public against anything that strengthens that enemy. With best regards, I am, etc." The "accompanying letter" had already been addressed to Mr. John White, President, National Educational Television, New York City, New York. "Dear Mr. White," this letter began. "*The*

New York Times states that National Educational Television plans to show Felix Greene's film 'North Vietnam—A Personal Report' on January 22, 1968. Is it possible that NET's management is unaware of Mr. Greene's record as a propagandist for Communist China and Communist North Vietnam? . . . We have not yet seen the film by Mr. Greene which NET plans to show, but Radio Hanoi's description of the film clearly indicates that it is nothing more nor less than Communist propaganda. . . . If this is NET's concept of serving the public interest, then the public has a right to ask that the NET management be turned over to men who understand that the public interest is not served by the dissemination of half-truths and lies. . . ." Twenty-seven Republican and six Democratic representatives, none of whom had seen the film, signed the letter, which was then sent on to Mr. White, and was also inserted by Representative Ashbrook in the *Congressional Record*. Representative Omar Burleson, a Texan, and a member of the Foreign Affairs Committee, sent in a letter of his own. "This film," wrote Representative Burleson, who had not seen it either, "is purported to be pure and simple propaganda of North Vietnam. . . . I respectfully protest further consideration for showing this film in the United States." Well, now. It seems they are trying once again to keep us safe. *The castle sleeps:* Ah, Burleson! What shapes are hiding out there in the darkness? Bad words? Bad books? Bad movies? Bad thoughts? The heavy footsteps of dutiful men pace up and down atop the battlements. Each night we sit exposed before the little screen, and they watch over us and keep us safe. Or try to. NET showed the program anyway, which was called "NET Journal—North Vietnam" and ran for two hours on the evening of January 22. The network used Greene's film—or, rather, some of it—but the program didn't turn out to be quite the way those representatives and Dr. Judd had visualized it. I think "visualize" is the word. In its entirety, Greene's film runs for eighty-five minutes. NET used forty-nine minutes of it and devoted the remaining hour or so to a sort of debate or discussion between David Schoenbrun, who represented the anti-war side, and Professor Robert Scalapino, a political scientist from Berkeley, who stood up for the administration's policy.

It was a good program, although Greene's film is obviously one-sided. To look at some of it, you'd never think that *any* military targets existed in North Vietnam, or that any non-civilian targets had been bombed, or that any bunch of people were more loyal, sturdy, plucky, obedient, clean, reverent, wise, etc., than the North Vietnamese. But NET went to some pains to make Greene's partiality explicit, to explain that he was not allowed to visit "military sites," to quote him at the start of the program as saying that he was personally "opposed to the war," and the fact remains that a lot of his film was really very moving. He didn't, after all, fabricate *all* those scenes of bombed towns and villages, of leveled huts, and craters, and silent children, and even if Saint Peter himself, and all the other admirals, should one day explain and make meaningful these scenes, these facts of life, it seems that they are indeed facts of life and that it is better to glimpse them now, even through prejudiced eyes, than not at all. The discussion afterward was interesting too, if it's still possible to be "interesting" about Vietnam, and I guess it is. (One wonders sometimes what those panel discussions in the ninety-eighth year of the Hundred Years' War were like. "Oh, sure, I grant you they legally *own* Aquitaine, but if you're speaking now about a question of *control* . . . or is it, um, *we* who, ah, legally own, and they who, um . . .") There was a good deal of talk about the origins of the National Liberation Front, and about the plausibility, or implausibility, of the South Vietnamese government, and about what China's role really is and whether we should worry about it. That sort of thing. But it was carried on intelligently, and with a certain amount of dispassion, which may well be a first for this particular debate. Schoenbrun's side of the argument seemed less arresting, partly because the anti-war position has been stated so often that it has begun to take on the hypnotic rhythms of a litany, and partly because Schoenbrun has a tendency to answer questions as if God might never give him breath again. Scalapino, the administration defender, was fine—

holding on to the thorny side of the stick, palms all bleeding and everything, while Schoenbrun tried to throw him around the room. But he said intelligent things, and seemed *interested* (not very many people on either side really seem interested any more), and helped to lift what is supposed to be this great national debate above the level of a squabble between two taxi drivers. It seemed like a good program, and a useful one, and the kind of thing that NET could stand to do a whole lot more of.

I called Representative Burleson the next day to ask him if he'd seen the program and what he'd thought of it. He said, Unfortunately, no. It's been a busy time in Washington. Representative Ashbrook was away from his office, said his special assistant, who then volunteered that "we think NET's choice of films in the past leaves something to be desired," and added, rather ominously, "Now that the Corporation for Public Broadcasting has been established, we are most keenly aware that it will become eligible for federal funds." It's probably been a busy time in Minneapolis, too, where Walter Judd used to live. There are 133 stations on the NET hookup at the moment, and 131 of them carried "NET Journal—North Vietnam" that evening. The two that didn't were in Buffalo and Minneapolis. The temperature in Buffalo and Minneapolis that night was 34 and 17, respectively. But it must have been comfortable and warm and safe indoors.

It's been a cold and snowy winter everywhere, except possibly in Seattle, where it rains most of the time. Yesterday it was 38 out there, according to the *Times*, and this sounds nice except for the rain. God knows what it was like the other day when a man called Frank T. Roach walked into the office of radio station KRAB. Mr. Roach is one of several people who work in the office of the Federal Communications Commission in Seattle. KRAB is a small, joky, intelligent FM station that operates out of a converted doughnut shop on a hillside above Seattle, employs five people, hopefully claims forty thousand listeners, exists by virtue of its license from the FCC and of small contributions sent in by the faithful, and beams a consistently high level of music, poetry, talks, readings, jokes, and assorted nonsense out into the wet Seattle nights. At 6 p.m., according to a program guide: "Anton Bruckner Still Lives (Symphony No. 6 in A Major)." At 6:30: "For the Children ('Dink Stover Crosses the Bar into Puberty and Cries,' a reading by Delphine Haley)." At 8:45: "Clinical Varieties of Sexual Apathy." At 10:30: "A Talk by Ken Kesey." KRAB also gets into politics now and then. It has scheduled a panel discussion on the subject of a new ICBM site that is about to be set up in Seattle. Last Saturday, it played a taped report about Greece under the new regime, which it borrowed from New York's WBAI. And one day in mid-December it ran a tape of a speech that had been made by the Reverend James Bevel at the University of California. Bevel is an eloquent and passionate (and political) Negro who back in 1965 was Martin Luther King's right-hand man in Chicago and who has recently moved over into a much more militant position, and the speech he gave to the Berkeley students was a strong one, filled with what is by now the inevitable phony-street-talk rhetoric of the "movement," and with the nearly as inevitable flashes of honest heat and poetry that make the rhetoric worth listening to. He talked a good deal about emasculation—not of the Negro but of the white man as a result of his dealings with the Negro—and he used rough language a bit. He said "goddammit" twice. And "bastard" once. And he said "balls" a couple of times. Frank Roach apparently didn't like any of it much. "He came into the station that morning and demanded the Bevel tape," says one of the KRAB people, a young man called Lorenzo Milam. "We mentioned something about our lawyer, and about its being an original tape, but he demanded in that rather *special* way, and so one of us went and got it out of the back room and gave it to him. He pocketed the tape, and took the program log showing that it had indeed been played on the date, and—with all his righteous anger and sense of power—scared hell out of us. He came back the next day to scare us some more. Nothing very much. He conducted an 'official FCC inspection' of the premises, which he's entitled to do. He poked around at the transmitter. And looked at our licenses. He looked at our maintenance log. Then he gave us back the Bevel tape, which he said he had had copied and had sent off to the FCC in Washington, and started to express his personal sense of outrage that the program had been carried by us at all. 'Why isn't KRAB more like KJR?' he asked at one point—KJR being the local rock-and-roll station. 'We never get complaints about *them!* They're very careful.' We told Mr. Roach something about how running the Bevel tape was what free radio was all about—or, rather, we made sputtering noises to that effect. The truth is, we weren't feeling very articulate or brave just then. We don't run this station on much of a margin, to say the least, and here is this guy standing on our feet with all the shining armor of bureaucracy, and with all those license renewals in his pocket. He told us curtly that there had been lots of 'other complaints' about KRAB; and left us—left us with the feeling that we'd be hearing more about it, and other matters, from them."

I don't know how this story ends. The KRAB people apparently got pretty spooked by Mr. Roach, because they canceled a replay of Bevel's speech that had been scheduled for later in the month. But lately they seem to have become unspooked, because they ran both the tape and a commentary on it last week. "The swords are drawn," says Milam gallantly, "but I hope the swords will turn to noodles." Mr. Roach's present position with the FCC is that of an engineer.

Perhaps you think that the role of the FCC in regulating broadcasting right now is purely negative. Perhaps you think the FCC merely gets in the way, obstructs—a little band of willful men, or some such. Not so, not so. The FCC does positive things too. The FCC renews broadcasting licenses, for example, deriving its authority from Section 307D of the Communications Act of 1934, which states, in part: "Upon the expiration of any license . . . a renewal of such license may be granted . . . if the Commission finds that the public interest, convenience, and necessity would be served thereby." There are roughly seven thousand radio and television stations in the United States at the moment, and the FCC renews licenses for roughly two thousand of them each year. Only last week, it renewed Iowa and Missouri—over two hundred licenses. The public interest, convenience, and necessity, one gathers, have been served in Iowa and Missouri of late.

The FCC also grants broadcasting licenses—a somewhat smaller end of the business, deriving its authority this time from Section 309A of the Communications Act, which states, in part: "Subject to the provisions of this section, the Commission shall determine . . . whether the public interest, convenience, and necessity will be served by the granting of such application." A few weeks ago, on January 4, the seven commissioners of the FCC filed, as is their custom, into the courtlike commission meeting room in the new FCC headquarters in Washington, where they swiftly granted—or, rather, approved—the "assignment of license" of FM radio station WMDE, in Greensboro, North Carolina, by Mr. Herman C. Hall to the Piedmont Crescent Broadcasting Company, whose president is Mr. Robert R. Hilker. The price the Piedmont Crescent Broadcasting Company paid Mr. Hall was $147,000, which is of no special interest here. What seems interesting is that Mr. Hilker already controlled nine radio stations, both AM and FM, six of which are in North Carolina and the three others just across the border in southern Virginia. WMDE makes his tenth—an even number. What seems especially interesting is that in the space on the application where the prospective licensee is asked to state his programing intentions, Mr. Hilker had stated his intention of programing no news and no public affairs—that is to say, zero minutes of news and zero minutes of public affairs. To assist Mr. Hilker in arriving at this intention, an FCC staff memorandum explains, an officer of the Piedmont Crescent Broadcasting Company had surveyed "local leaders in education, religion, civic affairs, and law enforcement" in Greensboro, eight of whom were quoted in support of the contention that there was no need of either. The final vote of the commission was three to two in favor of the assignment, which amounted to a majority. One commissioner abstained. One "did not participate." Commissioners Nicholas

Johnson and Kenneth A. Cox dissented, pointing out, among other things, that the proposal had landed on their desks at 5 p.m. of the day before the matter had to be decided—had to be decided, it turns out, according to another FCC memorandum, because the contract of sale was due to expire on January 11, and the parties would be "greatly inconvenienced" if the commission did not approve the sale forthwith. There are 120,000 citizens in Greensboro, North Carolina, at present count. WMDE will now play country-and-Western music.

I was speaking with someone at the FCC the other day and asked him if the commission ever got around to investigating this public-interest business much.

"Oh, we never investigate *that*," he said. "Most of our investigations are technical—generators, transformers, that kind of thing."

I asked him how many nontechnical investigators the FCC now had at its disposal.

"For the whole country?" he said. He thought for a moment. "We have three."

There are only a few thousand citizens around Tasley, Virginia, a small farming community in the eastern part of the state, and on May 24 of last year the owner of the one AM station in Tasley applied for a license to operate the first FM station in town. On his application he wrote as follows: ". . . Applicant further states that in order to fulfill its obligations to the public and maintain its economic health, the proposed station will find it necessary to increase the percentage of commercial time during special occasions such as before elections, Christmas, Old Timers Days, Thanksgiving, during vegetable harvest time, and during periods immediately after an outage due to equipment failure; however, during these periods, the commercial time is not normally expected to exceed about 55 per cent in any hour." In plain English, this means a permissible thirty-three minutes of advertising per hour. The commission voted five to two to grant the license, Commissioners Johnson and Cox again dissenting.

Watchman, what of the night, indeed! The night is nearly gone, or turning fast to noodles. What of the watchman?

AN ILLUSTRATED HISTORY

OF THE TET OFFENSIVE

Oh (I tell you, lad), the enemy kept pouring in that night, out of the hills and valleys of the central highlands, higher lowlands, lower uplands, wearing their sneakers, sandals . . . concealed sometimes in flowers, disguised as friendlies . . . bicycles streaming out of the farms and prairies, hills and valleys, all night long, all week long, all month long, past elements of the 25th Division, the 1st Air Cavalry, Frank McGee, the South Vietnamese police force, Walter Cronkite, Les Crane, the Smothers Brothers. I sat with Grigsby on the floor that afternoon and watched the shelling of Cholon, the Chinese section. "Oh, God," said Grigsby, "the element of surprise! Oh, God, observe the camerawork!" Our people brought up tanks and pistols. Grenades. Automatic weapons. Brap-brap-brraaapp. Women and children ran here and there. This way, that way. Hither and yon. The loss of life was hideous to imagine, to say nothing of the disruption of public services. Our President appeared around twilight and spoke to us softly about the war. "On the other hand, there have been civilian casualties and disruption of public services," he said.

A convoy rumbled along the road going north out of Phu Bai. Route 1. The VC blew a bridge along the way. I don't know how our boys got through. Five trucks. Two tanks.

Miranda hovered in the doorway, wearing that bandanna thing around her head and clutching sprigs of oregano. "Sniping, I hear," she said, "continues on a scattered scale in outlying districts of Saigon."

Grigsby looked up. "Major units of the 1st and 25th Divisions," he said, "have been drawn sixty to ninety miles north of the capital by a series of North Vietnamese and Vietcong attacks."

"The surprise element," said Miranda, "seems to have been total, or nearly so. I understand they came in silently on speedboats—"

"No, sneakers," said Grigsby.

"—during the NBC Golf Classic—"

"No, *Flipper*," said Grigsby.

Miranda bit off a piece of oregano. "I'd rather not think *that*," she said.

A squad of soldiers was running down the side of a road. The gunfire was very loud and sharp. The three of us sat down side by side and rocked back and forth with each explosion. "Spread out! Spread out, my buckos!" yelled Grigsby above the noise of the guns. He turned to us. "The point man keeps too close," he said. Two tanks appeared. Miranda rose to her feet. "The cassoulet . . ." she said. Grigsby looked puzzled. "*My* cassoulet," she said, "Sauce Prince de Ganay . . ."

"Street fighting is about to begin," said Grigsby.

Miranda sat down again. Some helicopters came in low overhead, guns blazing. More tanks came up. A wounded Marine was carried by. "Oh, God," said Miranda, "the cruel tanks. The sound of mortars. The airplanes dying like wounded bison on the great airstrips."

Harry Reasoner appeared and spoke briefly to us about the situation. "Troops of the United States 1st Air Cavalry Division are reported to have retaken Quang Tri," he said.

"Thank the sweet Jesus for that," said Grigsby.

More tanks appeared. There was a loud noise. "What's going on?" said Miranda. "My cassoulet . . ."

"They're shelling the walled Citadel of Hué," I said.

Miranda slumped into a chair. "The beloved walled Citadel of Hué," she said after a while. "So it's come to that, has it?"

"The hostiles are plainly entrenched behind its ancient walls," Grigsby explained. "The unfriendlies are already hidden within the cavernous corridors of the rather marvelous Imperial Palace, home in bygone days of a weary succession of imperial emperors. How else to blam them out of there?"

"How else indeed," said Miranda in a flat voice. The recoilless rifle crunched. The machine guns spat and crackled. A handful of South Vietnamese troops advanced down a street, rifles raised. Gunfire everywhere. The sounds of buildings tumbling. Women. Children. "Why were we not told," Miranda said, "about their streaming out of the hills and valleys? About the bicycles and sneakers? About the speedboats and the Geneva agreements? Where was the NBC Golf Classic when we needed it most? Where the Smothers Brothers, who truly care?"

"They *do* care," said Grigsby. "I know they do."

"That only seems to make it worse," Miranda said. "All those dark valleys. Those dark pajamas. All those unfriendlies. Did *none* of you notice anything at all . . . *unusual* . . . in the hills and valleys . . . during the *Late Show?* Did Captain Kangaroo not spot the bicycles? Where was Joe Pyne? Did Roger Mudd not hear words spoken secretly behind bushes? Plans? Intrigue? Surely some messages exchanged. A slip of paper. A sign. A hint?"

Two planes came inland, flashing low over the rooftops, dark shapes, dark snouts. "Navy," said Grigsby. "*Malheureusement,* too low for napalm." A helicopter hovered, landed. Men rushed out. Two wounded Vietnamese ran by. More Vietnamese. A crash. Another crash. "Oh, God," said Miranda, "the beloved walled Citadel of Hué." The sounds of gunfire stopped. Our Secretary of State came into view. He wore civilian clothes, looked straight ahead. "I have no doubt," he said, "that there are some people in South Vietnam who are grumpy." Jeeps and motor scooters sped down the big main street of Saigon. Policemen ran forward, backward. A Vietnamese in a checked shirt was walking, being walked, dragged, held between two soldiers. The soldiers took him over to another man, holding a pistol, who held it to the head of the man wearing the checked shirt, and shot him. Miranda began to cry—short, sniffly sobs. She blew her nose, then wiped her eyes on Grigsby's shirt, looked up. "I don't like any of this," she said. "My home is sacred. My kitchen floor is blessed. I wish no mortal harm or hurt or bruise or injury or other bodily damage. Tell me." She clutched at Grigsby, who was checking body counts. "How is it that Walter Cronkite didn't know? About all those unfriendlies? About the bicycles and speedboats?"

"It's hard to say," said Grigsby. "They evidently met in jungle fastnesses invisible to the naked eye, and poured out of them in ways no man can now envisage. Their plans were clearly laid between commercials on *The Dating Game*. They hid their weapons during 'Raymond Burr in Vietnam.' Their leaders sent out inflammatory messages and sneakers at key moments in the course of Superbowl Sunday. I'd rather not talk about it any more."

Vietnamese Rangers started to run across open ground. Gunfire was coming in from all sides now. Miranda put her hands over her eyes, but seemed to be peeking. A large helicopter landed. Men poured out. One man, small face in a big helmet, flopped right down on the ground beside the helicopter and began firing. "The Vietcong attacks," said Grigsby in that drawl of his, "have hit nearly every important province capital in the country, scores of district capitals, and many airfields." Some smoke was rising in the distance. "The ammo dump," I said. Grigsby shook Miranda by the shoulder. "They hit the ammo dump at Cam Ranh Bay. It's going to blow." Miranda got to her feet. "Huge military complex of Cam Ranh Bay, I salute you!" she said. "Massed transports, workhorses of our logistics command! Slender, sharp-nose fighters poised for takeoff!" She turned toward us, her soft, shy face now streaked with tears and flour and bits of parsley. "But did not General Westmoreland know?" she said. "Or William Paley? Dr. Stanton? The King of Sweden? I mean, there were so many of *them*—and *so* unfriendly." Three Vietnamese women walked down a city street carrying their possessions. Ron Nessen said the things they were carrying were their possessions. "They met at night," I said, "in darkness."

"In blackness," said Grigsby, evidently angry. "They walked for hours and months on tiny trails, their footsteps silent, avoiding twigs. They lived in holes, like mice."

Miranda looked up. "Like moles," she said.

"They slept in fields and wells," I said.

"In waterways and ditches," said Miranda.

"Their birchbark canoes slipped slyly down the jungle waterways," said Grigsby. "It was impossible to see. It was impossible to hear."

Out in Dalat, a South Vietnamese platoon moved forward toward the center of town. The Vietnamese moved warily. There were snipers on the rooftops. A man came out of a doorway in the distance, the camera shaking just a little, ran sidewise, there were shots, he fell. "Sweet Jesus," said Miranda. "One sees everything today." She took off her bandanna and let her hair fall down. "It is so *good* to see everything in modern life." A Vietnamese woman walked down a street, carrying a child. The child was bleeding. A tank rolled by. "Ah, God," Miranda said, "the immediacy . . . the communication . . ." "They literally lived in tunnels," said Grigsby, "*underground*. . . ."

"I know, I know," Miranda said. "I hear"—she turned to Grigsby, took his arm—"I hear the networks have now flown in men across the world in order to best communicate the conflict. I hear that bands of cameramen have already started to sweep inland from the China Sea. I hear the processing labs in Tokyo work overtime, and that in Saigon today the water boys tell tales of film transshipments that would eat your heart out. I hear—"

I took her other hand (it is a way with her I have). "Easy, old girl," I said. "The President is about to speak." The cameras switched. The fighting stopped. The grass was green, deep green, and stretched for miles on either side. The sky was blue. President Eisenhower stepped forward to the microphone. He seemed confident, relaxed. He wore a light beige suit. He turned to

Arnold Palmer. "It's a special pleasure," he said, "for me to be able to present to you this trophy," and handed Palmer the Bob Hope golf award.

The sky outside that night was black as ink, but clear. Some stars. Tom Dunn was on at eleven o'clock. Strong government forces, it appeared, had broken into the walled Citadel of Hué. A young Marine ran forward, hid behind a building, peered around, and fired his rifle into the distance.

In the days when *Life* was turning out those gorgeously illustrated, simple, simple, simple picture stories about the Decline of the West, or the Rise of the East, or the History of Man from Ape to Atom, on the wall of the managing editor's office there used to hang a little plaque, a sort of bronze engraving of a candle burning, and beneath the candle was the inscription "It is better to light one candle than to curse the darkness." Back then (this was about fifteen years ago), I remember admiring the positivism of this inscription a good deal—a good deal more, anyway, than I really like to be reminded about. Back then, one's friends were all at law school, or writing verse plays in farmhouses, or were in some other faraway, obviously out-of-the-mainstream environment (all the while feeling free to *criticize*, if you will, the "superficiality" of fourteen-page photographic essays on the History of God), and here was—well, a bunch of decent, intelligent, hardworking men and women who were at least trying to *do* something instead of sitting around being *merely negative*. There is surely nothing in modern life more useless and disagreeable than someone who is sitting around being *merely negative*. I thought so then. To some degree, I think so now. It's hard, after all, to unlearn all that positivism that has been dinned into the race by generation after generation of ark-builders, field-tillers, tracklayers, and missile-makers. It is better to light one candle than to curse the darkness. It is better to do something than nothing. But, hell, I don't know. One looks around the country now at a land-scape already jagged with pieces of metal and brick and rhine-stone and concrete that are simply *there*—and one knows that they will stay *there* for years, sometimes for years and years and years, and that one is stuck with them. One is stuck, for the fore-seeable future, with these structures we have caused to be placed upon the horizon line, that now sit there limiting and diminishing our field of sight. One is stuck, for the foreseeable future, with the structures we have built so much of our lives around, and with the concepts, ideologies, points of view, and whatnot that we have so firmly programed into our minds (not the least of which, perhaps, is that we are "free" and can change all this) that nothing can really be expected to take *their* place, either, despite all the adult-education courses this side of Eden. One speaks grace-fully about candlelight to guide us. One sees in fact a room, a lot of rooms—dark chambers filled with shapes, and ciphers on the walls, strange pictures on the ceilings, obscure algebra, everything dark, dim, difficult to make out—and inside each room a candle burns, and now and then the door is opened and people stick their heads inside. A guide is with them. (He says he is a guide.) See how well lit the room here is, he says. Observe what you will. Read what you can. Ah, yes, they say, a well-lit room. And glance about them for a minute or so, take snapshots into the gloom, and go out—and rarely, it would seem (after all, they've "done" that room), come back again. I'm not so sure, really, about this com-parison between candles and darkness. I'm not so sure that it isn't sometimes better to leave the damn place dark, so dark and spooky that someone will eventually come along and light it properly—or at least to take the risk that someone will. I mean, if the town of Agamemnon, Iowa (I made that name up), feeling the need for such things, gets itself a cultural center, but, because of the politics, machinery, and limitations built into that center, the citi-zens of Agamemnon are taken further away from life and reality and the possibilities of man, will Agamemnon then get itself a second cultural center to replace the defective one it has? Built on top of the first? Next door? If the citizens of this country, feeling the need for such things, get a Corporation for Public Broadcasting, but, because of the politics, machinery, and limitations built into that corporation, the citizens of this country are etc., etc., is someone likely to set up a *second* Corporation for Public Broadcasting? Built on top of the first? Is something automatically better than nothing? Is *some* Public TV automatically better than none? There is an old Turkish saying (is there not?): "It will be a damn sight long wait, effendi, before they tear down the Pan Am Building."

A couple of things have happened recently in the saga of Public Television (as it progresses, or perhaps descends, from the grand scheme of last year's Carnegie Commission report toward its forthcoming incarnation as a corporation) that I think might give people some cause for distress about it all—if anyone, that is, has the time or the lack of distraction to be distressed about such a matter, on top of all the other distresses. The first development was a meeting that took place in New Orleans recently of an organization called the National Citizens' Committee for Public Television. The second was the announcement by President Johnson of the fifteen-man board he chose to direct the Corporation for Public Broadcasting and to select its operative head. The *fact* of the meeting of the Citizens' Committee was really quite a fine thing. It numbers about a hundred and twenty people, and they seemed an able and intelligent group—a number of journalists and other writers, some university people, some lawyers (always lawyers), some Educational TV people, and so on. The meeting was chaired by Thomas Hoving, which seemed auspicious—as it seemed auspicious that such citizens as Kingman Brewster and Whitney Young, and Lee DuBridge of Cal Tech, and Shana Alexander of *Life*, would hie themselves off for a couple of days in New Orleans out of a serious concern for Public Television. But then the meeting started, and everybody talked about money. "Funding," it's called. Should the Congress be badgered to appropriate the whole $9 million for 1968 that the Public Broadcasting Act of 1967 had authorized, or should it be badgered to go along with the $4 million that the President had actually mentioned in his budget request? Should the Congress be badgered at all? And so forth. This is called "the realities." Sally Smith, a college girl from Denver, stood up at one point to say something about how Public Television, whatever it might turn out to be, should somehow concern itself with trying to communicate with young people, and she was listened to politely—rather too politely—and then everyone went back to talking about "funding." It may be a precious thing to say, and I feel myself in no position to condescend to the people who were at the meeting—or, indeed, to "the realities" of American life—but it seemed so damned *sad*. All those brainy, effective people (and many of them were) so bloody distracted by the sheer busyness of their own important lives that it seemed physically impossible for them to make the sort of energy leap that it would take for them, especially in so short a time, to even try to take hold of the concept of Public Television—that it would take for them to do anything beyond surrendering to the routine techniques of American problem-solving. Committees. Compromises. Funding. Congress. The realities. Well, who is to knock American problem-solving? It gave us pollution. It will shortly give us anti-pollution. It gave us Work. It will now give us Leisure. Wonderful. But the trouble with trying to handle television this way is that television just isn't altogether what it must seem to a lot of people to be. Or, rather, it *is* what it seems to be—a machine for dispensing "entertainment" and "education" and "information," and consequently something people think can be improved by the construction and attachment of other machines (a machine system of broadcasting "educational" television, for example, in order to increase the volume of "education"). But it's also something else: it's perhaps the chief contributor to an enveloping substance of pictures, images, ideas, words, facts, dreams that increasingly surrounds us, and as such traditional navigational fixes as God and home-based "identities" disappear, this enveloping substance, this Other Voice of communications, does more and more to determine who we are and how we are—and *this* doesn't seem at all so improvable by technical methods, by "funding," by beefing up already existing structures such as Educational Television, and so forth.

It's not so much that people don't get "content" from television, or that the content isn't important. They do—movies, information, spy shows, good, bad, indifferent—and the content is terribly important, unless, of course, one chooses to compress the sum of all one's energy and will into one of those McLuhanesque shrugs. But what people really and mostly receive from television, it would seem, is a sense of themselves—the same sort of sense, perhaps, that people once received by looking into the faces of their neighbors, when people still had neighbors, when neighbors still had faces and in turn looked back. On the surface, television now gives us isolated facts. Some fun. Even, now and then, a tiny morsel of the world. But what it mostly gives us is some *other* world, the world we dream we live in. It tells us nothing, almost *nothing* about how life is and how we are (connected, as most of it is, inextricably and pragmatically to the sacred mainstream), and I don't see how Public Television is ever going to be worth a damn if it can't somehow be brought to a point of being at least *willing* to break through the dream. And I don't truly see how *that's* ever going to be. Commercial television is what we live with. Commercial television provides the reflection that we all live with, and commercial television, no matter what anyone says, is irredeemably and unalterably, implicitly and explicitly, a system for moving goods—with various lures thrown in, so that people will be attracted to it. Some of the lures are better than others. Some are "good" or "interesting," but the system is what it is—not really concerned with providing a truthful reflection of life, because we've never required it to do so. Public Television *could* be something, but right now I just doubt it. I suppose a lot depends on what one thinks of "the mainstream of America." If one likes it, if one thinks that it ennobles and enhances the life of the people, then a system of Public TV that is keyed to the "mainstream" (that will, in its present conception, probably amount to a sort of funded-up Educational-TV network) will be a satisfactory advance. My own feelings—my own feelings (he mumbled) are that the divinity of man was a rather nice thing while it lasted but that we are now all so well along on the road to a life of metal and organization and technique and cultural technology and educational technology and sexual technology and all the rest of the morbid paraphernalia of modern life that it will take a few exertions of nothing much less than a kind of anarchism of the soul (well, that's a floaty expression for you) to even postpone the desert for a while. Well, hello, Corporation for Public Broadcasting, whoever you are. Hello. Good-by. Hello.

Oh, yes. About President Johnson's fifteen-man board. I'll just give the names of the members, if you don't mind. John D. Rockefeller III, chairman of Lincoln Center; Joseph A. Beirne, chairman of the United Electrical and Communications Workers; Robert S. Benjamin, chairman of the United Artists Corporation; Roscoe C. Carroll, general counsel for the Golden State Life Insurance Company of Los Angeles; Michael A. Gammino, president of the Columbus National Bank of Rhode Island; Mrs. Oveta Culp Hobby, president and editor of the Houston *Post;* Sol Haas, chairman of station KIRO, in Seattle; Joseph D. Hughes, vice-president of T. Mellon & Sons; Erich Leinsdorf, conductor of the Boston Symphony; Carl Sanders, former governor of Georgia; Jack Valenti, president of the Motion Picture Association of America; Dr. Milton Eisenhower, president emeritus of Johns Hopkins University; and Dr. James R. Killian, Jr., chairman of the corporation of the Massachusetts Institute of Technology. The man who is going to run this bouncy little outfit is Mr. Frank Pace, Jr. Mr. Pace was at one time Secretary of the Army and later chairman of the General Dynamics Corporation. Now that I think of it, while he was running General Dynamics, that company had the distinction of losing more money (a hundred and forty-three million bucks) than any American corporation had ever lost before, so maybe Mr. Frank Pace, Jr., is the secret swinger after all. It seems a long shot, I grant you, but right now that seems to be about the only shot available.

SUNDAY

Night. Saturday night. The curtains blowing. The curtains flapping. Sunlight through the curtains. Sunlight? No no no no. Saturday *night*. It *is* Saturday night. It is *still* Saturday night. Buses grunt and gargle beneath the windows. Some chapel bells. I keep my eyes tight closed and start up the dream again. The girl is wearing nothing at all, next to nothing. She runs down the beach. A great white beach. I run toward her. Nearer, nearer. An airplane appears a few feet above us, stops. (Damn the airplane.) My uncle leans out of it. (Damn, *damn* my uncle.) He is dressed in red and has grown a peculiar beard. He reaches down and hauls the girl up with him. "Sound common stocks," he says to me in a thoughtful manner, "are still an excellent investment for the long pull," and he flies away. The beach turns to stone. A garbage truck starts grinding next to the bed. A taxi horn sounds. A strange buzzing of voices is everywhere around. Eyes open. Eyes way open. I am standing in the middle of our living room. Sunlight is coming in through the windows. Clearly, it *is* Sunday morning. Objects inside the room are blurred, drift slowly toward me and recede. I try to move my feet. They seem stuck to the carpet, possibly webbed. I suddenly remember Harry Pollock's blank pink face. I am arguing with Harry Pollock. I said *that* to Harry Pollock late last night? The pain inside my head is very fierce. The buzzing sound continues, is localized, defined: a small gray screen. My children sit in front of the television screen in their pajamas. I am a grown man, after all. My head hurts. My feet *are* webbed. I argued half the night with Harry Pollock. I am standing in the middle of my living room early, early Sunday morning without knowing why—but *I am fully in control.* I speak to the children softly. I am their father, am I not? The great patriarch. "Why are you yelling at us?" a small voice asks.

"I am not yelling," I say. "What are you watching?"

"A movie," another child says. I look at the movie. It seems to be about a couple of men in prison. One of the men is beating the other with a chain.

"Here, now," I say. "Isn't there anything better than this?"

The first child looks at me sweetly. "No," she says.

"You . . . are . . . a . . . damned liar," I say with my lips, being careful not to sound the words. I flip through the stations. On Channel 2 some clergymen are talking earnestly about the Newark riots. On Channel 4 Eugene H. Nickerson, Nassau County Executive, is being interviewed about the Long Island Railroad. Bugs Bunny is on Channel 7. Thank God for Channel 7. Bugs Bunny is somehow involved in the Second World War. Bugs Bunny is doing a humorous imitation of Mussolini. Mussolini?

"We've seen that," say several children impatiently.

"See it again," I say vaguely. "It will do you good." And stumble off, hunting pathetically for coffee, understanding, the book section of the *Times,* wisdom, stray scraps of myself that I seem to have left somewhere in the course of the night.

My wife appears. Some coffee is made. "That was a nice party last night," I say with an attempt at affability that nearly splits my skull, "but we seem to have left rather late."

"You were arguing with Harry Pollock," my wife says.

"About what?" I ask casually.

"About optical scanning," she says.

"Oh," I say. I want to stand up right then and there and phone Harry Pollock and ask him to a nice lunch and send him tulips and tell him I don't know anything about optical scanning, and never did, and never will, but I sit there instead and drink coffee and listen to the sounds of children fighting. Children fighting? A small child in fact appears, tear-stained.

"What's the matter?" I ask in my best fatherly manner.

"Edward hit me," says the child.

"Why?" I ask. "What were you doing?"

"Nothing," says the child.

"What happened?" my wife asks.

"Edward hit her," I say.

My wife looks at me. "There is no child called Edward in this house," she says.

Sounds of squabbling grow louder in the distance, draw closer to us. "What's on the TV?" my wife asks. I hunt up *TV Guide*, grope for the right page, and read aloud. " 'The Face of the Pharisee,' a story of a domineering woman and her emotionally and morally crippled son. Host is Ralph Bellamy. *Inquiry*: Dr. Ruth Fox discusses the emotional problems of alcoholism. *Way to Go*: Lois Anderson, of the National Council of Churches, and Charles Brackbill, Jr., of the United Presbyterian Church of the U.S., discuss promotional religious films. Host is Ormond Drake. *Anima e Corpo*, an oratorio in the form of a morality play. The Soul asks wherein lies eternal joy, and the Body, Intellect, and Blessed Spirit offer replies. 'Youth in Revolt—Why?' is discussed by Camilla Ohdnoff, minister for—"

"They must be crazy," my wife says. The sound of a large piece of furniture being overturned is heard. She takes the magazine, glances through it. "Here," she says. " 'Unchained': At the California Institute for Men at Chino, California, hardened criminals are rehabilitated." She gets up, goes out, and turns it on.

A strange silence descends. Coffee is drunk. "We should do something," somebody says. It must have been me. "We should do something," I say again.

My wife looks at me. "*Late Sunday mornings,*" she declaims in a peculiar dreamlike voice, "*Charles and I betimes would break-fast in the solarium before sallying over to Lady Hesketh's for an amusing lunch. . . .* Do you suppose," she says to me in a thoughtful way, "that there was *never* such a thing as *late* Sunday morning? Do you suppose—"

"Well," I say. "Times change, of course. The family-formation period, and so forth, which we are so fortunate to be participating in at present instant."

"Do you suppose it was all a lie?" she says. "I mean, the *concept* of a late Sunday morning, of amusing lunches?"

"Not at all," I say. I feel we are both very close to tears. "One of these days we too will have a late Sunday morning and amusing lunches. I promise you." It is a tender moment. There is the sound of several bodies hitting a wall at once, and crying.

"We should take them out," my wife says. "We have to take them out."

"Why *out?*" I say. "Why do people always take their children *out?* If God had wanted children to be taken *out,* he would have made them—"

Some children come racing by. "We're all going to the park," my wife says.

"The park?" the children say. "We've been to the park. Why can't we watch TV?"

"You've watched enough already," I say. "When I was your age I didn't watch TV all day long."

"Why not?" one of the children asks.

"*Because,*" I say. Wretched children. "Because when I was your age we learned how to live without this constant need for artificial stimulus."

"You did?" say the children, as if I were some kind of freak. I look to my wife for support.

"Your father, I want you to know," my wife says benignly, "saw *Rebecca of Sunnybrook Farm* as a first-run feature."

"Nobody," I say, "will watch any more television in this house for the time being. There are other things to do in life besides watch television. We will now all go out to the park and have a wonderful time."

"We will now all go out to the park and have our bicycles stolen," says a child.

"We will now all go out to the park and catch emphysema," says another child. Boring children.

An interval of several hours or days elapses, during which everybody gets dressed.

"Governor Romney is on television," a child runs in to tell me.

"What do I care for Governor Romney?" I say.

The child looks hurt. "You said he is going to be the next President," the child says.

"I did *not*," I say. I look in the living room. The children are sitting around the set with the sound turned off, looking at Governor Romney. "Last *Christmas* you said," the child persists. "I *heard* you say."

"Everybody ready?" my wife calls. A March wind is now bowling down the avenue outside. The children are all rolling around on the floor, pulling off each other's socks.

"You know," I say as she comes in, "this seems to be a rather interesting program about Romney."

"With the sound off?" she says.

"Well, I mean, it looks like a rather interesting program. I thought maybe I might just—"

"Stay in and have a little peek?" she says. "Not on your damned life."

New York. A Sunday in March. Observers of the Central Park social scene were not surprised to find the park deserted this particular day, owing to the extraordinary cold, the rotten wind, the gray skies, and the promise of rain, hail, snow, or worse— except, as it turned out, for the presence of an unnaturally aged thirty-seven-year-old man, who was seen leaping and jogging about in the middle of a field, surrounded by several small children, and uttering cries that only from a distance could have been taken for merriment.

"I'm very cold," I say. "I want to go home. I'm very cold. I am thirty-seven years old. I am jaded with parks, park-weary. I have been to all the parks. I have experienced all the park experiences. There is nothing I can learn further from parks. I am going home."

We go home. Deftly, with apparent casualness, I turn on the hockey game. The children come in.

"Who's ahead?" one of them asks.

"The Black Hawks," I say. Hull takes a pass from center and is about to shoot.

"Where are the Yankees?" a small voice asks.

"The Yankees play baseball," I say. "This is hockey. Please be quiet."

Chicago moves down the ice.

"What's hocking?" another small voice asks.

I glower at the child. Goals are streaming into the net.

"Hocking," my wife says, "is one of those artificial stimuli your father can simply take or leave alone."

The children bring out a pad of paper and some crayons and proceed to rip the pad of paper into little bits. Somebody cries. Somebody scores another goal. Wild cheering. The hockey game is over.

"Can we watch one of our shows now?" one of the children asks.

"No," I say.

"Please," they say. "A nature show. Miss Bookmaster says it's very good to watch shows about nature and animals."

I flip casually through the stations. A golf match. Some basketball. Ah, yes, a fish. A marlin, it looks like. There is a marlin leaping in and out of the water, and there is a man in a large power boat holding a fishing rod that he is reeling and unreeling. The marlin dives. "When a marlin goes deep," an announcer intones, "the moments of waiting are extremely agonizing." The marlin comes up again. Wonderful pictures of the poor damned marlin. The marlin is hauled into the boat. "I never realized these babies were this strong," says one of the men in the boat to his friend. "It's the end of a great day," says the other. We are watching, apparently, a program called *American Sportsman,* on ABC.

"I don't think I like this," says one of the children. "I don't like people who kill animals."

"You like eating well enough," I say.

"I like eating ice cream," the child says. "You don't have to shoot ice cream in order to eat it. That's why I like it."

"Can we have some ice cream?" says another child.

American Sportsman continues. We are in Alaska now. We are in Alaska with Cornel Wilde. "Come here!" I call to my wife. "Cornel Wilde. You loved him in *The Bandit of Sherwood Forest.* You thrilled to him in *Forever Amber.*" Cornel Wilde is panting up a slight incline, carrying a rifle at the ready. He is hunting bear. "Ooh, boy, this is mighty spectacular country," says Cornel Wilde. "It sure is," says his companion. Cornel and his companion do a lot of walking around, holding their rifles up, and finally they spot a big bear way way way way in the distance. But our TV camera has a zoom lens that brings him in close, and Cornel's rifle has a telescopic sight, and so he plugs him one. "Good shot," says his companion. "Hit him again." Cornel takes aim and plugs the bear again. "Oh, beautiful, Cornel!" calls his companion. "Beautiful." They both run pantingly toward the dead bear. "That's a nice bear," says Cornel's friend. "Boy, oh boy, oh boy," says Cornel. "Wow," says his companion.

"You mean they killed that bear?" one of my children asks.

"That's right," I say. "The law of the jungle. The bear was probably stealing their ice cream."

"That's not true," the child says.

Meanwhile, Cornel and his pal are peering over the dead bear. "We did it," says Cornel. The friend says, "Give me your hand, Cornel." The two men shake hands over the dead bear. "That's a beautiful fur," Cornel says. The camera shows the fur of the dead bear. "Look at those claws," says the friend. The camera shows the claws of the dead bear. "Look at the eyes," says Cornel.

"Small eyes," says the friend. "Excellent hearing, though," says Cornel.

"Everybody take baths," my wife says.

The children wander off in silence.

"What's going on here?" my wife asks.

"The Bandit of Sherwood Forest shot hisself a bear," I say.

"For God's sake," my wife says. "You made them watch that?"

"When are they going to have dinner?" I ask.

"I don't know," she says. "They told me you said they only needed to have ice cream."

"I didn't say that," I say. "I said the reason Cornel Wilde shot the bear was because the bear had been stealing all his ice cream."

"You said that?" she says.

"It was a joke," I say.

My wife looks at me. "Well, if that's your story," she says, "you go right ahead and stick to it."

I go out and make a drink and sit trying to read *Harper's* with my left eye and watch the end of the golf game with my right. Dinner. Kids eat dinner. Cutlery is dropped from incredible heights onto plates. Plates leap up and collide with mugs. More drinks.

"What are we going to do today?" one of the children asks.

"That's a ridiculous question," my wife says. "You've been up for nearly twelve hours."

The child looks puzzled. "How could we be up for twelve hours if we didn't do anything?"

Dinner over. "Do we watch *Lassie*?" one of the children asks.

"No," I say. "You've watched enough television. Why don't you read a story?"

"I don't know how to read," the child says. "*You* read us a story."

A strange feeling of unbelievable tiredness suddenly sweeps over me. "Well, I don't know," I say. "It seems to me I've read you all the stories."

"That's pathetic," my wife murmurs.

"Read *Charlotte's Web*!" the children call.

"Well," I say slowly. "Yes. Well. Maybe later. Right now, why don't you watch TV for a bit?"

The children leave. I make another drink and make my wife one. The house is quiet. The living room is quiet. Suddenly the sounds of gunfire, bombs, airplanes. I go in. The Japanese are bombing Wake Island or somewhere. "For God's sake," I say, "what kind of a thing is that to be watching?" I flip to another channel, find something that looks likely—*Voyage to the Bottom of the Sea.*

"What are they looking at?" my wife asks when I return.

"Some kids' show," I say. "About a submarine."

"That's nice," she says.

More strange sounds. The oldest kid brings the youngest kid in looking distraught.

"What's wrong?" I say.

"That show you made us watch," the oldest kid says. "The captain of the submarine turns into an ape."

The youngest kid starts to cry again. We go in to where the TV set is. It's the damned truth. The captain of the USS *Seaview* is indeed turning slowly into an ape. He crashes about in the submarine and shoots at a few people. Then he turns back into a captain. "Have you got the hypodermic handy?" asks somebody who is referred to as "the admiral." "Close collision screens," says somebody else. "Magnification factor of four," says the admiral. The captain reappears, looking pretty and well shaved. "Maintain your trend," he says into a tube. A commercial comes on.

"Is that a true story?" one of the children asks.

The children are directed to bed. The children are redirected to bed. Threats. Whines. Mutterings. The children are re-redirected to bed.

The children are in bed. Spasmodic heavy drinking takes place in the kitchen. Fragrant smell of food. Fragrant smell of food is from nearby apartment. Casserole is served in time for regularly scheduled, just-in-time-to-catch-them-at-dinner, emotional phone call from sister in California, who is active in the peace movement and concerned about contraception, or vice versa. Hard to tell. Good night to sister. Good night to casserole. The children asleep. The house is quiet. Some brandy in the living room amid the scraps of paper from the drawing pad, some toys, a bright pink woolly tortoise. *After supper betimes, Lady Cynthia and I would often take a small liqueur with friends in the Green Room.* Sir Edward P. Morgan swims into view on PBL. Sir Edward Morgan looks smooth and vague, and seems to be surrounded on all sides by eminent Negroes who are all talking at once about civil rights.

"I thought we saw this last week," my wife murmurs.

"It's a *continuing* crisis," I say. I flip, anyway, to the Smothers Brothers. A big, ungainly Negro woman is stumping about on-stage. A colored woman? Negress? Black woman? I feel a brief seizure of liberal-fatigue, and go out to see if there is any more brandy. There is. I come back in. The sky is dark outside the windows. The rooms of the apartment building opposite us, across the avenue, glow eerily where the television sets are on. We are back with PBL. A sociologist is speaking. He is talking about "structures."

"It's very good," my wife says. "Jimmy Baldwin was just on."

I sit down beside her and look into the set. The sociologist speaks on. The screen is gray. The beach is very white. The girl wears nothing, next to nothing, runs down beside the water, nearer, nearer . . . I blink, look out the window. There are almost no lights opposite us across the avenue. Monday hovers somewhere out there behind the buildings, waiting for us. Monday? Then this was Sunday.

It's hard to remember sometimes that television is machinery—bits of equipment, consoles, cables, lenses, little black boxes—and that when you turn it on one day (most days, in fact) and get *The Flying Nun*, you think of it as junk, as if the junk were somehow built into the equipment, and that when you turn it on another day and get, say, Dean Rusk and the gang down at the Foreign Relations Committee, or Bobby Kennedy announcing his Reassessment, or Eugene McCarthy watching Bobby Kennedy announcing his Reassessment, you think—well, what do you think? *The Flying Nun* is interrupting Dean Rusk? Dean Rusk is interrupting *The Flying Nun?* This country seems to include both, in some mysterious, lunatic balance, and television includes both too, although commercial TV has generally managed to push the balance so far out of whack that the country is barely recognizable to itself most of the time.

What's been so good about the presence of television these last few weeks is that what one has been able to see on the screen, to some degree, seems to reflect American life—seems to reflect more of it, rather than less of it or none at all, which is usually the case. It's true, of course, that there's a considerable "non-event" quality in a lot of this so-called actuality coverage. At this very moment, doubtless, in some abandoned factory seventeen miles west of Duluth, newspaper editorials are already being patched together by Old World Craftsmen about how political conventions aren't "real" conventions any more ("When I was a lad, I walked sixty miles to school each day . . .") but are held only for the purpose of being certified as "real" by television. And I guess some of that is perfectly true. A politician indeed doesn't seem to exist—can't, in fact, exist—until he has somehow gone through the symbolic liturgy of incarnating himself by television. And then, ironically, after 107 years of public service, he himself doesn't believe that he's achieved any "reality" until he's got a $9,000,000 advance from Harper & Row and published a book about it. Well, sometimes fussing around about other people's "reality" is more worthwhile than at other times, and right now, since a bit of life does indeed seem to be stirring, albeit dimly, beneath the great gray dank cloud that covers this country, it seems good just to be able to watch some of it— event, non-event, reality, unreality, what you will.

Speaking of events and non-events, I think NBC did especially well by all of us in deciding to cover the Rusk hearings live and in full. It's true that RCA, the parent company of NBC, is less dependent on earnings from NBC-TV than CBS is dependent on CBS-TV. CBS had a bad earnings-per-share dip last year, and when Richard Salant, the head of CBS News, insisted that the reason CBS wasn't covering the Rusk hearings live had nothing to do with economic considerations and was only the result of not wanting to duplicate NBC's coverage, all the savvy people started making all those elegant savvy motions with their razor-trimmed eyebrows. CBS, after all, is hardly famed in song and story for its spendthrift managerial habits. In fairness, I'd guess that Salant was in a spot. He works for a company that has this healthy, normal American tendency to break out in hives every time the earnings go down, and, besides, if CBS *had* run the hearings, who's to say that everybody wouldn't have watched them on NBC? The thing is, unfortunately, it's not a question of fairness. If you take yourself seriously as a transmitter of news, you run the damn hearings anyway—that is, if there is a "you" who is capable of feeling seriously about such matters, and not just a piece of machinery gulping down profit-and-loss statements.

In the current and increasing coverage of the political scene, the networks have made a number of useful strides lately in terms of equipment and technique, and also in terms of loosening up (a little, anyway) their news formats, and this might be a good time for them to go the rest of the way and try to do something about what those of us down here in the Personnel Dept. call "the human factor." The other day, for example, CBS had a good takeout on Bobby Kennedy announcing his candidacy in Washington, and then switched to Green Bay, Wisconsin, where Eugene McCarthy had been watching Kennedy on television with CBS's David Schoumacher. The Kennedy announcement, needless to say, had been quite an event, and the switch to McCarthy was good. There was a lot of drama in the air—tension, excitement, ill-feeling, most of it obviously real— and there was McCarthy sitting in the chair, and David Schoumacher leaned toward him . . . and guess what he asked? "Senator McCarthy, what's your reaction as a politician?" Old Gene looked a bit blank for a moment, so Schoumacher added, "Can you take him, I guess, is the best question." "Well," said McCarthy, "I haven't really been moved to withdraw at this point. I think that I can certainly win in Wisconsin, and I see no reason to believe that I couldn't go on and win the other primaries to which I'm committed." I don't wish to be too heavy on David Schoumacher, whose work for CBS in Vietnam has been among the best to have come out of there recently, and who handled the rest of the interview with McCarthy well, but when you think of the months and months of interviews that stretch ahead, of all these candidates and events and non-events and drama and so forth, and when you think that each one of these moments of drama will be accompanied—or, rather, connected to us—by a well-scrubbed network newsman sticking his head between the camera and the Personage and saying at the crucial instant, "Well, Archduke, how does it *feel* to have been shot three times in the thigh and shoulder?" or "Well, Astronaut Pilch, how does it *feel* to be the first man to make a complete circuit of the universe as we know it?"—you wonder if this mightn't be a good time to set up some sort of night study course in the Art of Not Asking Empty-Headed Questions of Important People at Key Moments. Or, to put it another way, if time is running short, and you have cornered the man who has just thrown the convention over to Oscar W. Underwood as a result of having bought up a hundred and seventeen votes from the State of New Jersey during teatime, "How do you feel?" or "What's your reaction?" might be fairly far down toward the bottom of a list of the thirty-seven most useful questions you might ask him at that point. In these circumstances, what in hell is anybody going to say except, "Well, Buzz, I feel real good." And there is old McCarthy in Wisconsin, and he is being asked if he can "take" Kennedy. What is he supposed to say? The thing is, a lot of the best actuality stuff on TV is admittedly in the form of people just talking—"being themselves"—but at that particular point, of all the ways to *keep* McCarthy from being himself, one of the surest was to ask him a question that he couldn't possibly answer straight. Someday, no doubt, out of the hills, or maybe out of the woods, will come riding a politician sufficiently joky and anarchical so that when the newsman says, "Claude, do you think you can take the Big Guy?" Claude will shuffle his feet in the hot sand and mumble, "Well, golly, Buzz, now that you put it that way, it seems kinda hopeless to me," and that will be that, and maybe all those thousands and thousands of previous questions will have been worth it. But right now it seems like soft space—and especially so in a medium that keeps telling us it is continually short on time, at least for showing us the world beyond *The Flying Nun*. I mean, the "how-do-you-feel" stuff would be okay if it led anywhere, if it were something people could respond to. But they don't, they can't—it's too much a part of a tradition of synthetic connectives. "How are you?" "I'm fine." "How's Martha?" "She's fine, too." "How are the kids?" This is barely okay in passing-old-Fred-on-the-street conversation, but in a professional interview what it really amounts to is a sort of marking time while the reporter thinks up some real questions, or maybe while he hopes that this one time the

Personage will actually include a bit of genuine information in his inevitably mechanical reply, which the reporter can then happily pursue. Newspaper interviews, admittedly, aren't always so great, either. Newspaper interviews have a lot of soft space of their own. (I think the *Times* is still telling us that Haiphong is "the port city of," as a small example.) But when the *Times* or any other good paper reports that a Personage said this or that, the fact is that the Personage usually said this or that in response to questioning by the *Times* reporter. When TV news breaks a big story, though, as it increasingly does, any useful information revealed seems more a matter of the Personage's convenience than the result of any particular probing on the part of a TV interviewer—more a matter of the Personage's using the medium, and the dignifying ritual of the "interview," to publicize some view or statement of his own. There are plenty of exceptions to this, to be sure, especially on the Sunday-afternoon interview shows such as *Meet the Press*, although even then most of the better interviewers seem to be newspaper or magazine people. Standard, everyday television news, though, too often just collapses around the interview: too many soft questions, asked less out of interest or any sense of the person interviewed than out of a sense of filling time and a misplaced sentimental desire to somehow achieve a personal rapport—the same sort of hopefully "personal" rapport, I guess, that the networks have in mind when they insist that the best way of transmitting actuality is through the reassuring physical, on-camera presence of a newsman. Sometimes, especially after watching television reporters converge on a political convention, I have this picture of the last great interview: The polar icecaps are melting. The San Andreas Fault has swallowed up half of California. Tonga has dropped the big egg on Mauritius. The cities of the plain are leveled. We switch from Walter Cronkite in End-of-the-World Central to Buzz Joplin, who is standing on a piece of rock south of the Galápagos with the last man on earth, the water rising now just above their chins. Joplin strains himself up on tiptoe, lifts his microphone out of the water, and, with a last desperate gallant effort—the culmination of all his years as a TV newsman —places it in front of the survivor's mouth. "How do you feel, sir?" he asks. "I mean, being the last man on earth and so forth. Would you give us your personal reaction?" The last survivor adopts that helpless vacant look, the water already beginning to trickle into his mouth. "Well, Buzz," he says, gazing wildly into the middle distance, "I feel real good."

MC CARTHY IN WISCONSIN

There was that moment in so many of Adlai Stevenson's campaign appearances—around ten o'clock at night, the giant auditorium in Pittsburgh, Cleveland, Denver, where you will, packed with expectant people, buttons, bunting, everyone hunched forward on those hard wooden chairs, smoke curling upward, the air electric, murmuring, the candidate not yet arrived—when, from down toward the front, from amid the rows of chairs and tables where the press was sitting, one would see Harrison Salisbury's tall, lank frame rise, and he would stuff some papers into his pocket and walk diffidently toward a nearby exit and out, his tall back disappearing through the doors, and walk down the auditorium corridor, upstairs, downstairs (every auditorium was different), to the telephone to file his story for the morning's paper. The candidate would enter the auditorium some twenty minutes later, having been delayed by bad weather in Buffalo, bad scheduling in Cincinnati, or by a meeting with a mayor uptown or a labor leader en route. *The New York Times* waits not for candidates. *The New York Times* waits not for Harrison Salisbury, even. I thought of this a little while ago in Madison, Wisconsin: a truly huge auditorium filled with people, young people, old people, colored shirts, more comfortable chairs this time, less smoke perhaps, but everybody waiting, waiting, the minutes ticking by; ten o'clock ticks by, and then, not quite so lankily, not quite so gracefully, perhaps, as Mr. Salisbury (it is now twelve years later, is it not? Mr. Salisbury is assistant managing editor of the *Times*), Ned Kenworthy of *The New York Times* gets to his feet and, twenty minutes before Eugene McCarthy arrives, goes out to file his story, to get it there in time for tomorrow's paper. Once McCarthy has arrived and given his speech, Kenworthy phones again and adds a few paragraphs, but it is still a low-key story. Alas, the candidate was late. Alas, the candidate was not tuned in properly to the demands of the press. I think of McCarthy as particularly like Stevenson in maybe just this one way, because both men not only succeeded in preserving an individuality into middle age but seemed so prideful, almost willful, in retaining it against all comers, which in a Presidential campaign usually means against the newspaper and television reporters who are always in attendance, hurrying beside one at airports, waiting in hotel lobbies, seated at those tables beneath the platform as one speaks, putting microphones in front of one's face as soon as one is finished. The question is: What does it matter that the candidate is not properly attuned to the demands of the press? The answer is—it's hard to answer. The candidate, if he is himself, should stay himself. The press is us. The press is a rumpled, partly bald, overtraveled middle-aged reporter asking a rumpled, partly bald, overtraveled middle-aged candidate some wild, surreal question about urban ghettos, housing programs, the NATO alliance, in the middle of the night at the Sioux City airport, and the outcome, on the front page of the *Morning Blat* ("'An urgent need for more middle-income housing' was voiced last night by the Candidate on his arrival at Municipal Airport"), is the smoke of "politics" that swirls around us and determines our deepest feelings about the men who run for office. One wonders, really, what sort of national nervous breakdown would take place if all the media were suddenly removed—made to disappear today—and from tomorrow until November 5 one had to take politics and politicians at face value, had only their actual physical presence to go by, had to listen to their words as words rather than as symbolic sentences imbedded protectively in media.

People talk much these days about the unfortunate decline

of real politicking (whistle-stop campaigns, old-fashioned conventions), and feel cautious about the growing role of media in somehow monkeying around with the reality of politics, but I should think that if there is anything to be learned about media and politics it may well work the other way around. In other words, perhaps the role of politics in our lives has in truth become progressively *less* real almost in proportion to the seriousness with which we claim to regard it; perhaps the ability of purely political acts to alter the true nature of our lives has in fact diminished since the time of, for example, Teddy Roosevelt and all the florid faces, whistle-stops, and whoop-de-do; and we now use media, use them on *ourselves*, in some senses, more than the networks or "they" use them on us, in order to transform and, especially, enlarge not so much what politics and candidates really are but what the possibilities of politics and candidates are. I get struck, anyway, by the wariness that people increasingly feel about the relation of politics to media, as if there were something wrong somewhere—something they ought to be wary about—but they can't quite figure out just what it is: Candidates can be "made up" to seem not what they are. A propaganda film can be used to exploit the least reliable or attractive of people's emotions. An incumbent President can command an unfair quantity of press and air time. A candidate can be elected on his "image" alone. This, especially, seems to terrify people, as well it might. It especially seems to terrify people, one sometimes thinks, in relation to the role that images, pretense, illusion play in their own lives. Old Fred and Nancy, such a stunning couple. Nancy drives an Isotta Fraschini because Elsie Domino does, and wears a B. H. Wragge into Bohack's because—well, *because*, and has just packed two boys off to St. Mark's for the good (she says) of their education, and recently bought a marked-down Frank Stella because she says she has come to care deeply about art, and Fred—well, old Fred can't, unfortunately, come to the phone right now, because he is dressed in some amazing Egyptian suit and has had those charming little touches of gray hair inked right out of his forelock and is down on his hands and knees making a presentation of a disgusting new campaign for National Sweatshirt that is going to clear him a cool forty thousand, and at some point in the evening we will all be discussing the alarming fact that television is now so powerful that it could actually elect, make us elect, almost, some movie star, or something, just on *appearances*.

People seem to be willing to put so much on the tube. People put so much on anything out there that they can touch, as long as it's out there. Four years ago, I remember conversations that went like this: "Rockefeller doesn't stand a chance." "You mean because of the divorce?" "That's right. Who'd vote for him?" "But—well, I mean, you've been divorced eight times. Divorce can't be that big a thing for *you*." "Oh, yeah. Well, I mean, *I* don't mind. I *like* him, actually. But imagine what all those other people think." Nowadays—a few weeks ago, anyway—the conversations were often like this: "Oh, yeah, well, I like McCarthy. He's very intelligent. But Kennedy has this great organization, and he's very sexy." "Yeah, well, I know that's what some people think, but, I mean, you being a professor of government, and a minister besides . . . is sexy really . . ." "Oh, well, um, I'm not thinking of my *own* view, which is, well, ah, well, anyway—I'm thinking of what these other guys are thinking." I don't really want to get into one of those casual street brawls with Professor McLuhan on the subject of "hot" and "cool" media, but it seems to me that the main tendencies in life among American bipeds as they march distractedly into the future are a gradually disappearing center (within the biped) and an increasingly desperate projection out (ah, information, ah, facts, discussion groups, newspapers, parties, transistor radios, the eleven-o'clock news) to any place that you can touch—and maybe find something out there you can haul back in—and that television doesn't really do anywhere near as much to us as we do to it. Oh, sure, they now have fifteen or something time-outs a game in the National Football League for razor-blade commercials, and that is something television does to us—it chops up the football game a bit—but we who look at football, who look at it more and more, we look at it more and more only in part because it is available and because TV does it well. Mostly, we look at it because the act of passing through this society has done things to us to make us want this kind of mechanical, brute, disconnectedly physical spectacle. We demand it, and television, which is such a key part of our brave, pioneering engulfment in technology, gives it to us: the unrebellious perfect slave, possibly rebelling at moments only to create an illusion of human relationship between it and us; and a slave really only in the sense that in the country we now seem to be heading toward, where the strictures of organization are on their way to reducing the possibilities of behavior to the computer's binary alternatives, o or 1 (one thinks of the literati's happy talk of "polarization")—where there is no choice, in other words (o or 1. "On" or "Off." For human beings, "Off" is still not yet a choice)—there are no masters, either.

On the subject of covering the Wisconsin primary, which I seem to remember prattling cheerfully along about before I fell into some kind of bear trap, it seems to me that the only TV outfit that did any kind of solid job about it was the CBS crew, under David Schoumacher. CBS didn't put an awful lot of Schoumacher's stuff on the air—there being sexier things going on around the country than Eugene McCarthy canvassing Wisconsin—but Schoumacher stuck close to McCarthy most of the time, covering what there was to be covered, and I don't know that you can do much more than that in the circumstances. Despite the *très grande gravité* and seriousness with which we Eames-chair activists invest politics, most of the people who have to do the covering know that nothing much ever happens in a political campaign, nothing of much interest ever gets said, and what it mostly comes down to is not getting beaten by the other fellow. On the night of President Johnson's combination bombing-pause-and-ascension-into-heaven speech, NBC's Elie Abel had chosen to stay in Milwaukee and do some end-of-the-line punditing for NBC's New York newsroom. Schoumacher decided to take one more blessed drive into the blessed Wisconsin night with McCarthy and cover a speech he was giving at some small college in Waukesha, in order to get his reaction to what was supposed to be a bombing-pause announcement. McCarthy had literally just finished speaking when the President's non-candidacy was whispered into the hall, and Schoumacher and cameraman and soundman leaped onto the stage, with a dozen or so newspapermen, everyone yelling, talking, pressing around McCarthy. Schoumacher squeezed through the crowd, pressed up close to the Senator, popped up his microphone. McCarthy said a few words. Nothing memorable, but it happened and was recorded. Schoumacher made the 30-minute drive back to Milwaukee in 15 minutes, and got the 20-second interview on the eleven-o'clock news, which was literally just beginning in New York. "The other announced Democratic candidate for President, Minnesota Senator Eugene McCarthy, was on public view, campaigning in the Wisconsin primary, when he first learned of the President's decision," purred Harry Reasoner, in New York. "CBS News correspondent David Schoumacher reports from Waukesha, Wisconsin." And there it all was, the organization whirring smoothly along, not a hair out of place. Elie Abel, meanwhile, had been sitting in his studio in Milwaukee listening to Johnson's speech and minding his own business, when Johnson suddenly finished and NBC's big pundit Edwin Newman appeared on the screen and Edwin Newman cleverly said, "And now we switch you to Elie Abel, in Milwaukee, for a reaction." And so there was Elie Abel, and *there* was Elie Abel, and Elie Abel sat there, and he looked out at us, and we looked back at him, and his lips slowly began to move, and after a while he said, "And now back to Edwin Newman in New York"—which, when you think about it, seemed as straightforward a response as any.

LIFE AND DEATH IN
THE GLOBAL VILLAGE

He was shot in secrecy, away from cameras. No strange slow-motion scenes, as when the young Japanese student, sword in hand, rushed across the stage to lunge at a Socialist politician, or when Verwoerd, the South African, was shot at and for whole crazy moments (it seems so long ago; so many people shot at since then) the cameras swirled and danced around the tumbling, stampeding bodies of the crowd—and then John Kennedy was killed, his life made to disappear right there before us, frame by frame, the projector slowing down, s-l-o-w-i-n-g d-o-w-n, s—l—o—w—i—n—g d—o—w—n as we watched (three consecutive days we watched), gathered in little tight-gutted bands around the television set, meals being cooked somehow, children put to bed, sent out to play, our thoughts of abandonment and despair and God knows what else focusing on the images of the television set, television itself taking on (we were told later) the aspect of a national icon, a shrine, an exorciser of grief; we were never so close (we were told later) as in those days just after Dallas. It could not have been quite close enough, it seems, or lasted long enough. The man who was shot in Memphis on Thursday of last week was standing on a second-floor balcony of a motel, the Lorraine, leaning over the railing of the balcony in front of his room, which was No. 306. (We have been told it was No. 306.) He was shot once and killed by a man who fired his rifle (a Remington 30.06), apparently, from inside a bathroom window of a rooming house some two hundred feet away. The address of the rooming house is 420 South Main Street. There was no film record of the act, no attendant Zapruder to witness for us the body falling and other memorabilia, but most of us found out about it by television, and it is by television that most of us have been connected with whatever it is that really happened, or is happening now. Television connects—the global village. We sit at home— We had been out, actually, a party full of lawyers, and had come back early and turned on the eleven-o'clock news. "I have a dream . . ." young Dr. King was chanting, "that one day on the red hills of Georgia . . ." CBS's Joseph Benti said that Dr. King had been shot and killed, was dead. The President was speaking. "I ask every citizen to reject the blind violence that has struck Dr. King, who lived by non-violence," he said. They showed us pictures of Dr. King in Montgomery. They showed us pictures of the outside of the Lorraine Motel.

The telephone rang. A friend of my wife's. "Have you heard?" she said. I said we'd heard. "It's so horrible," she said. And then, "I can't believe it." And then, "I feel we're all mad." I held the phone against my ear, mumbling the usual things, feeling, in part, her grief, her guilt, her sense of lunacy—whatever it was—and, in part, that adrenalin desire we strangers have who have been separate in our cabins all the long sea voyage to somehow touch each other at the moment that the ship goes down. She talked some more. "I'm keeping you from watching," she said at last. I mumbled protests, and we said good-by and disconnected. We will all meet for dinner three weekends hence and discuss summer rentals on the Vineyard.

All over the country now the members of the global village sit before their sets, and the voices and faces out of the sets speak softly, earnestly, reasonably, sincerely to us, in order once again (have four and a half years really gone by since Dallas?) to bind us together, to heal, to mend, to take us forward. The President appears. His face looks firmer, squarer, straighter now than it has looked in months. "We can achieve nothing by lawlessness and divisiveness among the American people," he says. "It's only by joining together and only by working together we can continue to move toward equality and fulfillment for all of our people." The Vice-President speaks. "The cause for which he marched and worked, I am sure, will find a new strength. The plight of discrimination, poverty, and neglect must be erased from America," he says. Former Vice-President Richard Nixon is expected to release a statement soon. There are brief pictures of a coffin being slid onto a plane. The Field Foundation, one hears, has just undertaken to donate a million dollars to the civil-rights movement. Dr. Ralph Bunche asks for "an effort of unparalleled determination, massiveness, and urgency to convert the American ideal of equality into reality."

The television sets hum in our midst. Gray smoke, black smoke begins to rise from blocks of buildings in Washington and Chicago. Sirens whine outside our windows in the night. The voices out of Memphis seem to be fainter now; the pictures of that little nondescript motel, the railing, the bathroom window are already being shown to us less frequently today. Down below us on the sidewalk, six blue-helmeted policemen are gathered in a group. Three police cars are parked farther down the street. The television beams out at us a Joel McCrea movie. Detroit and Newark have been remembered. Responsible decisions have been made in responsible places. The President is working now "to avoid catastrophe." The cartoons are on this morning. The air is very bright outside. The day is sunny. All day long the sirens sound. The television hums through its schedule. There is a circus on Channel 4. Back from the dime store, my daughter asks one of the helmeted policemen if anything has happened. He seems surprised. No, nothing, he says. A squad car drives slowly, slowly by. A bowling exhibition is taking place on Channel 7. Another movie—and then the news. Great waves of smoke, clouds, billowing waves are suddenly pouring out of buildings. The sounds of bells and sirens. Mayor Daley speaks. Mayor Daley declares a curfew. Six Negro boys are running down a street, carrying armfuls of clothes. Police cars streak by. More smoke. The news is over. We are re-enveloped in a movie. We sit there on the floor and absorb the hum of television. Last summer it inflamed our passions, did it not? This time the scenes of black men running past the smoking buildings of Chicago are handled briefly, almost dreamily—a light caress by cameras and announcers. The coffin—one wonders where the coffin is at present, who is with it. Boston University announces that ten new scholarships for "underprivileged students" have just been created. The Indian Parliament pays tribute. The voices of reason and reordering rise out of the civic temples of the land and float through the air and the airwaves into our homes. Twenty-one House Republicans have issued an "urgent appeal" for passage of the new civil-rights bill. "With whom will we stand? The man who fired the gun? Or the man who fell before it?" Senator Edward Brooke, of Massachusetts, asks. The City Council of Chicago meets and passes a resolution to build a "permanent memorial." Senator Robert Kennedy deplores the rise in violence.

There was a moment the other evening when (just for a few seconds) everybody stopped talking, when (just for a few seconds) the television stopped its humming and soothing and filling of silences and its preachments of lessons-we-have-just-learned and how-we-must-all-march-together—and (just for a few seconds) Mrs. King appeared; she was speaking about her husband, her dead husband. She spoke; she seemed so alive with him—it's marvelous how that sometimes happens between people; he really had been alive, and one knew it then—and for a few scant moments, just at that time, and afterward, sitting there looking at the set, that very imperfect icon, that very imperfect connector of people (will somebody really have the nerve to say this week that we are a nation "united in grief"?), one could almost hear the weeping out there, of real people in real villages, and the anger, this time, of abandonment.

And then the sounds came back—the sounds of one's own life.

The weather man came on. A Negro minister on Channel 13 was talking about the need to implement the recommendations of the President's new Commission on Civil Disorders. He *had* been alive . . . hadn't he? Later that night, one could hear the sirens —very cool and clear—and, somewhere nearby (around the corner? blocks away?), the sounds of footsteps running.

KENNEDY IN CALIFORNIA

Los Angeles

I was out somewhere on West Jefferson Boulevard in Los Angeles a few days before the California primary, arguing with Dan Taylor, the well-known image-manipulator, who was then working on radio commercials for the Kennedy campaign. You've heard about these sinister image-manipulators, haven't you? Sleek gentlemen in shantung suits and Italian shoes. Gorgeously tacky offices in Beverly Hills. Nubile secretaries. Charts. Graphs. "I think we'd better get the candidate's hair a little shorter," the image-manipulator purrs. "And maybe trim those eyebrows a bit . . . and have him stop wearing those light-up neckties . . . and talking to voters in the street . . . and, hell, let's just paint him blue and try to swing the Eskimo-American vote. . . ." Actually, Dan Taylor isn't an image-manipulator at all—at least, not much of one. Dan Taylor is a friend from New York (or was, at any rate, until now), a nice man in a rumpled shirt, who at the time was standing before a tape-recording machine in a place called Associated Tape Duplicators on the far reaches of Los Angeles, throwing switches and spinning dials and trying to extract thirty- and sixty-second sections from Kennedy speech-tapes to use as radio advertisements in the campaign. "What the hell do you people mean by *manipulation* anyway?" Taylor was saying. He was very cross, which may have had something to do with the fact that he had been sitting in that office listening to and cutting tapes since nine that morning and it was now around two the next morning. "Kennedy makes a speech, and we take sixty seconds out of it and use it as an ad. And ever since I started doing this thing back in April press people have been calling me up, and, for God's sake, calling my wife up, to find out what this *sinister* business is I'm up to." Taylor threw a switch on the machine, and a radio announcer's voice was saying "Lodi, eight-thirty a.m.," and then there would be the voice of Robert Kennedy talking to the citizens of Lodi, California. "I don't think we can ignore the rest of the world," Kennedy was saying. "I don't think we can pretend that other nations don't exist. But I don't believe we have to be the policeman of—"

Taylor stopped the tape and then ran it back again. "The voice quality just isn't good enough," he said. "Our guy was probably holding the mike too far away." He flipped another switch and the tape played on. More Kennedy—some of it in a voice so unclear you could hardly make out what he was saying. Then the announcer came on. "On the train to Stockton," he said. "Ten-thirty a.m. I have here a Mrs. Louis Miller. She understands that this is to be used as a commercial. I am giving her address as follows for release purposes." The announcer repeated her address, and then a clear, intelligent woman's voice came on. "When do you want me to begin?" "Begin now," the announcer said. Pause. "How do you feel Senator Kennedy compares with the other candidates you've met?" he asked. "Well, I've met—" "I *have* met," the announcer said. "I have met Senator McCarthy," Mrs. Miller's voice began, "and frankly he does not impress me too much. I can't quite take him seriously. He seems likable enough, but frankly he does not seem to me to have real leadership qualifications." The tape went on like that, with Mrs. Miller giving her impressions of McCarthy and Humphrey, and then Taylor stopped it and played that section back with a stopwatch in his hand. He played it back three times with the stopwatch, stopping the tape suddenly, then switching it back. He called a girl into the office—a Kennedy volunteer. "I think we can use some of this," he said. "It works pretty well as a sixty-second, or you can split it into a couple of thirty-seconds."

"Are they going to use it today?" the girl asked.

"I don't know," said Taylor. "But do it now, and then I'll play it to Al and we'll find out."

The phone rang, and Taylor picked it up. "You're in *what* kind of a section?" he said. He put his hand over the phone. "She says she's in a blue-collar Mexican-American section," he repeated. "It's *what*?" he said into the phone. "It's *labor*ish. . . . Yeah. . . . Well, we got some stuff with Cesar Chavez, but it's mostly in Spanish. Oh, you want Spanish. Okay. We'll get out a couple of Chavez spots. Yeah, just find out the size of your tape machine. That's right. Find out the size, and then send somebody over here to pick up the tapes." He put the phone down. "Some little volunteer out in Lynwood," he said. "She's found a section of Mexicans who haven't been reached and wants to send in a soundtruck. I think if I hear the word Mexican-American once more in this campaign I'll scream."

Another girl came in. "The announcer is ready to do the Evers tape," she said."

"Okay," said Taylor. "Just a minute."

Still another girl came in with an armful of tapes and placed them on the table. "From up north," she said.

Taylor pointed toward a large cardboard box, beside the wall, that was already overflowing with little white rectangular boxes. "Look at all that damned stuff," he said. "Indiana. Oregon. Nebraska. California. Now New York. . . ."

No doubt about it—there is a lot of political tape in the boxes these days, a lot of political film in the can. This time around, in the contest for the Democratic delegate votes in the State of California in 1968, American political candidates for the first time began to try really seriously to *use* media rather than do the sort of fooling around with it that has usually been the case before— when one man, perhaps, on a candidate's staff might be aware that TV is a great force or something, and with everyone else traditionally wary of it, or unknowing, or untrusting of the agency and media people who do know. The fact is becoming increasingly clear that a political candidate *must* use media, because the media are there to be used; and the corollary to that is that a candidate must then necessarily take onto his staff the people, the technicians, the ad men, the scriptwriters, the cameramen, the space-buyers who know how to do things, and the presence of these technicians in itself changes the shape and play of political candidacy. Dan Taylor, for example, is just a man in charge of editing radio commercials. He is a private citizen, in real life a businessman, and now a Kennedy volunteer, and when he finishes a spot he calls Al Gardner on the phone. Al Gardner sits in a room in the barnlike Kennedy headquarters on Wilshire Boulevard and is the account executive in charge of the Kennedy radio-TV campaign in California. Al Gardner really works for Papert, Koenig & Lois, the New York ad agency, but Kennedy hired the agency to do his advertising, and so now a whole crew from the New York office, including Fred Papert himself, are out in Los Angeles doing—well, what they are mostly doing is what is called "handling the logistics." Buying the newspaper space. Buying the television time—figuring out when you are going to need exposure in what city and arranging to have a TV time-slot already signed up. When Dan Taylor finishes a tape, the tape has to be run off into 140 separate copies for the 140 separate radio stations in California that have been signed up to carry the Kennedy commercials, and then these tapes must be picked up from the tape-duplicating office out on West Jefferson and somehow delivered as soon as possible all over the state, to little stations in Stockton and Fresno and south to La Jolla and God knows where else, and this must be done every day, and has to work right. You hire technicians because you need things to work right, and the trouble with that is that technicians often bring with them their own rhythms and devotions. At this moment, in fact, Al Gardner is on the phone to Dick Goodwin, Kennedy's aide, who is with a roomful of top Kennedy people at the Fairmont Hotel in San Francisco—and what they are talking about is a newspaper ad that has just appeared for McCarthy which makes what the Kennedy people consider to be unfair and unjust allegations about Kennedy's role in the Dominican crisis. McCarthy will in fact later retract the ad and say that he had no hand in it, which is doubtless true, but the fact of his denying it, and having to deny it several times, will cause him a certain amount of grief, will not have helped him, in any case. The ad was placed by McCarthy's technicians, a Los Angeles ad agency called Norman Lewis & Associates, a small outfit, as it happens, that has not had much experience in political campaigns.

The media side of political campaigns these days involves a tremendous amount of work, of planning—of money, necessarily —and it also seems to increasingly involve a recognition by the candidate that he has, to some considerable degree, to turn himself over to the professionals. It is not the Svengali-Trilby, the Machiavelli thing that people are always looking for, and not finding, because who the hell is going to play Trilby at the Cow Palace? It is a technical thing, one of those technical things that we sort of *evolve* because we want things to work right, and which later sometimes seem to take on an almost independent existence of their own. This business of turning oneself over to the professionals—one can make too much of it. But it is probably a truth of some sort that, in order to run a maximally effective campaign, a candidate nowadays must needs somehow surrender himself to, if not an actual member of his staff, at any rate, a process outside himself. Eisenhower, in that respect, was an ideal candidate, serving himself up bodily to Jim Hagerty, who would then carve the general into appropriate servings for—what was in *those* days the prime concern—the five or six daily wire-service deadlines. Hagerty always had something new, or something that seemed new, to give to the press—the wire men would come badgering around Hagerty whenever the plane landed, or the train pulled in to a station, and Hagerty would give them the mimeographed handouts (the general had chicken salad for lunch, the general salutes Brazil), and little pieces of the general would go clicking out across the country and be received into the changing deadlines of the daily press. Stevenson, on the other hand (a man much like McCarthy in this one respect), seemed to be constantly aware that he had successfully retained his individuality up to the moment of his candidacy, and seemed not merely unwilling to surrender it, to have himself carved up for anyone (for Clayton Fritchey, for Bill Blair, even), but to be almost aggressive in keeping himself to himself. McCarthy started out this way—very Stevensonian in his determination to keep himself whole. He would, like Stevenson, madden newspaper reporters by never, or rarely, sticking to the advance text, which you might say is of no great consequence by itself—I mean, one maddened newspaper reporter more or less—but the fact is, if Ned Kenworthy of the *Times* doesn't have an advance copy of what you're supposed to say in Spent Bullet that evening at eleven o'clock, it doesn't matter how perceptive, or aggressive, or amusing, or whatever your views on this or that are, because nobody except the citizens of Spent Bullet will have a chance to hear them.

McCarthy, anyway, began his campaign by being very offhand toward the press, and it was interesting to watch him veer more and more toward trying to use it. In Oregon, for example, McCarthy finally began using his speechwriters—much more so, at least, than he had been doing until then, and although that may not seem like such an automatically marvelous thing, since McCarthy could write his own stuff better than most people could write it for him, the fact is if you are doing a campaign that way, and speaking your own stuff twelve or fourteen hours a day on the road, you just begin to run out—you don't even say the things you'd thought of saying yourself. And in California McCarthy really began to exploit a new technique—well, not exactly new, or even a technique, but he would take whatever opportunity was offered him for free interview time on radio or TV. Kennedy almost never did this. I think in the whole California campaign Kennedy accepted only two or three local interviews—I mean, the kind of thing where you are speaking in

Sacramento and the local station asks you to come in and tape a ten-or-fifteen-minute interview with the local Cronkite. Kennedy, to be sure, had much more money to spend on ads than McCarthy did. The official Kennedy staff explanation of this no-interview policy was that the candidate preferred to spend his time out with the people, which is doubtless partly true. But more to the point was the fact that he'd always been wary of exposing himself in this informal television-conversational arena—an activity that McCarthy was generally conceded to handle well and easily.

The thing about money—there is so damned much you can do with media if you can control it, if you can buy the time and put what you want to on the screen or over the air. Cutting, editing, sound, motion, pacing, all the developed and developing techniques of media play now upon politics, and produce almost a new language of political connection between the people and the candidates. And almost nothing about it is done by chance. McCarthy, for example, had a basic thirty-minute commercial which he ran about four times in the California campaign, and which had also been cut into three- and four-minute spots that were run more frequently. The short version went something like this. McCarthy appears (in what is obviously a scene taped from real events) walking among enthusiastic admirers. The camera is ahead and is looking up into his face. A voice-over announcer comes on. "This is Senator Eugene McCarthy. . . . His manner is very quiet for a politician. . . ." Scenes of McCarthy talking with people. "But don't be misled." Scenes of McCarthy speaking before a big crowd. "This quiet man toppled a President. . . ." Quick cutting to close-ups of McCarthy's face —he is speaking, looking forceful, stern. "Only this one man would come out and say that the war is not supported by the opinion of decent men." Scenes of McCarthy walking alone. "Only this one man . . ." Then more shots of McCarthy walking among crowds, and finally a single shot of his face, slightly smiling, and the voice-over saying, "On Tuesday, vote for Senator Eugene McCarthy."

The thing that seemed interesting to me was the voice, which was very low and aggressive and forceful—a voice that McCarthy himself does not have. The voice, plus the imagery of elections, of cheering crowds, of hurly-burly, of winning. Kennedy's ads, by contrast—his short ads, anyway—were very soft-spoken, quiet, seemingly unobtrusive. A full-faced picture of Kennedy would come on the screen, usually between ads for some prime-time show. Then his voice would be heard, speaking quietly, calmly—generally a couple of short sentences, such as, "As far back as 1965, I spoke out against what was happening in Vietnam. I'm not in favor of giving up in Vietnam. I'm in favor of having strong military forces. But [with great feeling] I'm in favor of using them with wisdom." And then the announcer saying, "In California, the people can choose the next President of the United States. Vote for Robert Kennedy." In this case the announcer was very soft-spoken, informal—the voice, in fact, of a young man I met one evening who was a bit perplexed that he had been chosen for the job ("Over Herschel Bernardi and people like that!") because his style of speaking, he felt, was so low-key. It's quite amazing the number of bases you can touch in a short period of time if you have control. From the opening line about speaking out, with its implication of authority, concern, leadership. The business of strong military forces (used with wisdom!), which tells the southern Californians that he's not completely a peacenik, and presumably also lessens the chances of his being tangled up with a lousy peace settlement in Paris. And the final little fillip about the "people" being able to choose a President, with its implications that any other candidate who says that money can buy an election under-estimates the folk-wisdom of "people," plus the notion, mayhap casually cast into the airwaves, that any Negroes or Mexicans who consider themselves people, and so might accordingly like to come in and vote on Tuesday, would be greatly appreciated.

One of the fascinating things about television advertising in politics right now isn't just the magic power (real and imagined) of television itself, but is also very much the changing relationship between people themselves and their candidates, parties—the electoral process. People, for example, don't really seem to give much of a damn about political parties. Oh, sure, I guess they do in certain parts of certain states. There are diehard Republicans in Greenwich and Phoenix, and cradle-to-grave Democrats in specific wards in specific cities. But the old lines of force and tension represented by political parties don't seem to count too much any more. Democrats say matter-of-factly, Oh, hell, I'd vote for Rockefeller if only he had the nomination. Candidates often run their campaigns in such a way as to blur or evade the political parties they actually belong to. The voter, in other words, is less and less held in place by the old allegiances, and now, too, there is a whole new breed of cat, the so-called independent voter, which often conjures up the picture of an amiable, thoughtful businessman sitting there on his back porch at twilight trying to make up his mind intelligently between Cadwallader and Havighurst but in reality is probably more often somebody who really doesn't have much of an opinion because he doesn't know much about it, and doesn't care much about it, although at some point he is generally made aware by media that he should.

In short, there seems to be a lot of floating going on in our country—there is a lot of floating anyway, but it seems especially noticeable right now in the relations of people to politics. Democrats voting for Republicans and nobody thinking that very unusual any more. Republicans voting for Democrats, and everyone by now just taking that for granted—kids doubtless unaware there ever was a time when whole families were lifelong dutiful members of a single party, and when the party affiliation counted for something in their lives. People float, adrift from their old ties of party, adrift in many instances from the seriousness that society wishfully attaches to their role as voters—and into this situation comes television, with its increasingly assimilated position in the household, with its already established authority as the dispenser and articulater ("I think that Arlene Francis is such a lovely person") of the realness in people. And television not only connects the mass of people to their candidates, but forms the relationship in ways that aren't always very evident. This seems especially true in the matter of "issues." When people identify with a candidate, they identify (they often say) because of his stand on issues. X takes a stand on unemployment, the newspaper says. Y takes a stand on China. A few days ago a beautiful round shiny man in Beverly Hills told me that he really liked Governor Reagan because he had risen above the "image business" and had "developed a real tough grip on the issues." Yes, well. A few generations ago, when this country was very different, when the admitted relationship of the government to the people was very different, and compartmentalized, in the old days when you could vote a party in or out on how it "stood" on silver—then you had a relationship with parties and with candidates that could more rightly be described as being based on issues. Even in the 1940s weren't some people saying angrily that Franklin Roosevelt had promised we wouldn't get into the war, as if this promise, this issue, was something hard and solid and tangible that Franklin Roosevelt had held out to us, and we had all reached out and laid our hands upon it, joined together, and that was that? Nowadays the political choices in national life have become so centrist and technologically connected to one another (slums, Negroes, riots, urban development, unemployment, education, riots, etc.) that it's become virtually impossible for one centrist candidate's program for administrating the life of the nation to truly and significantly differ with another centrist candidate's program. To be sure, there are certain non-centrists, certain black militants, New Leftists, certain people who would advocate abolishing utilities and painting everyone over thirty Prussian blue, and maybe they are right, maybe indeed Herbert Marcuse is more right than Arthur Schlesinger, maybe twenty years from now some Dayton, Ohio, police chief will be successfully nominated as the Democratic candidate on a platform consisting of the painting of everyone over thirty Prussian blue and compulsory walking on the grass at major land-grant universities. But right now we are most of us in the center (some Californians now bitterly complaining of how Reagan let them down on the issue of lowering taxes by raising them), and on an emotional level there isn't one hell of a lot of difference there.

This was one of the striking things, I thought, about that Kennedy-McCarthy television debate—not the fact that there didn't seem to be much difference between where they stood on the issues, but that people should be surprised and disappointed that this was so, as if they had looked in the traditional direction, in the direction of the "issues," for somewhere to place their emotions, and found nothing very much, nothing that would quite support what they wanted to put there. In California, people seemed to feel the "show" had let them down. "It just wasn't very much, it didn't grab me at all," said a young man who had moved out from New York a few years ago. There were issues, to be sure. There was the issue of whether private business was to rebuild the ghetto, as Kennedy has suggested, or whether the ghettos should not be rebuilt at all, as McCarthy has sometimes suggested. There was that "exchange" when McCarthy said something about the need to move the Negroes out into the white suburbs, and then Kennedy got very passionate about "fourteen thousand Negroes being moved into Orange County," and so this was finally an "issue"—to move Negroes in or out of Orange County—and the newspapers played around with it for days, both sides eventually denying that they had meant quite what they had said. Well, sure. This is an issue for the fourteen thousand Negroes, and for the people of Orange County, but beyond that it's not much of an issue that can affect anyone's emotions very deeply. Issues just aren't what it's mostly about any more—it's style, personality, image, all those dread, sleek, slick-sounding abstractions we recoil from because we are more serious than that, we care about substance. Well, ideally, it's more than style—it's the man, some live, glowing human being, on whom we can hopefully lay our emotions. But style is what we settle with in the rest of our dealings with people for the most part, and syle is what we settle with in electing our gods and princes—and we get most of our sense of this style from television.

Television reveals political candidates to us in several ways. It reveals them in the three- or four-minute film-clips on the evening news shows. It reveals them on the Sunday discussion programs such as *Meet the Press* and *Face the Nation*. And it reveals them by political advertising. In California the situation was fairly typical in regard to the news coverage and the Sunday discussion shows. It was an interesting and, because of the Kennedy aura, fairly glamorous campaign, and the coverage on the evening news shows ran true to form. McCarthy visits Chinatown. Kennedy visits Fisherman's Wharf. McCarthy speaking about Vietnam to college kids. Kennedy speaking about Vietnam to businessmen. Crowds. Confetti. Motorcades. Airplanes. Hoopla. Kennedy speaking. McCarthy speaking. There were a couple of "Sunday" shows, such as the so-called Kennedy-McCarthy debate, which was really just an ABC *Issues and Answers*, and on some of these the candidates, especially McCarthy, who seemed to be on more of them, spread themselves a little wider—being shown on television actually talking as human beings rather than only giving speeches.

What really was different was the political advertising, partly because there was so much of it (considering that it was only a state primary), partly because the advertising in the California campaign revealed that people are learning how to do this sort of thing very well. As to the money, few people will probably ever know how much was spent, no matter what the admitted figures are, because so much of the money goes out in untrackable ways. A man I know, for example—a free-lance cameraman—put in a couple of days' work for Kennedy and received $1500 by private check on a New York bank. A lot of money was spent, in any case. A lot for radio, and two and a half times as much for television. It was Papert, Koenig who had the idea for moving in big on radio for Kennedy. The other evening I heard Roger Mudd on CBS observing that California was a "television state," and maybe so, but as the man from Papert, Koenig put it, "This is the biggest radio state in the union. Christ, everyone's on wheels all day long. And the daylight lasts until eight o'clock and they don't watch TV until later on." The Kennedy people (courtesy Dan Taylor, etc.) turned out about seventy different radio spots in the space of three weeks for the California campaign. McCarthy, I'd guess, had about one-third that many, and maybe less, although in the last days of the campaign a whole lot of McCarthy man-in-the-street commercials began showing up on KCBA, the big jazz FM station that has a wide audience in the Negro sections—the voices in the interviews being explicitly Negro. And although both candidates, by previous primary standards, had big TV campaigns, Kennedy's was really something quite novel. McCarthy in this respect suffered from not having much money to spend, but also from not having people who were quite as effective and professional as the Kennedy entourage. The basis of the McCarthy TV campaign was really this one thirty-minute ad, which was professionally done but which hadn't been produced primarily for California, and, in fact, had virtually no references to California. It was mostly an image-building exercise, concentrating on such matters as McCarthy's having been the first to stand up against the President. "This quiet man toppled a President. . . . Now because of McCarthy's courage there are peace talks and a prematurely retired President. . . . Although our country was going down the drain, no one would go forward. . . . Eugene McCarthy changed the history of this nation in New Hampshire. . . . It took unusual strength." And all this against a gently moving panorama of McCarthy speaking to crowds, walking through crowds, talking to people. The Kennedy TV campaign—well, early in the game Papert, Koenig had hired John Frankenheimer, the TV-turned-movie-director, to direct. Dick Goodwin had turned himself into a TV producer. Frankenheimer and his crew would travel along with Kennedy— through Indiana, Nebraska, Oregon, now California, filming speeches, interviews, odd moments, Ethel, dogs, trains, Kennedy, anything, and then send the stuff back to Los Angeles, where Frankenheimer would later edit it into thirty-minute commercials. By the time Kennedy arrived in California to begin the

California campaign, he had three thirty-minute commercials already being shown on California TV stations.

The night before the actual vote—the last night allowed for advertising—Kennedy ran a new film, from eight-thirty to nine on CBS, and from nine to nine-thirty on NBC. The film was called "Let the People Choose," and what it was was an extraordinarily adept and artful editing of Kennedy's actual campaign appearances in California—all that boring stuff, in other words—into a well-paced film. "This is Senator Robert F. Kennedy. I want to show a small fraction of my travels across the country," Senator Robert F. Kennedy would say pleasantly, and then, for God's sake, there we were aboard a train flashing through the countryside (one of those Frankenheimer train shots), and Flatt and Scruggs were playing "The Wabash Cannonball," just like in *Bonnie and Clyde*. It was really pretty damned good—I mean, considering that it was just a political ad, that the only material they had to use was what was filmed pretty much in the course of actually campaigning. Kennedy's voice-over would be speaking selections from various speeches. "We have to make it clear in the United States that we cannot tolerate lawlessness, violence and disorder. . . . We have to see to it that those who live in our urban areas have jobs. . . . We have to move away from the welfare state. . . . Farming and agriculture are the root of economic progress in the United States. . . ." All the standard political stuff, all the semblance of issues, in other words—the mention of disorder and farming and unemployment—but what the film was really about was the pacing, the motion, the sense of expansiveness. In one really striking sequence there was a close-up shot of Kennedy, serious and thoughtful, seated by the window of a train, then a close-up of the land flashing by outside —then suddenly the camera is in front of the train on the tracks . . . the tracks, two great long silver lines, pushing like an arrow into the distance (into the future?) . . . we rush, keep rushing down this arrow—then suddenly again we cut to what is a big auditorium, all dark, except for Kennedy's name in lights, a huge name in lights, "KENNEDY," that's all one sees . . . then a big close-up of Kennedy's face . . . very close . . . closer . . . and Kennedy opens his mouth, the voice very soft, very, very soft. "I'm going to tell you what I think," he says, and proceeds to say something about draft-evasion.

It was thirty minutes, all like that—pre-empting the *I Love Lucy* show. And then it ran again on Channel 4. McCarthy's people had bought time that night but then had decided to show a replay of a CBS *Face the Nation* program of the previous Sunday—which seemed a disaster of a thing to do. The three aggressive CBS reporters nipping at McCarthy about whether he was going to switch to Humphrey, whether he was going to go with Kennedy if he lost—all negative questions, challenges, that McCarthy had to field. He fielded them fine, but fielding possibly wasn't the best occupational characteristic he could have been projecting at that moment. There was another McCarthy program later, on a local non-network station, which was okay in many ways. It was fairly straight, in the sense that it just showed McCarthy talking, but it didn't seem to be doing very much for the candidate.

What all this amounts to in the end I sure as hell don't know— the effect of television advertising on elections—and I wouldn't believe anyone who said he did. Kennedy won. He was supposed to win anyway. The thing is, I think my friend Dan Taylor, back in the tape studio, is both very right and very wrong. It may *seem* like a straight kind of thing to do—to take films of actual campaign occurrences, say, and simply rearrange them into an attractive end-product. It may seem, as many people engaged in the business of making political ads describe it, nothing much more than "bringing out the best in the candidate." But I think the propagandistic possibilities of film haven't really been touched yet, what can be done with imagery and consciousness— the sort of thing that Leni Riefenstahl did to such effect in the old Nazi films by the use of imagery, music, effects that seemed to be extraneous but weren't at all, were put there to have a deliberate effect on the viewer; the use of certain kinds of music, for example, and of natural settings, in order to move the viewer

out of his everyday reality. Wagner and dark clouds with Leni
Riefenstahl. Banjo music and two sharp sleek wild, wild rail lines
thrusting into the future with Frankenheimer-Goodwin. It's a
tricky business making movies out of real people and real events.
It's a still trickier business (I think even the most sinister image-
manipulator might admit this) watching them.

GRIEFSPEAK

When Robert Kennedy was shot, the reporters were already there—the cameras, the lights, the heralds of the people standing upon chairs and tabletops, trailing wire and tape recorders, the black tubelike microphones stretched out arclike into the room (that kitchen). He was shot, and it was real—a life, a death, the *event*, confusion, motion, people running, the man on the floor, young girls in straw hats crying, policemen, people pushing, yelling, the man on the floor, dying, dead, dying. It was all there for a moment, for a short while (it is perhaps this moment, stretching out forward and backward in our imaginations, that now remains), this event, this God knows what it was, and then the hands of people began to touch it. Inevitably, one will say. Inevitably. *Je suis touriste ici moi-même.* Soft hands, tired hands, sincere hands, oh those sincere hands touching it (and him), poking it, rubbing it, plumping it, patting it. The men in rumpled shirts, hastily buttoned coats, were on the tabletops (our witness-technicians), on sidewalks, in corridors, holding aloft their microphones and cameras. The other men, in better-fitting suits and serious expressions, were inside some room—it all seemed like the same room (some underground chamber), but it could not have been. They talked—to each other, out to us. "I suppose," said Charles Kuralt, "we ought to be giving some comfort to the country in times like this. . . ." Griefspeak. "I don't know about the rest of you," John Chancellor said, "but in the last few hours

I seem to have lost part of my self-respect." Somebody handed a piece of paper to Edwin Newman. "I have some new information here," said Edwin Newman. "Sirhan has ordered two books." He looked at the piece of paper. "One is by Madame Blavatsky. The other is by C. W. Ledbetter. We don't know the meaning of this as yet. Or whether it has anything to do with the alleged, the— we want to remind you that all this is tentative, because in this country no man is guilty until judged by a court of law." They talked of irony awhile. It was a time for discovering ironies. It was ironic about "the family." It was ironic that he was shot at the time of his "greatest triumph." It was ironic that "he had spoken out so often against violence." It was ironic that only yesterday he had rescued one of his children from the surf at Malibu. "Excuse me, John," said Edwin Newman. "We just got this on Madame Blavatsky. She lived from 1830 to 1891 and was a Theosophist—although I want to say that we're not yet sure what relationship, if any, this has to the . . ." "I just thought of another irony," said Sander Vanocur. "In a speech just a few days ago Senator Kennedy said, 'We were killed in Oregon. I hope to be resurrected in Los Angeles.' " A psychiatrist appeared at some point to say he thought the violence in our country derived from showing films like *Bonnie and Clyde*. There were discussions across the nation about brain surgery. "I think each one of us is guilty," Mike Wallace said. Telephone calls from prominent people to the family were duly logged and reported. CBS announced telephone calls from President Johnson, Vice-President Humphrey, Governor Reagan, and Senator Mansfield. NBC announced telephone calls from President Johnson, Governor Reagan, Robert McNamara, and Mayor Daley. The police chief of Los Angeles appeared before the press and spoke calmly and effectively. "I'll give you boys a moment to get your machines adjusted," he said before beginning. Prime Minister Harold Wilson was interviewed via satellite. The BBC announced "prayers for America." There were scenes of the coffin being placed into the plane in Los Angeles and being taken out of the plane in New York. There was an interview with Cardinal

Cushing. Lord Harlech said that violence in America had become "an international scandal." There were interviews by satellite with former Prime Minister Macmillan and Romain Gary. There was an interview with an old gentleman seated in a chair upon a lawn, who had once been Robert Kennedy's grade-school principal. "I remember him very well," he said. "One day he brought one of these animals to school with him. A little pig, I think it was." They showed us the inside of the cathedral. Norman Mailer was standing at vigil around the coffin. "I think Nick Katzenbach is there," said an announcer. "There is George Plimpton. Ed, is that George Plimpton?" "No," said Edwin Newman. "But I think Mayor Lindsay is now coming down the aisle." They showed us Ethel Kennedy. Mrs. Robert Kennedy was seated in church beside a child, her head bent low over the child. The camera zoomed in. "How does one comfort a child at a time like that?" asked Edwin Newman. There was a Chevrolet ad. A man and a girl were seated on top of a convertible singing about "the big new savings on all regular Chevrolets." The song ended. "And on Chevelles too," the girl said with a wink. CBS was running off a Western. A man and a very blond girl with frizzy hair were hiding behind some curtains. There were advance shots of the route to be taken by the funeral procession. There were shots of tree-lined streets in Washington. "He often enjoyed a brisk walk down streets such as these," a voice informed us. There were pictures of the White House. Leonard Bernstein, it was announced, would handle the musical arrangements. There were more scenes of Ethel Kennedy in church. There were scenes at Union Station. There were distant views of Hickory Hill. "He liked fresh air," said another voice. Jerome Wilson of WCBS had a number of people seated around him. "I realize it is hard for you to talk at a time like this," he said to a young man who had been a Citizen for Kennedy, "but what did you young people *especially* like about him?" The young man thought for a moment. "We especially liked him because he had leverage," he said. "I think I can say that business would have been happy with Robert Kennedy," said Roswell Gilpatric. They showed us the crowds lined up outside Saint Patrick's. "Young and old alike are joined in grief," an announcer said. They showed us the flags flying on the office buildings on Park Avenue. Some were flying at half-mast, some were not. "The flags fly at half-mast all across this mourning city," an announcer said. They showed us people filing by the coffin. They showed us the train on the way to Washington. They showed us the railroad stations. They showed us the train tracks. "What was it . . . what was the *mystique* that the Kennedy family had?" asked Johnny Carson. "Ethel Kennedy must now begin to build anew," Gabe Pressman said. The Red Cross, one learned, had already distributed four thousand cups of cold drink. They showed us the Lincoln Memorial. They showed us the Joint Chiefs of Staff. "As time goes on," said Louis Nizer, "the pain from his passing will diminish." They showed us John Kennedy's widow in church. I watched the television on and off those days, and the strangely disconnected people on the streets, in crowds, in the lines that rolled around Saint Patrick's down to Forty-fourth Street. "The people have come by to pay their last respects," the voices said. "The people file by . . . the people wait . . . the people touch . . . the people grieve. . . ." They showed us that throng of men and women waiting outside the station at Trenton—kids with American flags, parents in their shirtsleeves, the long train tracks, the crowded platform. "The question," the announcer said, "is how much the train has been slowed down en route from Newark." No. The question all along (we had known three days ago who had been killed) was who was dead.

MOON OVER MIAMI

Julian Goodman, the big boss at NBC, was up there in the big-boss observation room with Governor Reagan and his press secretary and a number of Secret Service men inconspicuously dressed for the Miami heat in their all-weather Secret Service black suits, nobody looking directly at the convention—most of them, except for the Secret Service (who were watching Governor Reagan and each other), looking twenty feet away through gray-lit darkness at banks of glowing television screens. The convention was there, all right, a few hundred feet away—go down the corridor, turn right, go past the convention guards, soft-drink concessions, smoke, state troopers, delegates, press, more Secret Service men, people in orange vests, hot lights, American flags. But Goodman and Reagan and the rest were inside now, in the small dark room with glass windows looking into other small dark rooms—a complex of rooms, paperboard walls, glass panels, dozens of television screens, cables, men in shirtsleeves, baseball caps. The air-conditioning was humming; lots of the men, in fact, had colds. A few feet below Goodman's booth, in the Master Control Room, was Reuven Frank, the head of NBC News, a youngish white-haired man in a white shirt, leaning over a small microphone, with two assistants on each side, telephones along the counter, an NBC News ticker behind him near the door—everything dark, glowing with gray light. To Frank's left, and behind three sliding glass panels, was the Outside Control Room, another dark room, but this one partially lit by a wall of eighteen television screens, which showed what the NBC cameras and reporters outside Convention Hall were doing. Right in front of Frank was the Inside Control Room, with twenty television screens, these watched by five or six men around a triangular desk—the images on the screens changing, flickering, showing what the sixteen NBC cameras inside Convention Hall were looking at, and showing the pool-camera pictures too, the pool cameras being the big cameras on the platform directly in front of the speakers' rostrum, staring straight ahead at the speaker, and used by all networks jointly. And to Frank's right was the Air Control Room, another dark room with a bank of TV sets, five men and a woman at a long table holding microphones and soft-drink cups, a man way over on the right seated, like an organist, in front of a machine that looked a bit like an organ, his hands gently tapping, stroking certain keys—the sound man, the mixer.

In the center of the bank of TV screens in Air Control were two big screens, one labeled "Air," which at that moment showed Chet Huntley talking live and on the air from the booth he shared with Brinkley—a booth that looked out over the convention and could be reached by stairs from the convention floor—and one labeled "Preset," which showed John Chancellor crouched on the convention floor beside Senator Karl Mundt. Mundt, seated, was fiddling with some papers on his lap. Chancellor was just crouching there, staring straight ahead, listening to the steady stream of NBC's coverage, plus periodic NBC directives, that was pouring into his right ear through the headset. The pictures started changing on some of the TV screens in the Outside Control Room. "Abernathy is coming in," a man there said into a microphone. The screen in the center of that bank of sets showed what seemed to be several dozen Negroes marching in front of the hall, and policemen, guards, confusion. A man in Outside Control got up and said something through the glass to Reuven Frank. The Negroes demonstrating outside the hall suddenly showed up on Preset in Air Control. Huntley was still talking. He was talking about the Republican platform. The woman in Air Control said, "Stand by! Stand by!" A man to her right asked, into his microphone, "What do we call them? Poor people's marchers?" On the bottom of a screen off to the side, labeled "Superblock," the words "Poor People's Marchers" appeared. A voice said, "Try 'demonstration.' That's what it is." The man spoke again into the microphone. To the left of the long table in Air Control, another man, in a coat and a yellow shirt, got to his feet and walked over to the glass panel near Frank. "Can we fit a short spot in about here?" he asked into his microphone. He was the liaison man for the Gulf advertising group, three members of which, also in yellow shirts, were sitting in an observation booth above and to the back of Frank, to the side of Goodman's booth. "No," said Frank. The man sat down again.

In the Inside Control Room, Eliot Frankel, one of Frank's producers, was speaking to Chancellor on the floor. "We're going to the Poor People's demonstration," said Frankel. "Then to you." Chancellor's picture was on several of the TV sets above Frankel. They showed him standing now, in the aisle beside Mundt, with people milling past him, as he held his microphone and talked to Frankel.

"Look, I can't keep this much longer," Chancellor was saying. "We were already interrupted once before."

"Three minutes," said Frankel.

A man beside Frankel was trying to reach Frank McGee. "Frank, Frank," he kept saying. You could see McGee on another of the screens. He was standing off to one side, also speaking into his mike, from which came a lot of static out into the control room.

"He must be getting feedback from ABC," said one of the men.

"We're holding Poor People," a voice suddenly said. "We switch to Chancellor in one minute."

In Air Control, the Poor People's image disappeared from the Preset screen, to be replaced by that of Chancellor, still standing. Then someone sitting beside Mundt got up and allowed Chancellor to sit down beside him. Huntley, on the Air screen, finished some remarks about a recent Nixon poll, then said smoothly, "This might be a good time to check around with some of the key platform-builders of the Republican Party to find out what sort of differences occurred in working out their positions. We now switch to John Chancellor, on the convention floor." Huntley's image disappeared from the Air screen, reappeared on a screen to the left—a smaller screen—which showed him rubbing his eyes. Brinkley, on still another screen, was smoking a cigarette. Chancellor and Mundt were now on Air. "Senator Mundt," Chancellor was saying in a relaxed voice, "one of the more interesting aspects of the Republican platform is its apparent success in working out a compromise on the Vietnam issue. I wonder if you'd . . ." Sander Vanocur showed up on Preset, standing beside Senator Charles Percy.

Nowadays the television networks don't cover a political convention so much as orchestrate it. I watched one night of the Republican thing on television—that is, on a single television set —but the rest of it I watched at the convention, and you'd really have to have been there to know what a controlled and dying, deathly thing it was. I mean, you sit there in your air-conditioned living room on Mulligan's Island—bare legs and summer dresses and nice drinks and lovely people—and the set hums along in a corner of the room ("I wouldn't miss it for the world," the hostess has said), and so there you are, participatory democracy in little Saks dresses, and now and then a couple of people will break off from a discussion of what they have heard about what someone has read about Norman Mailer's new movie, and go over and stand thoughtfully in front of the TV, turning it up a bit so that it can be heard, and sipping drinks and listening to John Chancellor ask Senator Mundt how come, if there were so many Republican hawks, the platform ended up so dovish, and to Senator Mundt reply, slowly and with great seriousness, as if he were thinking this all out for the first time, "Well, John, I really don't think those terms 'dove' and 'hawk' apply too well to basic Republican attitudes," and then we are over with Edwin Newman, who is standing beside big Leonard Hall, and Newman, who has been on his feet for seven hours already that evening—not only on his feet but walking around a Miami Beach amphitheater with a thing on his ear that keeps giving him the whole audio portion of NBC's national news coverage, whether he wants it or not—is saying, in quite an interested way, considering, "Well, Mr. Hall, I wonder if you'd care to comment about recent stories of slippage in the New Jersey delegation," and Leonard Hall looks over the top of Newman's head and says, also pleasantly, in the manner of a man who would be delighted to give information if only he had information to give, "I'm afraid that's just another of those rumors. Nothing is happening in New Jersey. New Jersey is holding fast." And so the drinks are sipped for a little while, and then a conversation about the vigor of some Rumanian rock group starts up, and the sound is turned back down.

Everybody seemed bored by the Republican Convention—the delegates, the press, the police. David Brinkley seemed especially bored. "There is *no* parliamentary reason for the nomination of favorite sons," he said briskly a number of times as Wednesday evening grew longer and longer with the nominating and seconding speeches. "They don't *have* to do it. They do it for reasons of their own." One wonders, really, if any of those people in Miami Beach, with the possible exception of an alternate delegate from Alabama who kept rushing up to one after another of the girls in Florida-orange vests and trying to embrace them, did much of anything for reasons of their own. In large measure, not only the outer shape—the timing and arrangements—of the Republican Convention but the inner shape as well was determined by television. It has been happening for some time, to be sure, this accommodation of the structure and scheduling of conventions to the demands of TV, which aren't, to be sure, demands as such but merely a mutual awareness of what will "work best." Yet somehow it seemed especially true in Miami Beach, where the apparent inner need of the Republican Party this year to "avoid divisiveness," to harmonize a platform, to give everybody a little something, seemed to coincide so smoothly and, in a way, beautifully with the structuring, the derumpling, effect of serving up an "event" such as this to transmittal, and thus reshaping, by television. I mean, once you determine that it is in one's best interests to transmit a political convention by television, then in the need to make it effective on television, to get it to work right, certain other things are more or less automatically set in motion, and Senator George Murphy on the speakers' platform, out of sight of the cameras, waving his arms, conducting some of the lesser speakers, keeping the pace up, is just a tiny, visible example of that, and so is David Brinkley complaining that the whole thing was taking too long, that the Republicans were being tele-genically ineffective by letting their favorite-son speeches go on at such length. The whole thing is full of small examples, and I guess that is all right, in a way. It is what the people involved seem to want, or nearly what they seem to want. It is hard to be really sure about these things. After all, is there any great virtue in nominating someone on the thirty-sixth ballot, as they nominated Garfield? Is the process that nominated Garfield more American, or better, than the process that nominated Nixon? I doubt it. The process that nominated Nixon seemed very American. And television's role in all this—well, it seems silly to be too demonological about it, saying that TV slicks everything up or makes politics gimmicky. The awful thing, in a way, is that television rarely has this sort of explicit sinister effect; there are few sinister people floating about in the upper reaches of television, pulling important levers, throwing significant switches. Mostly, the TV people are technocrats—they don't (when you think of those tense, efficient men in those dark rooms, and all those TV screens, and all those pictures flickering, changing, switching) have much time to be anything else. What TV really does with politics, it seems to me, is to accelerate the derumpling movement that is already well along in the rest of American life—the smoothing over, the melding together—and it does it even though the people who run the game don't really want it to.

The fascinating thing about the Republican Convention, in a way, was this conflict between the seeming facts of the con-vention—that Nixon had so many delegations sewn up that he would surely win it, probably on the first ballot; that it was virtually an open-and-shut case—and the evident desire of the people transmitting the convention, whether in the control rooms or on the floor, to represent it as "human" and "American," to make it real. All those press conferences dutifully covered—and not only covered but investigated for the least possibility of "something going on." Delegates solemnly interviewed as to their latest positions. Governors begged for their views on "erosion" or "slippage." And out at the convention, if you were there in the evening, what you mostly had, what you just about *entirely* had, was a succession of droning speakers droning on about things that either everybody knew about or nobody cared about. John Wayne woke some people up the first day. And Barry Goldwater caused a big stir, as stirs went. The television coverage was hardly exciting; there so obviously wasn't anything a reasonably intelligent person could get excited about, except, at the very end, for that brief flurry over the talk of Lindsay's Vice-Presidential nomination. But, for example, on Monday night Senator Brooke addressed the delegates for twenty minutes, and if there was anyone in the hall listening to him after the first five he couldn't be detected with the naked eye. In the hall, in other words, you stood there, and Brooke droned on and on, and guards in blue uniforms and wide trousers pushed you around, and delegates chatted with each other, or went out to get Cokes, or scribbled notes, and nothing happened, nothing, nothing, absolute zero. . . . But on TV—well, it was a bit different. Joe Benti of CBS was interviewing Governor Romney. Senator Tower of Texas was talking to Mike Wallace about the Vice-Presidency. "This is the eleventh hour for Reagan forces in the South," said John Chancellor. Sander Vanocur was getting the head of a Southern delegation to say that several of his delegates had wanted to switch away from Nixon. It all makes for a curious kind of actuality coverage—the actuality in this case being Senator Brooke's monotonous speech that was being barely listened to by a vague, bored audience, the coverage (in itself accurate as to detail) implying not only that there was a good deal of dynamism in the hall, in the party, in the event, but that more was going on than met the eye. It was true, of course. More *was* going on than met the eye, which was next to nothing. And probably less was going on than the coverage implied. And, in any case, I'm not sure that it matters very much. It seemed to me that the network coverage of the convention was very good. I mean, it was boring as all hell. But then the convention was boring as all hell, and it seems to me there are plenty of things to fault the Messrs. Stanton and Sarnoff on without giving them the rap for trying to cover the Republican Convention with ten billion rupees' worth of electronic equipment. After all, it wasn't NBC or CBS that issued an edict some indeterminate number of years back that politics henceforth was to be fascinating and sexy and exciting and naturally very American and wonderful and where it's all at, etc., and that suddenly let the side down last week by staging a mind-numbing convention and making us watch it. I think the networks did very well, and the correspondents—especially the ones I watched on the floor: Vanocur, Newman, McGee, and Chancellor of NBC, and Wallace and Benti of CBS—did as good a job as they could. The trouble is that these things get out of everyone's hands. The trouble is that although it's true that TV can really expose and reveal people, or people and events, it's also frighteningly true that what is revealed can be controlled and arranged, and that the people out there who watch and defer to these revelations very rarely know the extent to which this is so.

Out on the convention floor, it was late, very late. Frank McGee was standing beneath the girder tower that held the pool cameras, trying to get his equipment to work. Some of the NBC people inside thought the difficulty was a feedback from ABC. Others thought he was getting jammed by the one hundred or so Secret Service men and their walkie-talkies. He had been out of action for an hour and a half. His headset started to sputter. He spoke into his microphone. "Eliot Frankel! Eliot Frankel!". he called, an aircraft lost over the Andes. The headset sputtered aimlessly. A man in a blue blazer came toward him and beamed and held out a program and a pencil. McGee looked at him, managed a brief smile. The man held the pencil farther out to him, and McGee took it and signed his name on the back of the program and gave both back to the man, who said, "For the wife. She watches you all the time." McGee started again to try to reach Frankel. A woman came nearly running over to him. "Oh, Frank McGee!" she said. "I can't believe it!" McGee managed to look friendly. She too thrust a piece of paper at him to be autographed. "I just love your show," she said. "You know, I think of you as a real friend of the family. You're always welcome in our living room."

Vanocur walked by across the aisle, followed by his floor director. A whole cluster of TV people were gathering around Romney. McGee's headset started to buzz again. "Okay," he said. "Can you read me? . . . Yes? . . . Okay. Move where?" He started to walk. He stopped. John Lindsay came down an aisle toward the New York delegation. McGee followed, carrying his microphone in one hand, a clipboard in the other. In a little while now the men and women in the hall—men in orange blazers with oranges on the crest, in shirtsleeves; small businessmen in business suits; bright-faced women; young, young men, crewcuts, little white collars—would join to name the once and future king. Perhaps he was already named. (It was a complicated process.) One thought so, anyway; the air in the hall, a bit complacent, a bit dead, seemed to say as much. The men and women from the various states sat in rows beside and behind one another. New Hampshire. Iowa. Georgia. Vermont. Maryland. The sovereign separate states—one had read in books that they were once sovereign and separate—brought together. Everyone together now. "Mutual interest." Common consent. Laced together by the railroads (even the names of the railroads are now merged). Bonded by highways. "Marketing." Airplanes. Wires and cables. Walter Cronkite. "But what if Maine and Texas have nothing to communicate?" the wise man had asked many years ago. He was not so wise, really. Maine and Texas, using the same toothpaste, have somehow managed. They all sit together now—closer together, one would imagine, than they know. The cameras look down on them. Fifteen cameras above the floor of the hall, if you have a taste for statistics. Out there in the night somewhere a Procter & Gamble factory hums, dispatching identical cakes of soap to Bangor and Fort Worth. A wide-track Pontiac sleeps in each garage. How boring it is to talk in the clichés of "standardization," "technocracy." The smooth universal soul. Boring. Pointless. The TV correspondents—good people, for the most part, engaged in a kind of guerrilla warfare—scurry around the hall in a last attempt (for this event, anyway) to scratch the skin in a way that will reveal *differences*, blood. *Differences*. We have read, too, about differences—about those rumpled men in rumpled suits who smoked cigars in the back corridors of Cleveland hotels and dealt whole states away at four o'clock in the morning. Now the correspondents work against the clock. The clock is nearly always ticking above our "actualities," our rites of passage. Prime time. Spots. Preset. Air. Inside Control. Outside. One minute to standby. Three minutes to Vanocur. Seven minutes for the governor's speech. Twelve minutes for the senator. Eight congressmen are presented—choreographed, in fact—up on the platform, for the precise eleven minutes agreed upon in the schedule. It is very well done. It works very well. It really does work very well.

Back there in the dark, glowing rooms, back there in Inside Control, Eliot Frankel taps on the glass panel near Reuven Frank. A button is pushed. McGee appears on Preset. He is standing beside Representative Melvin Laird and fiddling with his microphone again. David Brinkley's picture disappears from Air. McGee and Laird stand there instead. He is an able man, Frank McGee. Kind face. Glasses. A friend of the family. "I wonder if you see any greater possibility now of a shift to Reagan on a third or fourth ballot?" he asks.

"I have my own preferences," says Laird, "but, frankly, I don't think anything is really nailed down tight in this convention."

A WEDNESDAY EVENING
IN CHICAGO

Chicago

It was one of those cool evenings you don't usually get in Chicago this time of year. "You don't often get it nice like this till after Labor Day," the cab-driver had said. The air clear. The night breeze blowing in off the lake. There were boats at anchor in the marina. Dozens of small white boats. White boats floating on the dark water. The boy beside me, a dark-haired boy with a scraggly mustache, was dressed in Levi's and some kind of T-shirt and was called Dave, and blood was running down one side of his face and he was sitting in the gutter holding this girl, and people were screaming, really screaming, and the kids were standing in the middle of the road between the Hilton Hotel and the Blackstone, and then a tight-packed gang of about thirty cops came out of a side street, more or less on the run, holding their clubs out, rushing, pushing into the kids. One kid turned to go by the cops, get out of the way, and one of the cops grabbed the kid by one arm, spinning him off balance, and hit him on the back of the neck with his club. The kid yelled, "Hey! God*dam*!" and the cop, who wore a blue helmet and a wide belt, shoved his club hard into the kid's belly, and the kid sort of doubled up, and the cop grabbed him by the arm again and pulled him down the street toward where a white paddy wagon was parked in the middle of the road—one of three paddy wagons, or white armored trucks, with their back doors open. The cop and the kid went by me. The kid, who was tall and skinny, looked about nineteen. The cop seemed young too. He kept dragging the kid by the arm, and then another cop came over and took the kid by the other arm, and they brought him up in front of the door of the paddy wagon, and when the kid hesitated a moment before climbing in, the second cop shoved him with his club. Then the kid climbed up into the wagon, and both cops pushed him forward so that he fell into it, and then the cops slammed the door closed and went back on the run, clubs out, to find more kids. The kids were everywhere about. A television cameraman was standing in the middle of the road, in front of a bunch of them, taking pictures of the line of cops advancing on them. The cops were walking in tight formation, striding, their clubs not raised but held against their chests. The cameraman moved back before them, and to one side—you could see him tilting his camera, a heavy thing, to get the picture right—and then the cops suddenly started to run, raising their clubs. The cameraman moved back again and aside more quickly, and then some more cops came in from right behind him, and you could see them all swirled in together—the kids, the cops, the cameraman, who was trying now to raise his camera so that he could see into the mob, then being pushed out, clutching his camera with one hand, a cop grabbing him by the other arm. The cameraman was wild with rage. He wrenched himself away from the cop and just stood there swearing at him, yelling at him, and then the cop took one step toward him, and the cameraman stood still, and the cop turned around and ran back in toward the crowd until he found a kid and hit him with his club on the shoulders and arms, which he had raised to protect his head. Oh, it was really rotten. You can have only a partial idea of how rotten it was. I kept reading in the papers about how "demonstrators" had been "thumped" or "thwacked" with "nightsticks." When you are six feet tall and weigh a hundred and seventy pounds and hit a man on the head with a thick piece of wood—a thick, hard piece of wood—you do not "thump" him. You give him not only hurt, which is finite, but something worse, something degrading, and this may be why the people who now advocate clubbing in our country seem to be the same people who have trouble understanding that the dropping of bombs on other nations is something more, and worse, than the "delivery" of "hardware."

And I think maybe this is as good a time as any to say something of the television people who tried to report what is officially known as the Democratic National Convention. People generally have the idea, I think, that television is such a big deal that it always gets in everywhere it wants to; nothing is sacred to the camera eye; everything is exposed; nobody has privacy any more. This time last year, I remember, I was standing beside some dust-blown Marine-helicopter pad with David Schoumacher of CBS, and listening to Schoumacher try to persuade a Marine information officer to let him and his crew fly in to Tam Ky, where, he understood, a big and costly battle was still going on. The Marine refused. He claimed they needed all their helicopters, and doubtless that was in a way true. "But what about the ones I can see in there empty?" Schoumacher kept asking. The Marine officer wouldn't budge. He had his orders. Later, after we'd gone back to the base, Schoumacher seemed quite calm about it all. "It's standard practice," he explained. "If a battle is going badly, they won't fly you in. Tam Ky, we hear, is going very badly. The UPI had a report out that some of the Marines turned and ran. Can you imagine the Marines allowing that to be caught on film? They'll let us out there when the enemy has gone and the Marines are engaged in mopping-up operations"—which is what they eventually did. The official Marine dispatches described Tam Ky as "a gallant action." I ran into Schoumacher here yesterday—Schoumacher in a business suit, rushing through the corridors of the Conrad Hilton with his camera crew, this time trying to buck Mayor Daley, the Chicago police force, and the official censorship of the Democratic National Committee.

It's common knowledge by now, to be sure, how Daley and the Democrats combined to cut down the television coverage of the events in Chicago by managing the electrical-workers' strike so that there wasn't any time left to provide the networks with mobile hookups—that, plus preventing the networks' mobile trucks from parking at key places on the streets, and making things generally as difficult and restrictive as possible. Still, it's hard to realize, just sitting there in one's living room and looking at the screen, the extent to which one's bird's-eye view of actuality can be diminished, altered, censored in this country, in the year 1968, by a combination of officialdom and sheer brute force. It has truly been very ugly here, and I do not mind being so personal about it because there was something very special in the air in Chicago this week and I have been reading the newspaper stories about it, with their now almost conventional narrations of "thumpings" and "thwackings," and I have been looking at the television, and even the television, which did as well by all of us as I think it humanly could have, couldn't quite give it out as it really was.

Just before going downtown toward the Conrad Hilton Hotel, where so much of the clubbing and tear-gassing took place, I watched the evening news in my hotel room. It was mostly about the convention. Would Humphrey really get it on the first ballot? Interview with Dick Goodwin. Talk about the Vietnam plank. And then a film clip just in from Czechoslovakia, about Dubček. And then—it seemed like something from an old, old movie, so familiar, so terribly familiar, by now almost obscene—a couple of minutes from Vietnam. A mopping-up operation, actually. And there we were once again, briefly—the scene now barely intruding on our consciousness, the same old cast of characters. This time a Marine sergeant—the same young, harrowed face, unshaven, eyes glazed—talking in a seemingly matter-of-fact tone about what had just happened. "Well, we weren't too worried," he said. "We knew we had the air power. But then a whole lot of them came up at night. Last night. They ran right over Mike Company. It was kind of bad then. That was when my buddy got killed." He seemed about twenty years old, and also had a scraggly mustache, and looked tired enough to fall right down where he was standing. And then the correspondent came on, standing there in his fatigues—a new face. I forget his name; there have been so many "generations" of correspondents in the last few years. Morley Safer, the CBS man who tried so hard to bring home the irony of the war at a time when only those weird people with long hair seemed to have the passion to hate it—Morley Safer, now elegantly sideburned, was reporting to us that evening from Czechoslovakia. David Schoumacher was, as I said, at the Conrad Hilton. John Laurence, who did such extraordinary work in Con Thien last fall, was over at Lincoln Park with the kids—"the young rebels," as he kept insistently calling them. Wilson Hall, whom I remember bouncing down a Danang road in the back of a jeep, his face quite scarlet from the sun, had been covering Richard Nixon in air-conditioned Miami three weeks ago. Dean Brelis, whom I recently saw from a taxi in New York, making his way up Madison Avenue with a bum leg, was also in Czechoslovakia. And the bloody, wretched war goes on. And kids in Chicago march in the streets. I find it hard to get that Marine sergeant out of my mind—all the more because he barely got into it. That familiar gray picture. Gray Vietnam. Gray Prague. Gray Chicago. Events on film.

When things had quieted down in front of the Hilton last night, I walked down one of the side streets, going no place special, walking partly to *do* something that seemed vaguely human, to get the tear-gas fumes out of the eyes and throat. There was a bar somewhere down Wabash—the Starlite Bar, or something like that. Small, dingy, the kind of bar that is the reason, I guess, one doesn't go to bars much any more. They had a television set on—an old Dumont set, for God's sake—up on one of those shelves above the bar, just like in the old days when you used to go around the corner to Corey's to watch the World Series. Governor Hughes of Iowa was nominating Senator McCarthy. Governor Hughes seemed like a good man, although not exactly a spellbinder, which is maybe just as well. Gene McCarthy also seemed like a good man, but none of that appeared to matter quite enough right then. A couple of the people at the bar were looking at the set but talking to each other about something to do with automobiles and payments. And then Governor Hughes stopped speaking, and the television switched to video tape and showed the fighting and clubbing that had happened an hour or so before, down at the Hilton. You couldn't see much, really, it was so dark. Blurred lights. The camera moving, tilting. Police running by. Kids milling, running. Maybe you could see enough. I sat there in the bar and watched a cop grab a boy by the neck, and the boy run off, and the cop run after him and hit him twice with his club. You couldn't see the boy's face, and you heard no sound, although you knew there had been a sound. I went out of the bar (one could still hear police sirens in the distance, smell the gas, the smell of tear gas seeming so much a part of the night air that it would never be without it) and walked up Michigan. A long walk, past the Art Institute and that big, shiny insurance complex and Bertrand Goldberg's Marina City, and back to my hotel room, which is all brown: brown walls, brown rug, brown lamps. Down below—fifteen floors below, on the sidewalk—some kids were chanting; you couldn't make out what it was. I switched the television on. The roll call of the states. Montana. Nevada. New York. The great state of Pennsylvania put Humphrey over the top. There was much cheering. That Marine sergeant on the evening news—he seemed so tired. And young. And Dave, the kid with the blood running down his head who had been sitting in the gutter by the Conrad Hilton Hotel. I knew he was called Dave because the girl he was holding kept stroking his face and saying, "Dave, just a moment . . ." It seems odd to think that neither of those two young men will ever know about the other, but before too long maybe somebody, somehow, ought to try to tell them.